# NAVIGATING NEW MARKETS ABROAD

# Navigating New Markets Abroad

## Charting a Course for the International Businessperson

**David M. Raddock**

*with contributions by*
Robert E. Ebel
Hermann Frederick Eilts
Guocang Huan
Felton McL. Johnston III
Francis Kornegay Jr.
Rensselaer W. Lee III

**Rowman & Littlefield Publishers, Inc.**

**ROWMAN & LITTLEFIELD PUBLISHERS, INC.**

Published in the United States of America
by Rowman & Littlefield Publishers, Inc.
4720 Boston Way, Lanham, Maryland 20706

British Cataloging in Publication Information Available


**Library of Congress Cataloging-in-Publication Data**

Navigating new markets abroad : charting a course for the international
businessperson / edited by David M. Raddock.
p.   cm.
Includes index.
1. International business enterprises—Management.   2. Corporations,
American—Management.   3. Country risk.   4. Cross-cultural
orientation—United States.   I. Raddock, David M.
HD62.4.N38  1993   658'.049—dc20   92–44668   CIP

ISBN 0–8476–7843–1 (cloth : alk. paper)

Printed in the United States of America

 ™ The paper used in this publication meets the minimum requirements of
American National Standard for Information Sciences—Permanence of
Paper for Printed Library Materials, ANSI Z39.48–1984.

*for Annette*

# Contents

**Part One: Assessing Domestic Conditions in the Host Country: Political, Social, and Economic**

**Part Two: Country Case Studies**

**Part Three: Calculated Risks**

# List of Tables

# Acknowledgments

This book represent years of study and contacts with academics, high-level foreign officials, journalists, and specialists in the U.S. government. Individual sources for this education are hard to pinpoint, let alone credit or blame.

I really learned my political science at Columbia University through my own efforts in reading for my doctoral examinations and through the practical experience to follow. However, one professor in particular, Michel Oksenberg, sensitized me to the key areas of exploration in political development and revolutionary movements. I also wish to thank the late Margaret Mead for helping me to break through cultural barriers.

My work at the Washington office of ENSERCH Corporation taught me a lot about corporate needs and corporate politics. The practice of applying social science principles to corporate planning problems gave rise to the sort of international environmental analysis construct that appears in this book. Widespread travel, for ENSERCH Corporation and earlier as an academic with the support of Columbia's East Asian Institute and the National Endowment for the Humanities, provided the critical seasoning.

I especially want to draw the reader's attention to the fact that my work on financial analysis in this book represents collaborative thinking with Fariborz Ghadar of George Washington University's School of Business.

*Introduction*

# The Business of Getting Global

Let's get *with* it! The world seems to be shrinking, and our own horizons should be expanding. Globalizing one's business interests ought to be a natural extension of the marketing process.

Territorial divisions now appear to be less of a barrier to the U.S. businessperson. The fact that the Berlin Wall can be dismantled, broken into small pieces, and sold as souvenirs at Bloomingdale's department store in New York is an invitation to all of us to redefine our operational boundaries. Enterprises in other countries have become more competitive internationally, and U.S. corporations must search for new markets and sources of supply or stagnate.

Terms like "globalization" and "internationalization" have gained currency in academic and business circles as a signal that our markets must be expanded overseas and as a proclamation of a new universality of doing business worldwide.

A science of business and management techniques, homegrown, has evolved and spread to other places and cultures and presumably drawn them closer to us. Telecommunications and computer technology have spawned linkages between country and country, bank and bank, terminal and terminal. But does this mean that, given an appealing business opportunity in this day and age, one should find Myanmar no less daunting than Michigan?

Even if it is now simpler to reach out and touch, one has to work harder at establishing a viable and enduring relationship with those whose cultures, organizations, and practices at bottom still vary so

1

much from our own. Although the world does seem suddenly smaller and more ideologically sanitized as we enter the last decade of the millennium, businesses should look before they leap.

Now indeed may be the critical time to look for offshore business opportunities but not without a sense of cross-cultural, as well as historical, perspective. What we must do is learn how to incorporate such a perspective into our international corporate strategic planning.

Historically, the era of ideologies has not necessarily passed. If the cold war has ebbed, the North-South polarity (the developing world counterpoised against less developed countries) still continues. And resurgent rivalries among nationalities portend more schisms, if not other "isms."

Cataclysms that threaten foreign-owned equity, expatriate lives, and the flow of normal international commerce are never farther behind us than the most recent local war, whether in the Persian Gulf, somewhere else in the Third World, or in the reborn areas of East and Central Europe.

## Political Risk Analysis: A Premature Birth

The year 1978–79 took all players by surprise. At one time, when things seemed simpler and aggressive energies in the world seemed more focused on a cold war, multinational corporations believed that they could cushion themselves against, or even transcend, most conflicts. In the United States, transnational corporate entities had followed the government's lead or worked in advance of the U.S. government to build economic bridges for the politicians to cross soon thereafter.

Before 1979, the relatively few U.S. corporations with heavy international commitments could count countries like Iran among their more reliable hosts and partners. Former Secretary of State Henry Kissinger had predicted that the Shah's Iran would be an anchor for U.S. security interests in the Middle East. That year, the social revolution that shook Iran sent a wave of aftershocks through the international business community and undermined a shared confidence that the U.S. government could show us the way.

The abrasiveness and inequities of Western-style modernization that U.S. foreign direct investment had helped create in Iran had led to social ferment. A pervasive Western presence that had cast a shadow on traditional values and had eroded a sense of identity that gave rise to a sandstorm that shook us out of our complacency.

After the dust had settled, a gaggle of experts, calling themselves political risk analysts, emerged to clear the way for a new sort of confusion in international strategic planning. (Even Dr. Kissinger eventually took his place among these consultants.) Making their impression at Washington cocktail parties and behind closed doors of major international corporations were new experts with a diversity of backgrounds in applied areas of international politics—former covert operatives and overt analysts from the Central Intelligence Agency, ex-journalists, retired State Department country experts and policy planning staffers, and even former expatriate marketing executives called in from the cold by their home offices.

Add to this list a small coterie of academics, persons with a critical formal training in comparative politics and international relations as well as in geographical area studies. What this latter group of specialists lacked for the most part was an appreciation for the businessperson's criteria for making decisions and formulating marketing strategies. Few seemed to grasp the international marketing executive's concerns and the pressures under which he or she must operate.

The new breed of "political risk analysts" as a whole were slow to make the linkage between political variables and their potential for direct or indirect impact on the corporate bottom line.

To be effective, such analyses needed to be predicated on a knowledge of the organization's specific needs and sometimes even the characteristics of a specific project. The reality is that corporations have different objectives and criteria for investment and financial exposure. Specific projects themselves, like nuclear power plants and joint production-sharing agreements for petroleum development, can vary in terms of their special conditions.

Corporate cultures too differ in their capacity to assimilate and utilize such information. Before the Iranian revolution, a senior executive at a major consumer products multinational told the author: "We were one of the first American companies in Latin America. What can anyone tell us that our marketing people there don't already know?"

If smug ignorance is an extreme and a defense against innovation, it is a hard reality that new techniques of planning need the push of the CEO and deliberate efforts toward promoting the service within the organization. Corporate leaders never proceeded far beyond the introduction of an innovation. They failed to help the analysts, inside and outside the corporate structure, develop a resonance with the varying

needs of the planners at the corporate center(s) and marketing executives in the field. Perhaps the greatest shortcoming of political risk
analysis itself in the 1980s was its pretense of attempting to predict the
future rather than getting down to the business of educating and
sensitizing.

As international corporations and commercial banks were affected
by events in Iran in 1978 and 1979, the need for a dimension of
international strategic planning to cover political intelligence and analysis seemed urgent. Those banks concerned with default on their
financing as well as with providing advice to their corporate clients
took new stock of their planning apparatus. Several corporations with
long gestation projects in Third World countries, such as oil companies
and large-scale construction and engineering firms, found themselves
hurt by the Iranian situation in particular. They could not even respond
properly to the crisis at hand.

For example, one petroleum-related company with some ownership
of equity interests in the Persian Gulf was in a quandary at its highest
planning level about whether to withdraw while it had a chance and
cut its losses. The Shah himself had fled at this stage of the revolutionary process, but this company wondered how it might look if the Shah
were able to return after all through some magical intervention. It did
not trust the intelligence mechanism that it had in place.

Corporations generally were unprepared for such extreme political
contingencies. Those with no involvement in the Gulf region at that
critical time suddenly realized that they had cause to be alarmed about
exposures in apparently less predictable areas elsewhere in the Third
World.

*What was to be done?* Many of these international business organizations—particularly the banks—already had economists or entire
economics departments studying the international business investment
climate. Lending institutions, concerned with default on financing or
servicing their clients properly, already had kept a watchful eye on
financial indicators. But by this time, economists who had been operating *in vacuo* or whose command of political and social conditions in
a given country was limited to a quick phone call to a Washington
office (normally simply a public affairs operation) increasingly had
come to realize that political or social factors were inseparable from
macroeconomic, and even nuts-and-bolts, commercial questions. The
social upheaval in Iran now provided an impetus for more sophisticated
intelligence gathering on the political side and for the recruitment of

political scientists, usually with backgrounds in specific geographical areas.

But such attempts at restructuring at bottom were reactive and not properly integrated into the whole corporate strategic planning and marketing thrust. In one large manufacturing company, the economist, an "old hand" working out of headquarters in Ohio now had a political scientist–counterpart working alongside him, that is, if one considers "alongside" to be in a Washington office. The choice of locating the political analyst in Washington is arguably correct in terms of closer access to certain sources of information. Nevertheless, being situated in a Washington office is not the same as being positioned at headquarters. The economist logically served as the fulcrum of the program, and yet he never became properly educated in international affairs. The political analyst was perceived to be out in left field. Contact between the two analysts was largely restricted to the use of a telephone, still a barrier in the age of communications. The operation failed within a few years.

One major bank, already heavily committed internationally before the events in Iran, proceeded to construct a full-scale political risk apparatus at headquarters. Nevertheless, the economists and political analysts remained separate animals—in a somewhat happier state of cooperation than peaceful coexistence but distanced from one another both by the "traditional" parameters of their disciplines, their physical locations, and lines of accountability in the corporation. And if such a thing as cross-fertilization between the disciplines ever developed, the offspring appear to have been stillborn.

By the mid-1980s, in a recession that took a particular toll among developing countries in the Third World, the international debt crisis emerged. Maxidevaluations, currency controls, import restrictions, delays in payment, expropriations of banks and bank-owned companies, and failure to meet repayments on private debt became commonplace from Latin America to Africa.

High-level management seemed inclined to swing back in the opposite direction. Some made statements to this effect: "What's needed these days is proper financial planning to alert us to the risks against which a corporation or bank really can protect itself."

Some corporations actually fired their political analysts or cut back generally on their staffs of geographic area specialists. The rationale might have been as follows: What good are they anyway? Even if they can identify a political problem, there is little that we can do about it. The people in the field say that what we consider political problems are no worse than the ones that we face back in the United States. And, besides, how often do social revolutions like the one in Iran occur?

## An Integrated Approach to Business Environment Analysis

The reality is that the disruptiveness of political and social problems is as persistent as the more identifiable financial clouds that we can sight on the horizon. (Ask the Russian-American friend of the author who smugly set up an office in Leningrad for his export-import business with the new "Soviet Union" a year before it was reconstituted and many of the critical rules of the game were being rewritten.)

If the corporate planner is wise enough to use such tools, he might as well be completely equipped. And one can use those tools in all sorts of constructive ways. They help a corporation plan before it enters a new market and serve the enterprise as it positions itself in the host country and integrates itself into the new environment.

At the initial stage of planning, one might think it simpler to forecast major economic adjustments in a Third World country than to become entangled in a seemingly complex web of political and social factors that may or may not have a direct bearing on a business enterprise. The potential economic risks are reasonably clear-cut and the statistical indicators exist in the open sources for those who know where and how to look.

The less-developed countries of the Third World and the nascent free-market systems in the former "Soviet bloc" of Eastern and Central Europe emit easy-to-read economic warning signals. They are operating under the measurable parameters of their own less-developed economies and often under the constraints of the multilateral lending institutions. Knowing with greater certainty that we might expect currency controls or major devaluations in a host country forces us to make choices, to keep options open in the negotiating process, and to leverage ourselves appropriately.

But the apparently greater predictability of macroeconomic outcomes within a defined time frame in a host country is not always free of significant political complications. Moreover, the relative precision of such forecasts provides real comfort only if one has yet to make a decision to enter that market. If a company already is well-entrenched, political resources and cultural-specific, political maneuvers—namely, political analysis carried to a more sophisticated level of ongoing, concrete adaptation to the environment—can be utilized again as the only recourse for minimizing the negative impact on one's position in the host country.

In actuality, a balance must be struck in international strategic planning and country risk management; economics and politics constitute an integrated equation for measuring the host country's environmental risk and disincentives to foreign direct investment, sales, or extending loans. Political/social analysis, a review of business climate or commercial conditions, and financial/economic analysis all have their own sets of variables. *But they are interrelated.* (Some of the ways in which the three categories affect one another will be demonstrated later.)

An integrated approach protects against the cyclical emphasis that the tide of world events seems to cast on one set of factors over another. It reflects an understanding of the persisting complexity of world conditions. We see that even as political uncertainties in the Third World seem to diminish and economic risk becomes more homogenized, challenges arise in the Second World. From the developing free market in Eastern and Central Europe to the new politics of a fully emergent European Community, fresh sorts of uncertainty are surfacing that demand an intertwined analytical approach.

It is important to remember also that the economic and political/social categories each are inherently relevant to the bottom line. In the political category, for example, it is not just a revolution or surge of nationalism that can threaten a company's assets. Terrorism, civil disorder of one kind or another, labor agitation, anti-Western scapegoating and foreign policy initiatives, populist trends, a breach in communications between the local level and the center, conflicts arising from tensions between parochial and modern institutions and attitudes, and now even how nations redefine their borders and institutional relationships—all these factors and more can have negative and sometimes disastrous consequences for a foreign business deal.

On the economic side of a good planning perspective, one must expect that hard-currency reserves, debt service performance, inflation, growth in Gross Domestic Product, subsidized prices, and (now more than ever) the whole question of the interface between the public and private sectors are among a host of variables that can lead to outcomes that could swallow an investment.

Any of these conditions—political or economic—could have a direct impact on the personnel, installations, remittance of profits, and effective operations of an enterprise overseas. The very survival of a foreign company's investment in a host country could be in question. And some misjudgments can even leave a trail of legal and public relations troubles behind the actual surcease of the business enterprise.

Even if a political factor (such as erosion of middle-class support for the government) or an economic variable (such as pervasive subsidies) does not have an immediate or direct impact on doing a specific type of business in country X, an analysis of all the relevant conditions and a discussion of various ways in which they might combine to produce a worst-case scenario will influence the content and style of one's negotiation and will educate the operations and marketing executive in the field.

For current and future use, the operations executive will have in hand not just a set of possible "outcomes" for his or her country of responsibility, but a framework for unraveling events as they occur on the spot. The analysis will serve not just as a background study replete with projections but as a set of signposts and a game plan—a map for careful observation and planning. And taken a step or two farther, as the company settles into a new market, this early research can become a building block for the enterprise's becoming an integral part of the host country's broader business environment.

## Environment Assessment: An Approach to Weighing Political and Economic Risk Against Opportunity

We accept it as a matter of course in our home country that new business opportunities carry concomitant risks or drawbacks. In our business expansion domestically, we look for attendant risks in the nature of the deal itself or in circumstances directly related to the business at hand. They are usually visible or easily identifiable to us. We live with such risks or cope with them, usually as part of the transaction itself.

In unfamiliar cultural, legal, and institutional environments overseas, the astute businessperson can take much less for granted. Time and money can be lost in greater measure just in pursuing and negotiating a given overseas opportunity. Before a company rushes headlong into what the pressured marketing executive perceives to be a golden opportunity, one must weigh this opportunity against the potential business environment problems in a host country and compare it to opportunities elsewhere.

Let's call this aspect of international strategic planning "country business environment assessment." What might hitherto have been cloaked in a veil of secrecy and dubbed "political risk analysis" can be explicated systematically and understood. If there is an art to relating political and economic variables to impact on business, it is not a free-form art. We offer the analytical approach below as a way to cut through the newspaper headlines to the bottom line.

All new environments—from Tuscaloosa to Tanzania—have singular characteristics that might be problematic for a business deal. Of course, the developing countries are stranger to us, have procedures for doing business that are either less formalized or less in conformance with our own customs and seem to be *less predictable*. Thus, the variables discussed here have a distinct Third World orientation. They are also meant to reflect problems for the investor that might accompany the changes of the 1990s in Europe, where formerly planned economies are giving way to free-market adjustments and where whole maps are being redrawn.

Our discussion is not really directed at more stable areas like Australia or the Netherlands. But if these variables are taken as a total inventory of environmental risks and disincentives, some can be applicable. For the more developed and culturally familiar markets, the business planner will be able to use the inventory selectively to identify problems with a minimum of reinterpretation.

The factors below should be considered from two standpoints. First, does the problem exist or what is the *probability* that it will occur? Second, what would be the *impact* of such a problem or turn of events on foreign business in general or on a particular project? No matter how serious a problem, if it does not have a markedly negative impact on a particular business deal, the matter is not insurmountable.

Consciously or unconsciously, one necessarily ascribes weights to the problems in a given environment. Although the quantification of cross-cultural scenarios can lead to oversimplification and can block the way to substantive understanding of what is going on in a country, the use of numbers as a means of manipulating the end user's attention is not discouraged.

If a country environment analysis is done in a comprehensive and structured manner, it can be useful to attach numerical ratings to probability and impact and then add a further weighting to each of the variables under consideration. This is not really a quantitative adaptation of the variables, but rather a deliberate manipulation to reflect the analyst's subjective judgment. It might help the user and decision maker at different levels to sharpen his focus and to generate questions of his own.

In the pages that follow, the reader will be guided through a host of factors—sociocultural, political, commercial, economic, and financial—that historically have affected the environment for international investment and trade. Included are myriad examples and case illustrations that can provide a framework for analysis—a prism through which the reader will be able to view events and situations as they unfold with the undertaking of fresh explorations of unfamiliar markets.

*Part One*

# ASSESSING DOMESTIC CONDITIONS IN THE HOST COUNTRY: POLITICAL, SOCIAL, AND ECONOMIC

*Chapter 1*

# Assessing Domestic Political Conditions: An Inventory of Variables

## Leadership Succession

In all countries, but particularly those with authoritarian political systems, leadership succession can be a critical political problem. It becomes a political risk to the foreign business entity when procedures for a smooth transition of political leadership have not been constitutionally established or have not gained legitimacy among the elite (particularly in some Third World countries where the masses are relatively naive politically) or among the people at large.

A leadership succession crisis, generated by an uncharted change in leaders, causes uncertainty and turbulence at different levels of society and can be disruptive to business as usual. In countries where military governments actually have overturned an established civilian political process through a coercive takeover and maintain their rule by means of top-down controls, it becomes imperative before too long to restore a normal electoral process.

Look, for example, at Pakistan's return from military dictatorship to democracy. As the projected elections of 1985 approached, the question then was whether President Zia ul-Haq, who had seized power in a military coup, would be able to manage local and national elections on a nonparty basis (the intention being to exclude the PPP, the left-leaning followers of executed former President Zulfikar Ali Bhutto)

13

and to integrate an indirect military control into grass-roots civilian government. If, after seven years, Zia could not successfully bring off the promised election, his own staying power might be jeopardized. In yet another scenario, if Zia were to maintain a behind-the-scenes hold on a transparently superficial constitutional system, what would happen when he eventually left? Would a successor, more or less imposed upon the people, be as remarkably adroit at managing the political tensions that wrack a government lacking legitimacy?

As it happened, the reemergence of the electoral process in Pakistan broke the unsteady grip of the military. The horse got away from the soldier, and we no longer have to wonder whether a military successor will be as able to stay astride!

In the longer term, the unimpeded evolution of participatory democracy in that country offers an institutionalized stability that promises to be more enduring than the concentration of power in the most competent autocratic leader. The reality is that civilian successors to Zia might have fallen far short of the idealized picture of service in the national interest, but they have been elected by the people through constitutional means. A shared commitment to the system (particularly from the middle class) contributes to the prospect of social stability and ensures a certain continuity at the level of government where doing business usually matters.

## After the Departure of a Charismatic Leader

In cases where the departed leader has established himself as a result of his or her own eminence in a movement or national liberation struggle and appeals to the people on the basis of personal charisma, the lack of institutionalized procedures for succession assumes an even greater importance. In parts of Africa or Asia, the death of an individual who has guided a country through independence and into modernity might not only cause a leadership vacuum but might lead to a social identity crisis. The inhabitants might fall back on tribal or traditional identities or become so psychologically disoriented as to resort to anarchic behavior or emigration. In Kenya, Jomo Kenyatta's successor, Daniel arap Moi, has been threatened with assassination attempts and holds onto power through increasingly conspicuous repression; Ghana's civilian rule has been unsuccessful since the death of Kwame Nkrumah.

When such leaders depart, their symbols and doctrinal writings alone often are insufficient to see the country through the transitional period in an orderly manner. In Indonesia, the late President Sukarno's "Five People's Principles" (Pancasila) ring hollow when sounded by an elitist soldier republic; in Burma, now called Myanmar, the name of the departed independence leader U Nu elicits a contemptuous response from a new generation of intellectuals and students to whom his "Burmese Way to Socialism" seems empty when it is invoked by a seemingly ruthless, corrupt, and unreasoning military regime. Indeed, in the latter case, a nascent popular rebellion has been simmering while a newly emergent articulator of the people's interest, a woman and Nobel Prize–winning poet, Aung San Suu Kyi, sits at home in limbo-like official detention.

A corollary to the question of a succession after the death or departure of an important leader (one who has a broad following and either a mesmerizing effect or terrorizing hold on his people) is the power vacuum that his absence creates. What other leader has the strength to take his place and to command the loyalty of a broad constituency?

For example, the withdrawal of Burma's powerful postindependence leader Ne Win to a behind-the-scenes role has left the chairman of the ruling committee Saw Maung to face the 1990s with the desperate and tenuous last resort to bribery and coercion. Ne Win had shunted aside his more able successors. The new leadership's power base in an international era of democratizing trends is the military alone, and political power in that camp most certainly will grow out of the biggest gun! When even the military elite is antagonized by being excluded from an arbitrary demonetarization (removing and not replacing certain denominations of currency without notice), the man on the platform easily can lose his footing.

The power vacuum created by the absence of strong and viable leadership can lead to one military takeover after another in the fashion of musical chairs. And even with the onset of civilian rule, if an election is won by a weak compromise candidate who is unable to reverse an economic decline or build a base of lasting support, the military conceivably will intervene again. Worse still for an investor, a sustained power vacuum can reinforce the generativity of an antisystemic, grass-roots movement that might radically rewrite the rules of the game. Of course, such an outcome is not necessarily undesirable unless a foreign investor already is in the game.

In very hierarchical social systems from Asia to Mexico, even local leadership becomes a factor in stability and can be of concern to a foreign investor. In such cases, the people's real interaction with formal government occurs at a village or county level, and their perception of formal state authority and the political system's intervention is shaped at the bottom of a pyramid. The foreign businessperson too must deal with these local-level leaders, whether for special permits or licenses or for the negotiation and implementation of a contract.

During the early Cultural Revolution in China in the late 1960s, the Western business presence was minimal. But let's look at what happened when local party leaders were discredited in the People's Republic of China at the height of the Great Proletarian Cultural Revolution. People were thrown into a state of chaos. With social uncertainty, a potential for disorder, and no certain locus of decision making at the grass roots, business undertakings of any sort became paralyzed. The social trauma in China was so great that in the south the Cultural Revolution precipitated a wave of illegal emigration to Hong Kong. Such migrations traditionally had been more symptomatic of economic disaster and famine. The apotheosis during the Cutural Revolution period of Chairman Mao Zedong might have been an attempt to steady and unify society by lifting the locus of all authority to the heavens. (Staring at a godlike statue of himself in Tiananmen Square, Mao told American journalist Edgar Snow that he felt like a Buddhist monk in the rain without an umbrella.)

## *The Bottom Line*

Change of any sort naturally elicits anxiety, but leadership change in a less-developed country is not necessarily cause for alarm. On the contrary, some types of radical change in leadership at the top do not represent crises at all. In some Latin American countries, for example, a coup d'état, or golpe, against an apparently legitimate government is not necessarily a departure from normality in the context of the country's historical political culture. *In such cases, there can be stability in instability.*

The international planner must focus on impact. What effect would a succession crisis have on the type of foreign business in question? Perhaps none, if the project is not closely linked to the person of a departed leader. But consider that major construction projects undertaken in Ghana to enhance Nkrumah's prestige were particularly vulnerable after his ouster. In Indonesia, the pet developmental projects of Suharto's cabinet ministers could also be shelved with the advent of a new government.

## Uncertainty in Thailand

The impact on foreign investment can be more generalized if an uncertain, incoming regime defends itself against international criticism by overreacting nationalistically or blames an economic decline on the nature of the foreign business presence. In Thailand in 1992, a quasi-military government with civilian trappings uncomfortably tried to fill an immediate power vacuum by displacing a popularly elected, if truly questionable, president-elect with a senior military person. A longer-term power vacuum in the real sense had existed since well before the military's coup against the elected government in February 1991. The existence of a government, five of whose parties in parliament are promilitary and whose ultimate authority rests with the military, might not have appeared to have major repercussions for foreign investment. After all, most military-backed govenrments tend to be rather conservative and favor private enterprise, and Thailand's military is no exception.

But in 1992, the military emerged from behind the scenes. The duly elected, civilian prime minister with an apparently drug-tainted background, was pushed aside for a military candidate, Gen. Suchinda Krapayoon. The Bush administration supported his selection over the duly elected candidate. Discouraged by the illegitimacy of the government and so many years of de facto military government, the students within months took to the streets. Thailand has a long history of student protest. What matters now to the foreign businessperson is whether the momentum of the popular outbreak will be sustained in the months ahead. The draconian suppression of this mass unrest by the military has not necessarily put out the fire. The students want more, and they want revenge for the brutality of the military. The foreign investment community now must ask itself: Will business proceed as normal with the government's resignation and a "political cease-fire" negotiated by the king? Will the students and intellectual elite accept a compromise government in which the pivotal locus of real power still is the military and promilitary parties in parliament? Is the king enough of a living legitimating symbol to see Thailand through to a sort of compromise civilian government? Will an accommodation truly satisfy the parties who would take to the street and those who would bash their heads? As the King of Siam declared in the celebrated play *The King and I:* " 'Tis a puzzlement!''

The major consideration for all businesspeople now, Thai and American, witnessing a possible strengthening of parliamentary government is whether the rules of the game for doing business might change. Nothing so radical would be either likely or in anyone's best interests. Be careful, however, of a latent tendency even among the military (a year ago, then–military commander Suchinda Krapayoon took a rhetorical swipe at the Bush administration) to scapegoat U.S. investors in the face of continued domestic economic and social frustrations. Nevertheless, all other things being equal, a military-civilian combination of interests could be expected to toe the line, that is to say, the bottom line.

### Venezuela and Peru: Populist Elements of the Military

Although the military usually sides with the private sector, it should not be taken for granted that the military as an interest group will always be favorably inclined toward an unfettered free market and will encourage foreign investment. In some cases, a movement within the military can react nationalistically against what it perceives to be a civilian government's betrayal of the expectations of the people. A subjective frustration of upward mobility in the ranks can combine with populist sentiment to propel a segment of the armed forces against an elected government.

The abortive coups against President Carlos Andres Perez of Venezuela in 1992/1993 is a good example. Comprising middle-rank and second-rung officers and led by a thirty-seven-year-old lieutenant colonel who previously had been an instructor at Venezuela's military academy, the uprising in the army hoped to win the support of students, intellectuals, workers, and the "progressive" church. Among its apparent objectives: the reversal of the Perez government's removal of free-market restrictions and its introduction of austerity measures that had left more than half the population with less than one daily meal.

Some elements of the military in developing countries inherently can be prejudiced against industrialization and the foreign investment that has provided its impetus. In Peru, for example, a sizable portion of the armed forces have poor and rural backgrounds and have risen through the ranks while retaining their ties to their roots. If this segment of the armed forces (particularly the navy) were to assume power, prejudice might be translated into policy and further complicate an already troublesome situation for foreign investors in that country.

### When the Military Government Hangs on by Its Teeth

When the military eschews the political process as in Burma and rules unreasonably through a combination of bark, bite, and bribery, it is not likely to hold together a country that is fraught with ethnic divisions and liberation struggles. Absent a stable social environment, how can business be carried on as usual?

In all cases involving leadership succession problems, the strategic planner must ask: Are efforts being made in a potential host country to groom successors? Autocratic rulers might seem to want to cultivate protegés, but they also apparently have singular difficulty in reconciling themselves to their own political mortality and in delegating power to others. It often happens that if an emerging figure in the political elite becomes too popular or appears to be developing his own constituency, he is consigned to obscurity. President Suharto of Indonesia has fashioned a pattern of demoting ministers of state who become too popular. Former presidents Ahmadou Ahidjo of Cameroon and Ne Win of Burma each have found it difficult to release the grip of power once a successor has assumed office. Ahidjo actually attempted coups against his overly assertive successor Paul Biya and brought the country to the brink of civil war.

Another question to ask: If there is a succession struggle, are some factions better positioned than others? In Indonesia, for example, where interpersonal relations and cross-cutting alliances are so important, it is crucial to tie into the right political group, directly or indirectly, through an informal network of friends and acquaintances. If the Indonesians with whom one works closely are linked to a high-profile group that is identified with the current leadership, such a position can be advantageous in the short term but might be a liability if an opposing faction were to take control. On the other hand, an alignment with Indonesians whose political linkages are middle-of-the-road might gain less in dollars in the short term but make more sense in the event of succession.

A final problem for the corporate strategist is to examine the evolving attitudes and policies of the key political protagonist(s) as they pertain to foreign investment and trade in the appropriate product or service area. The planning group in a corporation must also gauge the extent to which a consensus has developed for that particular perspective. In other words, after the faction(s) that are apt to come to power are identified and their positions with regard to foreign investment in general and the enterprise in question are considered, the support of their power base must be assayed. (What cannot be learned through published materials often can be obtained through personal interviews and the chatty and informal queries of your own local executives.)

### Turkey As a Case of Successful Transition

In Turkey, the military (which had come to power during the violence of the 1970s) allowed the reconstruction of a constitutional
civilian government through the election of November 6, 1983. We
correctly anticipated that the opposition Motherland Party's candidate
Turgut Ozal would be chosen prime minister. The military junta, or
National Security Council, resigned their commissions and remained
as a governing advisory council under President (formerly General)
Kenan Evren. The potential for a tug-of-war between the two ruling
bodies still exists but seems less likely. The military is more bureaucratic and interventionist, yet never evidenced a firm commitment to
induce foreign businesspeople to invest. The paucity of investment
before the new political system was set right indeed reflected a suspi-
cion on the part of foreign investors that they would encounter the
same hostility as in the past in government and bureaucracy toward
foreign capital. Foreign businesspeople too have had an impression in
their memory of the ability of political forces to arouse an apparently
natural antagonism toward outsiders among the people.

We predicted in 1983 that Turgut Ozal, who already was recognized
for his open-door economic policy and his creation of a foreign
investment department when he was serving as deputy prime minister
under the military, would initiate policies favorable to Western business and would work toward building a consensus among his constituency for liberal policies toward foreign investment. The key question
was not whether the former International Monetary Fund (IMF) officer
would approve of investment but whether he would be able to survive
the rocky road of leadership transition and be able to develop legitimacy for the new government and its policies. He seems to have done
well, and has also established himself as a regional leader cooperative
with the United States.

Other than undermining an enterprise (which can include nationalization and expropriation of a company or default on a debt), a
leadership succession crisis stemming from the regime's loss of legitimacy can impede business as usual and jeopardize company expatriate
personnel living in the host country. Your own installations, operations, and personnel certainly are at risk when a power vacuum in the
absence of proper leadership leads to anomic civil disorder and chaos.
Witness the case of mob violence in India by the Sikhs, who have been
on the rise since the assassination of Indira Gandhi and, later, her son
Rajiv.

The awareness that elite factions are competing for the rule of the country also can lead to an unreasonable assertiveness on the part of interest groups, including the staging of widespread strikes. And in a demonstration of the interrelatedness of politics and economics, a political leadership crisis also can cause a lack of confidence among the people that extends to a mass run on banks and capital flight. Concomitant currency controls would paralyze a foreign company's operations.

The question of leadership succession crisis usually has applied to Third World countries where leadership has been embodied in one person with whom the people have come to identify closely, where there are no established procedures for leadership transition, or where such procedures have not obtained sufficient legitimacy to ward off an interloper. Now, the emergence of a new political complexion and the creation of new nation states in the former Soviet Union and Eastern Europe pose an even greater challenge to the business planner and ought to become a prime focus of our attention.

## *Applied to a More or Less Developed World: Spain As a Case*

In a still more general sense, the "leadership succession" problem also can be applied to analysis of the more routine processes of change in leadership or party administration in relatively developed countries. Spain is an interesting case study.

Since the death of Francisco Franco in November 1975, Spain has developed into a democracy—in form, a constitutional monarchy. Although Spain has since withstood coup attempts by two groups within the military and security forces, the country's democratic institutions are still fragile and have not really gained a grounding in history. It is still too easily to be sure about the steadfastness of democratic institutions in Spain and its people's (particularly the military's) commitment to them. Felipe Gonzalez's socialist (PSOE) government won handily in the October 1989 election and the Cortes (parliament) is fundamentally centrist. The fascists per se, the extreme far right, have a constituency of only about 1 percent of the voting public; the communists (formerly the PCE), weakened after the 1986 election, joined forces with other far-left parties to form Izquierda Unida (IU), still garnering only a handful of seats in the Cortes. Therefore, the threat from either the left or the far right is negligible. A critical problem is that the earlier and almost charismatic appeal of Gonzalez has worn thin as a result of economic hardship and an austerity program, the party's veering to a more economically conservative hue, conspicuous corruption in the upper echelon of party and government, Gonzalez's own increasing aloofness, and a general perception of stagnation and despair that there is no alternative to the Gonzalez government.

In a hypothetical sense, if an economically desperate situation were to call for an immediate proactive agenda for the people, or if the government were to become bogged down in inertia with right-center or left-center parties unable to form a coalition to unseat Gonzalez, the military might intervene "for the sake of the country." In another scenario, if President Gonzalez were to be assassinated, the military certainly could take over. His persona has come to symbolize post-Franco democracy in Spain.

A short time ago, before the experience of the threat to Perez in Venezuela in 1992, such scenarios would have been considered unlikely even in a young democracy like Spain. If no coalition develops between left-center or right-center or between the remnants of the old centrist UCD and the right-wing Popular Alliance, the system will get stale fast. Fortunately, the memory of Franco still is imprinted on the minds of the Spanish people and militates against a military usurpation of power. But fascism could recur in a different guise. In any case, the future of the current political system is uncertain as long as the mantle remains unpassed. Although the PSOE government will continue to remain hospitable to foreign investment, the corporate investor needs to be prepared for political winds that might shift suddenly.

Thus, in Spain a matter of constitutional transition could become a constitutional crisis if no real transition in fact takes place. And this sort of crisis in the best of circumstances, where all viable factions favor foreign investment to a greater or lesser extent, still could have an indirect bearing on the psychological environment for the foreign business entity.

## Crisis of Legitimacy of a Regime

Whereas the previously discussed leadership succession question tends to revolve about the *uncertainty* of the process of change from one leadership to another, a legitimacy crisis occurs when the very form, procedures, and institutions of government fail to establish *credibility* among the people or lose that trust after protracted failure to perform the functions expected of them. In simple metaphor, to maintain itself effectively over time, a political system must build up a reserve in its bank. This is accomplished through outputs that serve the aggregate needs of society and justify the continued existence of a regime even in the face of adversity.

The legitimacy of a system is so difficult to measure and quantify (in part because culturally the limits of tolerance of a system's performance vary) that it is extremely difficult to convince senior management to limit or withdraw an investment from a host country or even to pay attention to what is happening. This was my experience when a professional colleague tried to convince his own company to pull out of Iran even as the Shah's regime was tottering on the front pages.

## Tunisia As a Case

Tunisia illustrates how legitimacy can come to constitute a problem. Although the December 1983–January 1984 bread riots raised the question of leadership succession in that country and indeed served as one catalyst for change, it was really the ongoing erosion of legitimacy of the Bourguiba government that led to an intervention. Habib Bourguiba, the nation's independence leader since 1957, had enjoyed a nearly charismatic hold on his people in earlier days. As he became progressively more senile with illness and began to lose credibility before his people, the grace he enjoyed began to lose its gloss. Mme. Bourguiba's meddling in "palace politics" with the prime minister, other cabinet ministers, and the head of the ruling Destourian Party was shaming the office and the image of the republic; the government's ineptness in economic management and inability to implement equitable, or at least politically clever, austerity measures had triggered riots; the largest trade union increasingly was appearing to be the handmaiden of the Bourguiba regime; and the nation's party system had been undermined by the apparent rigging of the election of 1981.

In 1986, we predicted either a grass-roots upheaval led by some militant Islamic movement or, more likely, a top-down military coup. What happened was that when Bourguiba sought to make martyrs out of militant Islamic dissidents instead of controlling them with some political adroitness, State Minister of the Interior Zine al-Abidine Ben Ali took the helm. The 1987 takeover was indeed constitutional, the cabinet exercising its right to intercede should the president's health prevent him from competent leadership. But what happened never could have occurred during the first decades of Habib Bourguiba's charmed, authoritarian presidency.

## Peru

Particularly in an era of trumpeted "democratizing" trends world-wide, the legitimacy of a government can be tricky to define. Western democrats tend to apply norms and value judgments that might not fit some political cultures or societies in their stage of development. When President Alberto Fujimori of Peru dissolved parliament with the backing of the military, his avowed purpose was to cope with corruption, with courts that would not mete justice to drug traffickers, and with the challenge of the ominous guerrilla organization *Sendero Luminoso* (Shining Path). The Bush administration and others were quick to condemn the action as a *golpe* (coup d'état) that would be self-defeating and would undermine the legitimate process. The foreign investors found themselves with as much to fear from an edginess in the host country (already in a state of crisis) as from international pressures and sanctions.

Arguably, a system's legitimacy ought to be culturally determined. Reports indicated that 70 percent of Peruvians surveyed approved of Fujimori's suspension of rules and freedoms as an alternative to uncontrollable social violence. Peru's regional neighbors like Colombia and Argentina had experienced an intolerable sort of chaos in earlier times. In another part of the world, a successful Turkish democracy emerged from military intervention to quell social violence in the 1970s, and effectively orchestrated the return to civilian rule. The results were salutary to stabilizing the business environment and bringing fresh investment into the economy. But in Peru, as long as the *Sendero Luminoso* continues to wage an effective internal war and legitimate government remains suspended, the political and social situation can be defined by its own frightening state of emergency.

## Colombia: A Case of Questionable Legitimacy

In Colombia, the key issue in past years has seemed to be the political system's legitimacy. This author recalls that American businesspeople interviewed in summer 1984 were sure they understood the situation because they had been situated in the capital city and could observe daily events. A representative of the U.S. Chamber of Commerce there argued that investment conditions could not be better because the economy seemed to be on a slight upswing (he had been charting long-term trends), an anticipated maxidevaluation had not taken place and did not seem imminent, and the recently elected government seemed to be resolving a long-standing and widespread problem of guerrilla terrorism.

During the years that followed, by conventional guidelines, these American expatriate commentators from Bogota seemed to have been mistaken. Their perspective was based on a proximity to separate events (they looked at the parts rather than the whole) and a natural bias that stemmed from the vested interests of the marketing executive. Guerrilla violence in Colombia increased, and the country's president announced that the treasury was on the verge of bankruptcy. For the shorter-term businessperson, the psychological uncertainty alone of working in a state of crisis was unnerving.

The erosion of the government's legitimacy increased as the country continued to be ruled by a tight oligarchy and the guerrillas and bandits remained untamed in spite of the best efforts of the military. Voter turnout for intervening presidential elections was averaging at about a 50 percent level. This apathy was compounded by the system's incapacity for some time to deal with worsening economic conditions. It began to gnaw away at the legitimacy of political institutions. Pervasiveness of the phenomenon of corruption from an illegal drug trade (narcotics are Colombia's biggest export), as well as ambivalence over suppressing it, served to discredit the political parties, state bureaucracy, legislature, and the judicial branch. In the late 1980s, we could envision the possibility in the future of a creeping military, or military-backed, takeover.

As the situation stands in the early 1990s, foreign business interests did suffer in the process, but the worst political scenarios never came to pass. Instead, as the case study on Colombia later in the book intimates, a new "narco-democracy" is evolving. The infusion of hard currency from narcotics into the Colombian economy corrupts, but it can also be regenerative in a sense, rescuing the balance-of-payments situation and strengthening the country's hard-currency reserves. The "narcoterrorism" in the wake of general protest over the assassination of a popular candidate for the presidency, an ardent democrat and an opponent of drug trafficking, in a tragic way made the government reach an accommodation with the narcotics cartels. It also induced a certain resignation among the people. A rotting system got a reprieve simply because people seemed to adjust their social values downward. Now, despite an atmosphere of generalized violence and the continuation of civil war, the new-found wealth has been properly distributed among the elite and the "trickle-down" effect from drug sales has made popular resistance more manageable. Illegitimacy seems to have been accepted as legitimate, and Colombia continues to "muddle through."

Every new political system accumulates legitimacy, or credibility, only gradually over time. Similarly, failures of the system to perform, such as our own Watergate scandal, or an inability to set right a foundering economy, are resounding faults that tend to diminish or at least call into question this legitimacy. Once a regime loses its "creditworthiness"—and this happens only after many failures to carry out the essential mandate of its constituency (sometimes this group comprises only the articulate elite and does not include a politically inactive majority of the people)—it may have to resort to force of arms. The more the regime must resort to force to quell riots or protests, quash an attempted coup, or suppress guerrilla activity, the more it demonstrates its weakness. And sooner or later, it is replaced. It is up to the international environment analyst, whether he or she works for a bank or international products and various types of service industries, to be aware of a political system's developing political bankruptcy, to identify those groups prepared to mount a challenge to the ruling order, to gauge their relative strengths, and then to try to anticipate the timing.

## Frustration of Rising Expectations and Hopes for Upward Social Mobility

As members of a capitalist society, most of us want and strive to better ourselves. Even members of societies that theoretically are more equitable want to be better than equal. What is at first an economic question of survival and comfort also assumes a psychologically competitive animus. Less-privileged people want to escape the dreariness of their lives. In Third World countries, a peasant's fantasies often embrace visions of the modern sector and the promise it might hold for him. In a world in which a radio or television can be found in almost every village and in which transportation networks make travel to the city a possibility, peasants are less inclined to stay on the traditional farm and eke out an uncertain living. Instead they move to the cities, often to discover that they are not easily employable. There they endure crowded neighborhoods of slums and hovels because they hope to become regularly employed workers. In many developing agrarian societies, a gainfully employed worker is considered part of the broader middle class. Once an individual has attained middle-class status, he moves to a better neighborhood and continues to look upward.

Frustration can occur at any point in the upward mobility of members of a developing society. It stems from the promise of economic and social rewards, or even the fleeting taste of those rewards, and then the failure to attain and hold onto them. Never to experience "progress" is less disturbing psychologically than to experience it and then undergo a setback. In the cities of developing countries, frustration of upward mobility is often compounded by such phenomena as psychological uprootedness, poor housing conditions, population density, and growing political awareness in the crowded urban slums and barrios. At bottom, it springs from inflation, layoffs, and denial of opportunity for advancement. When similar frustrations are shared by many, they can become political. The collective frustrations can be manifested through the legitimate utilization of the electoral process, or they can be expressed more explosively through "bread riots" (caused by the reduction of subsidies on staples), work stoppages, isolated strikes, or general strikes. The more compelling the sense of personal frustration and the less receptive the authorities to consider articulated grievances, the more likely seems to be the possibility of some sort of civil disorder.

What types of developments in a given country could alert the analyst to possible trouble? First, an example of a political act that could have been destabilizing was the promise of new housing that Belisario Betancur offered the people when he ran for the presidency of Colombia in the early 1980s. Ultimately, 1.45 million people submitted applications for a total of 50,000 units available.

In developing countries, as in the United States and the rest of the developed world, the middle class is particularly vulnerable to inflation and economic recession. In Nigeria, the firing of many government workers within months of Muhammed Buhari's coup in December 1983 contributed to the erosion of middle-class support for the new government. (In earlier years, it had become apparent how dependent an earlier military regime had been for its support on the middle class).

In recent years, "middle class" has come to represent a newfound status for a large proportion of people. In parts of the more advanced Southeast Asia of the 1990s, factories teem with *unionized* workers, and white-collar government employees suddenly are either unhappy about the uneven increase in wages or have the newfound latitude in their lives to pursue new nonmaterialistic goals, such as greater political participation. In sum, once people have something, it is not just a question of holding on to what they have achieved, but getting something more. In the 1992 riots in Bangkok, students, government work-

ers, and unionized workers were in the streets putting their lives on
the line for a greater say in the political process.

Rising expectations therefore gain momentum as new goals are met.
They are felt especially acutely among the educated in secondary
schools and universities. Many of these young people represent the
first generation in their families to obtain an education, usually at
considerable sacrifice to their parents. Their families share the expectation that they will enter the technocracy. In Cameroon, university
graduates in large numbers search for appropriate positions in their
homeland, but neither the bureaucracy nor the industrial base can
accommodate them. Could they not constitute a source of antisocial
or political instability in the system? In Turkey's transition to democracy, its economy is doing rather well. The irony is that because of its
progress and prosperity, Turkey will have to deal with a large pool of
educated people who will be seeking an important role for themselves
in the adult world. If they are frustrated in their search, they could
become a potent source of political pressure on the system.

### Disaffection of Middle-Class, Professional Support
### Toward the Regime

In developing countries suffering from economic and social deterioration, the middle class can be pivotal. And the question of rising
expectations, just discussed, is closely wedded to the development of
this class in a modernizing society.

Historically, in any prerevolutionary situation, this class has comprised waverers. Let the government overreact to mass violence with
violence of its own, and these equivocal supporters can become
radicalized. Any one of our readers who ever has stood on the edge of
a political demonstration as a neutral observer probably is aware of the
effect of a bullying and billying squad of police appearing on the scene
with the explicit mandate to break up the crowd; one can have one's
head turned easily with a few swings of the stick.

If this class can serve as the swing group in a politically confronta-
tional situation, it also is the pool from which a dissatisfied "counterelite" might emerge. Young, educated members of the middle class are
most susceptible as they attempt to carve a niche for themselves in the
adult world and improve the economic lot of their families of origin.
As revolutionists in China, Mao Zedong, Zhou Enlai, and Deng Xiaoping, if not strictly middle class in origin, all belonged to the group of

newly educated in their country. A student counterelite in today's China, tinder for the likes of the Tiananmen massacre, also persists as a spark for igniting protest at critical moments throughout urban China. Among the seriously alienated in the younger generation of Chinese must surely be individuals who, bereft of the ideological symbols of a previous generation, still await a new dawn economically for themselves and crave a more participatory political role.

The M-19 guerrilla organization in Colombia, antigovernment in the past, has comprised educated, middle-class students who feel excluded by age *and* class from the political process. These people hold great expectations both about advancement in economic status and participation in the political process; in many instances, able to look over their shoulders and see their own family's poor origins, they want to be part of a process of social change that will ensure a future for themselves and their children.

Just as a middle-class loss of confidence can indicate an erosion of a system's legitimacy, its forbearance can shore up an established order. In some Latin American countries, a conservative, Roman Catholic middle class might put up with infringements of human rights to avoid a period of extreme disorder and chaos. The majority of the Argentine middle class apparently was willing to endure the anti-Peronist police terror of the military junta for some time because the military seemed to be a preferable alternative at first to the tyranny of guerrillas and Peronist terrorists in the streets. Only very slowly, and under changed social and economic circumstances, did sympathies turn significantly in the direction of the families that had suffered seemingly unjustifiable and deplorable "disappearances" of their close relatives. It took not only the experience of being touched in some personal way by the regime's reign of terror, but the crunch of economic chaos and the humiliation of defeat in a war with the British for the Argentine middle class to abandon the military government.

Because the movements of a Third World country's middle class can be like shifting sands, they should not be overinterpreted. Nevertheless, the appropriate bank officers or operations executives of a corporation should try to gauge their sentiments, particularly at a time of significant social or economic change. Similarly, one should observe how well the regime is attempting to develop a consensus for major policy innovations among this ever-broadening social stratum. The untroubled implementation, for example, of an IMF-induced economic austerity program can hinge on the limits of middle-class tolerance. Even if violence erupts in the streets, a more reflective middle class can serve as the mainstay of the regime and support the argument for giving short-term hardship a chance to work.

It is not so difficult to gain an impressionistic sense of the support of the middle class for the political system. Intelligence information can be garnered from the newspapers targeted at this class, from conversations with university professors and informal chats with shopkeepers and, secondhand, from local journalists and other knowledgeable sources in the community. Even cab drivers now in Third World urban centers can serve as the same sort of barometer of middle-class alienation that New York cabbies have personified. Sometimes this shadowy information can suggest positive evolutionary trends within the political-social system. In Turkey, middle-class enthusiasm for the civilian system bodes well for its future. In economically strained Latin American countries like Venezuela and Peru, where the wealth has become still more inequitably distributed, middle-class and student disaffection with official corruption and skewed social and economic policies have given impetus to the consideration of more radical alternatives like the instrument of a populist military coup (in the case of Venezuela) or the inadvertent opening of a greater window of opportunity to a people's guerrilla movement (in Peru).

### Corruption

Corruption is a critical issue—and yet a tricky one—for the foreign businessperson. The businessperson from a Western country must approach the question of corruption in a host country from at least two perspectives. A moralistic strain in the American culture in particular, reflected in the Carter administration's promulgation of the Foreign Corrupt Practices Act, tends to carry over into the U.S. businessperson's worldview and behavior overseas. Therefore, it is important to make an analytical distinction between the sort of institutionalized corruption in host countries that serves as a traditionally acceptable income supplement and the other category of special payoffs, bribes, and kickbacks to officials that in sheer enormity exceeds the acceptable bounds of propriety in that country and jeopardizes the legitimacy of the existing political system.

In many societies, corruption *in a manner of speaking* (usually informal payoffs, direct and indirect) has been institutionalized, sometimes over a span of centuries. Informal practices took root for redistributing wealth or compensating for the low salaries of government employees. In premodern China, scholar-gentry who ascended to official positions were given prebends (state-owned properties) as compensation for their service to the Confucian state. In turn, they theoretically took care of even the poorest in their large, extended families. In more recent decades in Indonesia, active military officers have been permitted to hold positions in business, in part to ensure their loyalty but also to supplement their low salaries and militate against the possibility of excessive corruption. Only if we arrogantly project our own Calvinist values on other cultures can we regard any of these practices as reprehensible. Even bribes and "facilitators" theoretically ought to be treated as the way some societies work.

However, when the intensity and breadth of official corruption surpass the threshold of tolerance of a country's own people, venality must be regarded as a threat to the stability of the political system. It can pose a direct hazard to those foreign businesses that have become personally involved in projects developed under the aegis of highly profiled members of the political inner circle whose futures are uncertain.

As people become more politically aware, they become more critical of unbounded corruption. For instance, where the level of corruption among a narrow elite has risen in direct proportion to newly found oil wealth and has exacerbated already existing social inequities, the middle class may become more disgruntled and begin to identify more with the poor and disenfranchised, thereby placing the system in a state of disequilibrium. In cases like Thailand, over the years corruption increasingly has become a popular issue of attention and is now inciting protest from a broader cross-section of organized labor and the middle class. In Colombia, narcotics-related corruption pervades the political system at all levels and in the legislature, judiciary, and political parties. The phenomenon is as widespread as a quickly metastasizing cancer. The question becomes one of whether the convolution of legitimacy of the political institutions and the loss of the active support of the educated middle class can be offset by the "trickle-down effect" on the whole economy.

In those countries with a historical pattern of military coups, corruption seems to have had a special appeal as a rallying point for the military. Official misbehavior, compounded by other social and economic problems, can be an invitation for the troops to file out of the barracks.

## Secular and Sacred Ideologies

When either a secular ideology or a religion takes on the characteristics of a political force, it can become an organizing ethos for challenging the system—a sort of cement that can hold a revolutionary entity together. The very political and structured organization of the Shia Muslim sect and its eschatological appeal provided a cause, a goal, and a psychological identity for the Iranian revolution.

Political religion (both secular and church-related) can perform similar functions for smaller-scale social protests and civil disobedience, both of which at worst can target business installations and/or disrupt operations, and at best can be alarming to the members of families of expatriate employees of a given country. It is truly uncomfortable to have to take shelter from a hysterical mob driven by a sense of moral self-righteousness.

Such movements can have a traumatic effect on the existing political system. In the 1960s in South Vietnam, militant Cao Dai Buddhists organized demonstrations that had a very negative and psychologically destabilizing effect on the political mood and indirectly increased the effectiveness of Communist activities. In Algeria in January 1992, the military had to intercede to prevent an Islamic government from legitimately assuming power through parliamentary election. In what is still very much a garrison state, the military annulled the vote in the runoff elections just as the fundamentalist Islamic Salvation Front (FIS) was on the verge of winning a majority. Later, the court banned the Islamic Salvation Front from the political process. The fear was that a weakened and scandal-racked National Liberation Front, the one party in power since 1962, would be replaced by a reckless and unpredictable government that would interpose Islamic strictures on secular behavior and would discourage foreign investment as part of a general condemnation of Westernization. Even in Indonesia, which the average Westerner tends to link with an oriental mystique, Islamic militants pose a problem, staging riots from time to time. Indonesia has the largest Muslim population in the world, and more young Indonesians have been turning to fundamentalist Islam in search of meaningful values as an alternative to a materialist life style.

In the past century, Marxism-Leninism has been the most common revolutionary ideology in the developing world. In the formation of many Third World nation states, democracy *cum* capitalism did not provide a cogent thought system that could easily be communicated to lower echelons of leadership or to the masses. Marxism, the natural panacea, offered a centrally planned program of postrevolutionary economic development for the deprived. As many scholars have noted, it also served as a stick with which to beat the Western world and therefore was well suited to national liberation movements of various kinds. With the shattering of the Marxist-Leninist system in the former Soviet Union itself and the discrediting of centrally planned economies, only a few countries cling to its tenets.

But many so-called Marxist-Leninist movements still exist in the backwater areas of still-divided countries from Africa to Southeast Asia, posing a threat to foreign oil installations and other types of infrastructure and endangering expatriate workers and lines of supply. Both Marxism-Leninism and the more militant forms of Islam have been the two ideologies that have most frequently served as focal points for political unrest in developing countries. It is probably fair to say that as Marxism-Leninism ceases to offer any long-term functional appeal, or is simply retained in name by certain states just to define the revolutionary origins of the country, its impetus will wane. But the specter of the Islamic jihad will continue to move forward in stops and starts, posing a real threat to some critical aspects of modernization.

In Burma, the Buddhist religion has played a militant role, but Buddhism has never been the guiding force of a modern political movement. The Buddhist monks in Burma at one time might have aligned themselves with the Burmese Communist Party, representing a secular antiestablishment ideology, but the communists destroyed themselves through internal fighting and the politically active monks have attached themselves instead to the coalition based in rebel-held territory in Manerplaw on the Thai border. The "Coalition Government of the Union of Burma" is centered on the figure of the poet and charismatic social leader Aung San Suu Kyi.

An ideology—a denunciation of the political economic status quo, a set of goals and objectives, a presentation of the means to achieve those ends, and the promise of a utopia at the end of the rainbow—is an essential force for binding together an antiestablishment movement bent on either revolution or demonstrations of militant social protest. In societies where the economically disenfranchised and most politically frustrated people have been displaced from their villages and are leading isolated and psychologically dislocated lives in dense urban slum areas, or where traditional ethnic and religious differences have made persons naturally mistrustful of one another, political religion is an indispensable tool for organizing against the existing political order and social hierarchy. Too often, however, the foreigner and specifically

the foreign investor can become targeted in theory and/or practice as a
spoiler, an agent of corruption, and become a scapegoat for a panoply
of problems.

## Demographic Patterns

At a level deeper than focusing on the expressions of discontent with a
particular political system, the strategic planner can look at population
growth and distribution trends in order to pinpoint undercurrents of
tension within a social system. A good example of the burdensome
effect of population growth on the economic complexion of a country
is Kenya. Exceeding its own yearly increase in Gross Domestic Product, Kenya's annual population growth rate of about 4 percent is
among the highest in the world. More than half the population is under
the age of fifteen. Eighty percent of the country's people are for the
most part concentrated on the 20 percent of the land considered arable.
The population will double to 35 million by the year 2000. Because
procreation in numbers is a sacred testament to masculinity in Kenyan
society, politicians are timid about pressing the issue of population
control.

### *Unemployment and Rural-to-Urban Migration*

Land subdivision, drought, the pressures of subsistence living in the
countryside, and the appeal of what seems from afar to be a more
comfortable life in the cities have led to a constant stream of refugees
from the countryside to the urban centers. This problem is shared by
most developing countries to a greater or lesser extent, and it is
important to assess the various pressures brought to bear on the
system and how well the system seems to be withstanding them. First,
an extreme rural-to-urban imbalance can make inroads on the country's agricultural productivity, sometimes transforming a net exporter
of food into a country that is no longer self-sufficient in feeding itself.
Even people who are driven from the countryside by a temporary
natural calamity like drought or flooding are unlikely to return to the
land. Second, migration into the cities is socially and psychologically
dislocating. If, as in Algeria, whole families tend to migrate together,
the social problem is not as grave. But more often it happens that
family members are separated from one another, and the newcomers
to the big cities feel isolated, alien, and emotionally disoriented.

Frustrated by urban living conditions that do not measure up to their earlier fantasies, they can easily fall prey to antisystemic groups that offer friendship and identity through an appropriate ideology that reflects the cleavage between the "haves" and "have-nots." Third, the population flow from the outlying areas to the high-density cities puts pressure on the more modern sector of the economy to provide adequate housing and social services (most often it simply fails to cope with the problem) and to absorb the new manpower into the employment force. Some unique countries like South Korea, with successful social health care plans and a continually expanding industrial base, have been able to absorb the flow. But even Korea has found it useful to establish special economic zones in some of the outlying towns in order to forestall an even greater shift of the population to the major cities than the current proportion of 75 percent.

Throughout the developing world, unemployment and underemployment in the cities are on the ascendant because of the phenomenon of unrelenting waves of hopeful migrants descending on the cities and because of a continuing world recession. In some areas of Africa, unemployment and underemployment in the urban areas approach 30 percent of the work force. At the same time, the government cannot afford to increase its public spending, nor can industry expand at a rate fast enough to absorb this manpower. The disbanding of failed state enterprises in several countries has contributed to the large number of idle, unemployed men who can easily be spurred to civil violence.

### Migration from Beyond the Borders

Some countries have the added problem of immigration from neighboring countries, where either economic and social conditions are worse or internal civil war has made life unendurably insecure and unstable. A heavy flow of migrant workers exists in the Middle East between the poorer countries and the oil-rich states, posing a problem of different cultures intermingling in an uncertain manner and perhaps even infusing a new element of more militant Islam into the host country. In Mexico—already suffering from a serious population problem—the influx of Guatemalan Indian refugees has put enormous pressure on an economic system already sapped by its own population. North American Free Trade Zone aside, if social violence in Central America ever were to escalate again, this problem would be compounded. (This has been one very practical reason why Mexico has

worked so hard to persuade the U.S. government to decrease its
involvement in Central America and permit the civil war to ebb in
Nicaragua and El Salvador.)

## Age Demographics: Youth and Politics

Many countries in the developing world experienced a big bulge in
the rate of population growth in the 1960s. Even if the rate of population increase has decreased since that time as a result of the world
campaign concerning birth control and unilateral efforts on the part of
governments to educate their people and make contraceptives available, a large proportion of the total populations already is of working
age. In Colombia, although the population growth rate had declined
from 3 percent in the 1960s to 2.4 percent by the end of the 1980s,
more and more young people have flooded the work force as we enter
the 1990s. Still other countries that have been slow to limit population
growth have an even more disproportionate number of youth and
young adults who have been hard pressed to find a place in the active
work force. In the "more advanced" less-developed countries (LDCs),
where the secondary and higher educational system is now well developed, young graduates are looking for positions commensurate with
their training. In many cases, the bureaucracies are already swollen
and the industrial base has not developed at a sufficient pace to absorb
these young people, particularly the better educated among them.

Although these new candidates for the work force have the option of
expressing themselves through the vote, participation in the actual
"moving and shaking" of the political process and selection of programmatic priorities is usually not open to them. In so many societies,
a gerontocracy actually prevails in the formal and informal political
structures of society down to the grass-roots level. Adults, who have
been involved in the struggle for a while, can become inured to the
system. But members of the younger generation, exposed to modern
ideas and full of adolescent expectations about autonomy and proving
themselves in adult work roles to their families of origin, often become
frighteningly impatient with the impenetrability of the marketplace.

Look at the youth of China. In the decades following the Cultural
Revolution in China, educated youths were politically frustrated from
their earlier experiences and were wary of the risks to life or status of
making too great a political commitment. Many reportedly chose to
rechannel their efforts into economic pursuits when they had the
opportunity.[1] Educated youth in the China of the 1990s, still not

content with the lack of openness of the political system, could turn again to protest if thwarted in their pursuit of economic opportunity. Under such circumstances, they might find some common ground with the increasing pool of unemployed workers who have been laid off for being insufficiently productive.

In so many countries, young adults in effect are both economically and politically disenfranchised. Armed with an education and ability to communicate, and susceptible to new ideals ranging from Communism to the Koran, they are both potential leaders and recruits for dissident movements. Large numbers of bitter youth (educated and uneducated alike), who hang out idle and unemployed in the cities, are positioned to spark broader outbursts of civil unrest. This is a very real political hazard that can be monitored by operations executives on site.

## Manpower, Labor Agitation, and Worker Participation in Management

Over the years, the local labor question has been one of the greatest problems for the foreign investor. Is the labor force as a whole reliable, adequately trained, or sufficiently well educated to absorb special training for the tasks at hand? Will a new enterprise have to cope with absenteeism or various expressions of ineffective productivity by poorly motivated workers and lower-level managers? Will the foreign investor be put in the situation of negotiating for more expatriates on the job against a host country's disposition to have new job opportunities created for its own people? Will this version of technology transfer be feasible, and at what cost to the foreign investor? Is it not possible that in the end many of the local personnel, particularly executives, will be hired for appearance rather than performance? In Indonesia, for example, we have observed that in many cases the real enterprise, comprising expatriate managers, acts as "consultant" to the operating company.

Yet in this new era of globalization, the reservoir of educated youth who could not be absorbed by their countries' growth-stunted economic infrastructures now might be more adaptable to new technologies with proper conditions of cooperation in technology transfer between foreign and host countries. And in some countries in the less-developed world, the manpower force—increasingly well trained and less expensive than their counterparts in the most developed areas—

can be a critical determinant of choosing a new manufacturing or marketing location. Countries like Israel, with the national security imperative of having to remain on a war footing, have made great strides in training their young people in higher technology. This country makes an excellent site for members of the computer industry.

## An Activist Labor Force

Viewed from a more negative perspective, the work force sometimes can not only be unproductive but can act as a potential source of dissonance and disruption—a dagger in the side of any enterprise establishing itself in an unfamiliar overseas country. The threat to the integrity and smooth operation of a newly established company that could be posed by excessive agitation on the part of locally organized labor is almost self-evident. Work stoppages and strikes are capable of paralyzing local operations; moreover, if such actions have political overtones, they might become part of a much larger, nationwide social movement that could have an impact on international business or even the private sector as a whole. It is important to become informed about national confederations of unions in a host country, their links with the major political parties or the governing elite, and how effectively they can control their member unions at the grass-roots level. (Like our own AFL-CIO or Teamsters, some of the federations are not quite as effective at gathering input at the lower level of the rank and file and aggregating and articulating those demands before the political policy-makers as in manipulating and controlling their members.)

Only a decade ago in Tunisia, the UGTT was a militant movement whose leaders were jailed. By the mid-1980s, it was evolving into an apparent ally—if not instrument—of the government. In Venezuela, where once the powerful CTV had considerable influence over the Acción Democratica (AD) Party, presidents from Lusinchi to Carlos Andres Perez and the AD itself no longer have seemed to ascribe as much priority to labor's interests. As a result, either the union could ossify or there could be a resurgence of strikes. In any case, the advantage of one large labor confederation is that it is usually either controllable or already part of the established system.

Still another factor that might invite further analysis of the dynamics of organized labor is the extent to which multiple labor federations might be utilized by competing parties and politicians, or the extent to which unions themselves might compete for power and support. As in the early Peronist movement in Argentina in the 1950s, such labor federations occasionally are manipulated by dissident, fringe political parties to throw their massive weight against the established order. Demonstrations and general strikes can ensue to disrupt operations by paralyzing urban services. When politics and rivalry within the labor union movement become interwoven, the effect of the contest can have a direct impact on business operations. An example has been the contest in Spain between the communist-led union, Comisiones Obreras, and the socialist-controlled UGT. As Gonzalez has maneuvered to bolster his own socialist union's standing vis-à-vis the communists, management could be subjected to increasing pressures for more concessions.

Much less predictable is a situation in which the larger federations have become inactive or where there are no national unions at all. Under such circumstances, local unions can develop more autonomy; they are less hierarchical, more informal, and more united in purpose. In Morocco, the large UMT is controlled by the government, and the more militant opposition union seems to have been coerced into passivity. In such an atmosphere, scattered and localized wildcat strikes have occurred among taxi drivers, teachers, and some other groups. Under conditions of austerity and economic squeeze, local unions on both the left and right of the political spectrum are apt to become more aggressive. However, it is important to note that workers' strikes at mines and other extractive and infrastructural projects can be isolated and policed fairly easily.

A final factor to consider is that Western-style trade unions are now taking root among more skilled workers in countries like South Korea and Thailand. For these new middle-class Asians and for the governments, Western-style trade unions were at first uncomfortably foreign and have only been integrated into the organism of the host country after some disruption. South Korea, for example, experienced some serious work stoppages during the 1980s and early 1990s. The government will have to continue to be responsive to this new, activist pressure group.

## Worker Participation in Management

A trend is taking place among the political elites of both developed and developing countries toward worker participation in management decision making. It has been variously motivated. In some cases, it has represented a gesture to forestall greater wage demands through inviting worker participation in the decision-making process. Or, alternatively, it has constituted a genuine effort to complement the redistribution of wealth with a blurring of the distinction between management and labor. Still another consideration, probably in the minds of all advocates, is the notion that worker participation would increase the *esprit de corps* of a company and would spur productivity.

The European Community (EC), or Common Market, now based in Lisbon, is currently considering a series of directives that, if passed into law, would not only expand mandatory consultations between management and employees but would also set new guidelines regarding parent companies and subsidiaries in MNCs and would substantially increase the amount of information that companies would have to disclose about their operations. The Fifth Company Law Directive has been before the Community since 1972 and has attracted much public attention in recent years. Under such a directive, companies would be required to have worker participation in the board structure of all corporations and provide employees with information regarding local and worldwide plans. Reporting would be statutory, and penalties would be enforced for noncompliance.

Among the market economies of the developing countries, the staunchest proponent of worker participation in the management process seems to have been the Venezuelan CTV. Multinational corporations must closely monitor any universalized comanagement schemes in countries with powerful labor unions.

## Cultural, Regional, and Traditional/Modern Differences

In the developing world and the reemerging nations of east and central Europe, the strategic planner and operations executive must be mindful of tensions stemming from the heterogeneity of social political systems in just one country. Clashes between regions, cultures, and the traditional and modern sectors of societies are often interrelated and should be incorporated into planning, negotiating strategy, and consideration of the protection of installations and personnel. To multinational corporations and international banks, these societal divisions pose such difficulties as a lack of coordination between center and regional institutions (e.g., between central and regional banks), the potential for disputes over jurisdiction, the inability of the center to enforce law and order over a region, regional separatist movements, and even civil war. A further threat to foreign business installations exists in the potential for violent explosiveness of the contradiction between the traditional and modern sectors of a society and the festering rivalries of unassimilated cultural and ethnic groups. The foreign businessperson might have to adapt to different styles of doing business or brace himself for social disturbances that develop as people feel that the dominant culture, or even modernity itself, is overtaking them or threatening their identities.

The problems involving cultural, regional, and traditional/modern divisions that are prevalent in some of the central and eastern European countries of the former Soviet Bloc and in Africa, the Middle East, and South and Southeast Asia are caused by (a) the artificial borders and linguistic/cultural overlays imposed by a dominant group or an earlier colonizing power; (b) the efforts of newly emergent (or reemergent in Europe) countries to create strong nation states from a tapestry of ethnic groups; and (c) the attempt of these diverse groups to cling to their solidarity and to preserve their traditional ethnic or religious identities in the face of modern institutions and laws. Such rivalries within one nation's borders, whether in the Middle East or Balkans, often represent a resistance to a more generalized process of nation building and national integration.

## *Regionalism*

In dealing with the broad topic of regionalism, we must appreciate both its critical importance for operations planning in the earmarked host country and its far-reaching ramifications even for doing business in the relatively developed world. In the more developed world, the distinction is that the obstacles are not usually life-threatening. However, bureaucracy and conflicting red tape between one locality and another in areas as familiar as Canada and Newfoundland can seem as troublesome as the threat of ethnic rivalry elsewhere.

One of the first steps in actually getting operations underway in a new host country often involves regional politics. The foreign businessperson must obtain approval for a range of things from licenses to location site. (The oil company wishing to spud an oil well in the onshore Jiangxi Basin in China might find itself more directly impeded than would an oil executive operating in the Cabinda enclave in Angola; the latter might be surrounded by Cabinda Liberation guerrillas, but the former might have to deal with cutting through layers of bureaucracy at several levels, from Jiangxi Province to the central Ministry of Petroleum Industry in Beijing.) If the central government offers commercial incentives to invest in outlying areas for manufacturing purposes, the operations executive must weigh such incentives against the possible inconveniences of poor infrastructure, poor living conditions, and potential sources of regional unrest.

In other cases, a conflict might erupt among the central authority, provincial or state authority, and the local-level jurisdiction. Sometimes, as in the case of a developed country like Australia, disagreements are based on a legal or regulatory pretext. In Australia, a hydroelectric company being built for Tasmania was blocked by the central Australian government, which used provisions of an international convention on protecting wilderness areas as grounds for halting the project; the country's high court upheld that action. In Nigeria, because the state governments often stray too far from the central government's development plan, it is advisable for a foreign business enterprise to obtain payment guarantees from the Central Bank. The sort of intense business planning leads to important precautions. The close-in study of idiosyncratic regional conditions or conflicts with the center, like the analysis of basic market conditions itself, is as important as the broad-brush judgments about political and economic trends. The company's marketing and field operations officers should acquire a refined analytical perspective for this sort of approach, and at an early stage should consider retaining the services of local legal counsel.

The astute international businessperson ought to be aware that the differences between center and region might involve a range of complex and inconsistent procedures that might even impinge on the viability of the contract itself. In the People's Republic of China (PRC), for example, as many as three layers of bureaucracy may be involved, as well as the Party, which is the key decision-making locus at every level. In this case, proper planning at the home office will guide the operations officers through a snag by identifying an appropriate local agent or coopting a well-connected person who can guide his or her new employer on a course that will bypass such bureaucratic hurdles. In Chinese society, cultivating personal relationships with the right individuals *(Guanxi)* at the highest possible level (even above the relevant ministry itself) may do wonders! The process of developing relations should not be left to local personnel alone; rather, it is appropriate for key company executives to reinforce through personal contact the higher-level relationships that are developed.

If a central government cannot easily communicate its directives to the state level and then to the grass roots, the ensuing political paralysis is apt to affect business operations. In pre-coup Nigeria, in spite of the fact that power then had been diffused among nineteen states rather than the four old regional divisions that had permitted the major tribes to form political blocs, the lack of coordination between the president and state governors still had a crippling effect.

In some countries in the Middle East and Africa, nation states are still so fragmented into their traditional regional or tribal units that the central government is limited in its power to exercise law and order. This factor is an important consideration for foreign businesses contemplating a project in such a "frontier" milieu. In southeast Turkey, for example, where the oil fields and many large-scale infrastructure projects are located, the Kurdish population makes its own law and order. Banditry and killings are common, and the local police arrest whomever they please and treat them as they like. The central government can do little to intervene in this Turkish version of the "wild west."

Finally, regionalism in its extreme form can lead to wide-scale violence and civil war. The Ibo secessionist movement in eastern Nigeria in 1969–1970 fused a drive for tribal autonomy with economically motivated regional separation. The latent conflict in recent times in Nigeria between the Hausa-Fulani in the North and the Yoruba in the South represents a mix of regional economic imperatives, religious differences (Muslim and Christian), and tribalism.

### *Cultural and Traditional/Parochial Sources of Tension*

Cultural heterogeneity remains a source of tension in many countries seeking to forge an almost contrived unity from a diversity of languages and customs that in the Third World might have predated colonialism or, in Eastern Europe and the former Soviet Union, managed to survive (perhaps even as a psychological defense) the tyranny of central control and the imposition of a new ideology. Colonialism itself created artificial boundaries and entities. In Nigeria, the Ibo tribal structure, which spearheaded the Biafran secessionist movement of the 1960s, had been a product of the colonial era. Yet, comprising many smaller communities with similar cultures, the "Ibo" perceived themselves nonetheless as a culturally interrelated organization deserving autonomy from the Hausa-Fulani–controlled central government and separate recognition.

In the Cameroon in the 1980s, former President Ahmadou Ahidjo adroitly deflected a potential conflict between the northern and southern regions onto the "colonial" rivalry between the anglophones (English-speaking people) and the majority francophones (French-speaking people). Tensions have only increased, including disputes involving university curriculum and riots over the shooting by a francophone police officer of an anglophone citizen. These tensions, suggestive of problems in our own inner cities, can become serious against a backdrop of deteriorating economic conditions. In Burma, some twenty-six armed, dissident ethnic groups vie for autonomous control of their slices of territory and absorb the energies of the central government in the fighting.

Some countries have found ways to cope with such diversity, and the astute businessperson should ascertain just how well potential tensions are managed by the central government. One approach is simply the exercise of a modicum of tolerance. With the exception of periodic clampdowns on organized protest in Tibet, the PRC generally has been tolerant of the cultures and customs of its minorities as long as they have remained docile. A different approach is the utilization of coercion against ethnic assertiveness or employing a "carrot and stick" approach. The careful businessperson will examine how effective such postures have been in preserving social order and making it possible for the visitor to feel reasonably assured of safe passage around the country. One good test, for example, of the cleavage between Arabs and Berbers in Algeria in the early 1980s (outdated now because of the development in recent years of a more imposing threat from the militant Muslims) was the 1981 uprising of the Berbers in the Kabyle (eastern Algeria) against a trend toward Arabization of the educational system. The prospect of the government's substituting Arabic for the French language in the schools threatened the Berbers' economic mobility through the accustomed pattern of pursuing jobs in France. The government reacted quickly to the unrest by suppressing it and then by instituting a faculty of language and culture at the local university. A volatile situation was successfully defused during those years.

Where the idea of the nation state is still new, the conflict between central government and the modern elements of society, on the one hand, and the local ethnic or tribal political structures and practices, on the other, can lead to problems of control and paralysis of the decision-making function. In this author's opinion, Nigeria has been particularly vulnerable in this regard. The creation of about thirty states (nineteen was considered a lot in the early 1980s) that cut across the former tribal boundaries has militated against the recurrence of civil war along tribal lines. States separate now like amoebae under almost any pretext. And yet the strength of some 200 traditional cultural groups persists and makes the absorption of the groups into larger political bodies a long and difficult process. The recurrence of local riots, brought on by local emirs, Muslim militants, and other groups over the years has led to the crippling of government at local levels, particularly in the North, and would jeopardize any business operations that happened to locate in any of these potentially volatile areas of the country. Some consequences are indirect. One also cannot discount the possibility of an immobilizing impact on business throughout the country of multiple localized outbreaks that seem to undermine the central authority.

## Civil Disorder: Violence and Terrorism

Many of the issues that we have discussed can culminate in organized mass violence. This social violence indirectly can affect us by upsetting the political system and routine of business as usual. It occasionally *directly* explodes at our bottom line when our own installations, personnel, and flow of commerce are at risk.

When a businessperson evaluates a new market or host country, he must consider the prospects for organized mass violence (through unions, associations, political parties, or student vanguard organizations), anomic outbursts of social violence (such as the spontaneous crowd hysteria of overturning trains and buses), or a general state of lawlessness. If a society is given to organized violence, which under certain circumstances might escalate and spread, executives should be aware of the fact. In Colombia, for instance, corporations must monitor two countervailing trends: the spread of guerrilla activity and the gradual integration of the middle class into the political system. If successful, the latter would broaden the base of the existing political elite and could deprive the urban guerrillas at least of potential recruits.

Even if it falls far short of a social revolution, civil disorder, particularly when it spreads like wildfire from city to city, can disrupt international business operations and pose obvious hazards for expatriate personnel. Many countries in the Third World have histories of civil unrest. And in Yugoslavia, and some non-Russian areas of the former Soviet Union, one can expect ethnic conflict, compounded by other variables like economic inequities, to persist even after major squabbles over borders and cultural autonomy seem to have been resolved.

The threat of social violence should not be a deterrent to investing in a country or even expanding operations there, but the astute businessperson who evaluates the situation for his company should consider five factors that will help show him what to expect. A strategy can then be formulated on the basis of considering risk against opportunity in a fully informed way. Look into these conditions:

1. The history of civil violence in a given country (frequency, causes, pattern of locations);
2. The extent of the deterioration of economic, social, and human rights conditions, and whether a boiling point seems to be approaching;
3. Organizations (religious, political, student, labor) that might spearhead or manipulate demonstrations or riots;
4. The likelihood of an outbreak's being easily contained by the police or military through the effective threat or utilization of coercion;
5. The focus of acts of civil disorder: namely, would they deliberately target foreigners and foreign business installations, and why?

Outbreaks of civil unrest are so numerous and in many ways so redundant that it is unnecessary to go through a litany of them. The situation in Egypt provides a historic lesson through its cost-of-living riots in 1977 and the economic disaster that preceded them. Similar outbreaks were avoided in the 1980s because austerity programs were not implemented precipitously. It was not just the foreign investor who learned from the experience. A buffeting force against future mass demonstrations against the Mubarak government is the Egyptian cultural proclivity toward deference in the face of credible authority. In the 1980s, Hosni Mubarak consolidated his power vis-à-vis the military, strengthened his position before the Egyptian people, and learned to manipulate the Egyptian people's penchant for obeisance to authority. With a stronger domestic position, enhanced by a very positive international image, he now stands before a relatively compliant nationwide constituency. In the event of any social eruption, it is likely that President Mubarak would have little difficulty in bringing the disturbance under control. *An understanding of the mechanisms of control and their efficacy in a country is as important as the ability to identify potential sources of civil disorder and to predict volatility.*

Not only is the possibility of a given type of civil disorder predictable, but careful observation also sometimes can anticipate the timing of the event. In the months preceding the food riots in January 1984 in the Rif Mountains in Morocco, a first reduction in food price subsidies was undertaken. On December 17, King Hassan II appeared on television ostensibly to talk about a new census that would lead to a more equitable distribution of wealth among rich and poor; he implicitly was letting the people know that they were in for harder times under a draft budget that was then under consideration. At the same time, an exit tax was introduced that penalized the migrant workers in the North; a crackdown on contraband upset the small-scale smuggling operations among the poorer people of the region; the nucleus of the nation's police force was called up to provide security for the Islamic Conference meeting that the king was proudly hosting in Marrakech, thereby limiting their distribution throughout the country; and the king declared a national holiday and let the restless young people out of school. Any well-coordinated monitoring of the situation between the strategic-planning complement at corporate headquarters and an astute on-site field manager (observing, telefaxing corporate headquarters with an inquiry, and then further interpreting events) should have been able to forecast what was to be a limited period of popular unrest.

We should emphasize again that the excessive use of state violence to deal with social unrest can be the undoing of the political system. Indeed, the frequent use of harsh force to beat down popular protest can be perceived as evidence of the government's weakness; the very act of using brutal force can radicalize citizens who would otherwise be waverers or settle for the status quo. The successful exercise of control, a sort of manipulation of popular opinion and cultural disposition, is not the same as the resort to repetitive coercion.

## *Terrorism*

Still another variant of social/political violence is terrorism. Private consultants in the United States and Europe specialize in monitoring acts of terrorism that range from blowing up installations, to kidnapping businesspeople, to murders and political executions. Terrorist statistics are available to companies via on-line computer services. Often, as in Colombia, crime or banditry, kidnapping for ransom, and violence connected with the illicit drug traffic and political protest are interwoven. The purpose of political kidnapping can be (a) to gain the release of colleagues from prison, (b) to obtain a material ransom, and (c) simply to make a political statement by the harassment and/or execution of the victim.

If we live in a world of increasing globalization of standards and practices, violence also closes in on us from all sides. Often earmarked as its primary targets, businesspersons certainly cannot hide from terrorism. Nor can they create an effective image for themselves and their companies by going to work in a host country each day with gun turrets on the top of their vehicles. Since governments increasingly will refuse to meet political demands to rescue kidnap victims, and since host governments often forbid foreign corporations to make a transfer of money in kidnapping cases, a multinational corporation or international bank can best protect its expatriate personnel by monitoring terrorism in countries of exposure and by developing crisis contingency plans for such emergencies overseas. Concrete preparations can provide guidance to personnel and their families about being properly circumspect, traveling to work by different routes, defensive driving, and other means of evading would-be perpetrators on site. Comprehensive plans would also establish a crisis action communications network: a systematic program of response to a crisis between the local level and corporate headquarters.

In positioning themselves in questionable areas, strategic planners and field marketing executives must look for patterns that indicate *type* of activities, *locations* of prevalent acts of terrorism, and the *nature of the targets*. In Peru, several years ago the *Sendero Luminoso* guerrillas for the most part carefully targeted infrastructural projects in the southern Andes and left the people—and foreigners—alone. In the past few years, as the movement has escalated, the lives of civilian personnel have come to be at risk. Moreover, the *Sendero Luminoso*'s activities have spread from the outlying areas of the population centers. Colombia is notorious for its kidnappings—particularly in rural areas from Caqueta to the Magdalena Medio. In the cities too political elements are at work. Even if the M-19 guerrillas could be extirpated from the cities, widespread urban crime would continue to endanger foreigners living in Bogota who worry about the walk from their apartments in the luxurious high ground above the center of the city to their cars in the parking lot.

## Military Unrest

Countries with frequent military coups are often considered unstable. In cultures where political change is routinely wrought by military takeover, trauma and violence might well be minimal. Moreover, military interventions often restore order by deterring or reducing social unrest that could hamper the foreign businessperson. The foreign enterprise need be concerned only with the question of whether a particular type of military changeover can affect business as usual. Does an unusual set of new military usurpers have a bone to pick with the private sector, or will it leave the rules of the game alone? Will it meet the previous government's external financial obligations? In general, as we have stated earlier, a military government will continue to follow a tradition of conservative politics in such situations. The businessperson need be concerned only about the uncertainty and temporary paralysis that such a regime change might endanger and whether his particular project(s) might be too controversial and too closely linked to the previous leadership.

Can a military coup be anticipated? Some years ago we questioned an Africa expert on the likelihood of a military coup in Ghana. At the time, the civilian government of Dr. Hilla Limann was facing severe economic problems. The expert, who had in fact inadvertently allowed himself to become an advocate for democratic government in Ghana, said he considered a coup highly unlikely because no consensus for such a takeover had developed. Of course, no polls were taken when Limann was replaced by Flight Lieutenant Jerry John Rawlings. A general rule is that where there is a history of military control, the military might be inclined to rise again given appropriate and inviting circumstances.

It is useful to know whether the military, or part of it, regards itself as having political responsibilities; what general political, social, and economic circumstances would arouse its indignation? Does it see itself as an enforcer of morality and, like Nigerian Col. Muhammed Buhari's New Year's Eve coup of 1983–1984 or the 1992 attempted coup in Venezuela (the oldest democracy in Latin America), would its mission be to cleanse the Augean stables and to wash away official corruption?

Further analysis of the military, even in societies like Tunisia where the military does not perceive itself as any more political than perhaps in France or the United States, takes on particular importance in a time of political instability when the legitimacy of the civilian government might be called into question. If the alternative to social chaos is military intervention, nuances in the military's self-perception are important. The Moroccan military has generational differences. The most senior officers never developed a sense of separate identity since Morocco's independence; the younger officers, gradually working their way up the ladder in recent years, are more inclined to question the political order. They are also more likely to come from urban and Arab backgrounds than the preceding generation, are better educated, and tend to come from coastal middle-class families. They have become politically aware and might someday crave a political identity.

In anticipating a coup, it is also important to ask some fairly obvious questions. Are the troops happy? Do they have enough prestige, mobility (particularly junior to senior levels), pay, and other benefits? In Indonesia, both active and retired military officers are encouraged to take civilian and even corporate jobs. In China, the military— perhaps the one major source of instability during the past years of modernization—has been courted and restored to prominence at the same time as they have been professionalized and equipped with more sophisticated weaponry. In Algeria (a highly militarized society), not only is the president a product of the military, but the army is represented in the ruling party, state, and judiciary.

Finally, we must ask ourselves: If a coup, what then? In most cases, as we have discussed above, the most likely disruption would derive from the atmosphere of uncertainty surrounding the military takeover. To prepare optimally for such a contingency, a more focused analysis of the military is required. Published information might exist on dissidence within the armed forces of an unpredictable host country. Other insights might be shared on a personal level by State Department specialists and analysts and observers in other organs of the executive branch. One might discover, for example, a rivalry between field command and headquarters about reconciliation with communist insurgents, or learn that a markedly large number of the younger officers have come to embrace a militant form of Islam. A most important factor to consider in examining the ranks of the military in Third World countries is that elements within the armed forces might have poor, rural origins and adhere to a populist orientation that could prejudice them against multinationals and international lending institutions if they came to power.

## External Territorial Disputes

Territorial disputes have taken on some new importance since the Falklands/Malvinas war in Argentina and Iraq's efforts to grab oil-rich areas in Kuwait. Notwithstanding the importance of greed as a motive for aggressively pursuing some territorial claims, often such incursions beyond one's own unquestioned borders represent a means of diverting the people's attention away from its own domestic economic ills. A close examination of the political rhetoric, the way it resonates with the people's emotions, and the nature of the domestic problems on both sides can help the corporate planner gauge the importance of this dimension of political risk to operations.

Most border disputes in the Third World have their origin in colonial times when boundaries were imposed on them. What are the substance today of a nation's claims for territory against another, and how salient is a country's commitment to regain or retain the territory in question? Have developments occurred to defuse the emotional content of the contest? For example, by 1984, Guinea and Guinea-Bisseau had taken their dispute to The Hague for adjudication. Nigeria and Cameroon, which in the past had argued hotly over avowedly oil-rich border areas, were enjoying cordial relations because of a change of government in Nigeria.

In regions where local wars frequently erupt (such as the cluster of states surrounding, and including, Israel), a foreign company must be careful about operating in contested areas or major cities or strategic locations with concentrations of heavy infrastructure. The converse situation also obtains. Thus, although hostilities ranging from skirmishes to war seemed to be imminent between Syria and Israel for years, a foreign company did not necessarily have to be gun-shy. If an opportunity had presented itself to build a pipeline in remote western Syria, personnel and equipment would have been away from the line of fire.

External conflict also can be destabilizing to the domestic situation in a given country. Over the years, Moroccan King Hassan II's war in the Western Sahara won the applause of the people but drained the country's economic resources; yet, if Hassan were to quit now and compromise with the Polisario, his own people might force him from his throne. If Syria reacted to what it perceived to be an inadequate resolution of the West Bank issue and went to war with Israel, the country could fall into political disarray. A less-than-successful war could force Hafaz Assad out of power and leave a leadership vacuum that, given the situation that the military would be preoccupied with licking its wounds, could be filled by the Muslim Brotherhood or elements sympathetic to it. Such an outcome potentially could be more threatening to a Western business presence in Damascus than war itself.

Still another consideration for international corporate planners— particularly in the extractive industries—is the inadvisability of locating in an area disputed by two or more countries. In such contests, the U.S. government usually warns that it cannot be accountable for the safety of its citizens. In an area that was being offered as an oil concession in the 1980s off South Korea, sovereignty over the terrain was being asserted not only by South Korea, but by Taiwan, the People's Republic of China, and, of course, North Korea. In an earlier period in the East China Sea, the PRC once shelled the boats of a concessionaire affiliated with another claimant country. When the United States loosens its sanctions against Vietnam, the lower portion of the South China Sea including the Spratley and Paracel Islands, once the scene of bitter contention between China and Vietnam at the height of the Chinese Cultural Revolution, will be a promising offshore oil area of the 1990s. To penetrate this new area of opportunity and avoid risking whatever footing they might have in China, corporate negotiators will have to be sensitive to the volatility of the border dispute; certainly the consummation of any concrete deals will have to be predicated on a possibly protracted process of negotiating international agreements between the Socialist Republic of Vietnam and the People's Republic of China.

## Elites in an Elitist Country: Picking the Players

In examining the political stability of a host country or the ways in which policies might evolve to the advantage or detriment of a particular foreign enterprise, both corporate planners and marketing executives in the field need to identify the key actors or groups of actors within the political and social elites (quite often they overlap). Although sometimes the importance of interpersonal networks (who knows whom and who is related to whom) is overriding, it is usually of critical value to ascertain as well where individuals stand on the issues of direct, and indirect, influence on your business dealings. (The reader will see examples of the phenomenon in the country case studies on the People's Republic of China and Colombia.)

A still more refined planning approach would look more intensively at the less apparent divergences within one group of actors itself. Thus, within one country's military elite, it might simply not be enough to know that there is some sort of tension between junior and senior officers. Mix with them or talk to U.S. agencies that have looked into the question and try to determine how their origins and world views might differ and what the complaints are that might surface? Also, how well entrenched in the senior command are those officers who are less desirable from a foreign business standpoint? In the Thai army, and now in the parliament, Gen. Chawalit Yongchayut, who encouraged the left-leaning, so-called "Democratic Soldiers' Coup" in April 1981, is still in the 1990s a major military/political figure in Thailand. Since the uncertain recovery of parliamentary democracy in Thailand in 1992, Chawalit could well represent the "opposition" and be a prime mover among the more idealistic soldiers in the future should economic and social/political circumstances warrant intervention.

Among the civilians in either developing countries or even relatively developed societies like Venezuela and Taiwan, we would look not just at the different political parties or interest (special interest) groups but at the cliques and factions within them. We might ask: (a) Are these factions divisive? (In Syria, one could try to assess how well organized or fragmented is the political opposition Muslim Brotherhood.) (b) Can all factions be identified? (Not all are represented by a formal group.) (c) Don't distinct and even conflicted groups often comprise individuals whose allegiances within the same large group hinge as much on interpersonal relations as they do on the substance of the issues? (d) Do we find cross-cutting alliances among individuals who are linked to several groups, and do these alliances serve to ameliorate social and political tensions in general?

The latter two lines of questioning are particularly applicable to a country like Indonesia. Indeed one can make the argument that Indonesia is controlled by an interlocking directorate of elite groups, which run the gamut from the president's inner circle to the more vociferous dissidents and critics of President Suharto's leadership. In Indonesia, everyone seems to know everyone else personally, and the system appears to be virtually all-inclusive; in other words, even the "outsiders" are inside.

To prepare for a long-term stay in such a market, a company must learn who is who, who has "stabbed whom in the back," with what party and with what faction should potential business associates be affiliated, how might their particular group lend positive support to one's enterprise and, finally, how well situated would this political faction be in the event of a leadership succession crisis in the nation. Such information probably can be obtained on site in a very social way as one explores for partners and local allies. This sort of inquiry can be carried out openly as the logical and sophisticated extension of a corporation's normal check of local market conditions; it even can be integrated into a public relations effort to get to know one's local principals and associates more closely.

Making well-situated political friends for an enterprise and choosing

local principals and associates with attention to their influence and
standing is not only a critical safeguard for the welfare of the new
enterprise but a clever way for the foreign businessman to position
himself for a longer stay in the market. The initial advantage of
painstakingly investigating the place of local associates in a host
country's system of elites is that the process itself will constitute an
education about how the social and political system functions. Later,
if a foreign enterprise is victimized by the foul play of its local
principals or comes up against attempts at official extortion, the well-
positioned outsider can appeal to strategically well-placed friends in
the political system. Even serious bureaucratic roadblocks can be
cleared with the intervention of the right persons. In societies like
Indonesia or the Philippines, characterized by interpersonal networks,
important relations have to be cultivated continuously. High-level,
courtesy visits from the home corporation's executives will strengthen
the bonding.

## Nationalism and National Goals

In the process of nation building, it becomes necessary for a shared
value of nationalism to be inculcated among all the people within a
country's boundaries. Particularly at this seminal stage of development, nationalism should not be perceived as a threat to the outsider.
On the contrary, it is useful in the long run because it contributes to
the cohesiveness of entities often comprising many diverse ethnic
groups. However, some of the permutations of this unifying national
symbolism historically have proven to be dangerous and destabilizing
to the international community (either regional, as in Iraq's incursions
in the Persian Gulf area, or on a wider scale).

International business also must be wary of xenophobia, a historical
hostility to foreigners among the people in some countries. Often, this
nationalistic, ethnocentric, or perhaps just provincially naive resentment of outsiders takes the form of a proclivity to blame foreign
business interests or Western materialist values for corroding or con-
taminating the traditional culture or, at the bottom line, exploiting the
country, damaging the economy, or bleeding the country through the
austerity plans negotiated by the IMF and multilaterals.

Whether it involves an adventurous military occupation by Argentina of the Falklands/Malvinas Islands or a politically explosive domestic economic crisis that is alienating the people's support for the

political system, nationalism often can be effectively manipulated by the political leadership for the sake of self-preservation. If the leadership feels that its message will tap a xenophobic strain in the ingrained nationalism of the people, it might scapegoat foreign investors or blame the richer countries for the high-interest loans "forced upon them" by capitalist banks.

The Mexican leadership, in the last phase of José Lopez Portillo's term in the early 1980s, tried to turn its back on its external debt problem by manipulating what it perceived to be a shared "Yanqui go home!" attitude on the part of two other debt-burdened Latin American countries. But the others refused to cooperate, and it was only then that Mexico began to face its structural problems seriously in negotiations with the International Monetary Fund.

Mexico's desperate reaching out for a sort of extranational communalism, a regional cultural bond of South against North, suggests that in a shrinking world, strictly nationalistic sentiments can be stretched beyond borders in an effort to cast a net for regional loyalties. Thus, Mexico will not betray Fidel Castro rhetorically to the United States, and Nigeria in good economic times was able to put the squeeze on British Petroleum because of its interests through the 1980s in the then apartheid nation of South Africa. In the Third World in general, however, this is the weakest—and least amenable to mobilization— form of emotionalism. It is difficult enough for the average villager in a nascent developing country to identify with the concept of a nation state, much less look beyond it. On the other hand, the villager in a more modern developing nation (Morocco for example) can become fired with fury over a squabble over precise national boundaries.

As nationalism continues to develop, loyalties beyond the nation state tend to be thinner. While U.S. businesspeople were treated badly throughout most of Latin America for the U.S. position during the Falklands/Malvinas interlude in Argentina in the 1980s, no serious incidents occurred. Similarly, Nigeria's earlier militant position against companies doing business with the South Africa of apartheid in most low-profile cases was a matter of lip service; Nigeria could not afford to oust all multinationals and banks with interests in South Africa. National interest in reality came first!

The trend toward globalism indeed might encourage a shift away from parochial nationalism (although it is more easily discussed than accomplished) toward a greater investment in transnational economic and political cooperation. In the more developed countries, the phenomenon of finding commonalities beyond national borders was an animating force behind the early shaping of the European Community. In the still-developing parts of the world, we see some concerted efforts to form a regional economic and political bond before country-specific nationalism becomes too overpowering. The former "frontline states" of southern Africa, for example, are trying to implement an overarching union in the Southern African Development Community (SADC). But consider that in this era of a truly globalized universe of communications and economic relations, regional groupings will be more apt to become anachronisms than the historically rooted nation states.

## Social Revolution and Living with the Winners

The seemingly ultimate question is whether a social upheaval looms in the foreground—a successful rebellion that would bring in a new set of elite groups and perhaps even alter the rules of the game altogether. Such revolutions depend for their success on just the right combination of some of the factors already discussed and others yet to be covered, sparked by a catalyst that will bring about combustion and the rise of a new elite.

We already have discussed rising economic expectations. But no force can deal more of a blow to the political system or constitute more of a catalyst to mob violence than the introduction of political and social reform measures and then the reversal of these concessions. The old hypothesis that Czar Alexander III's freeing the serfs might have set the Russian revolution in motion certainly seems to have withstood the critical predilections of countless social scientists. As the citizens' access to the political system improves, their level of self- and political awareness usually increases. When individuals come to perceive that their horizons can be expanded and that common needs can be achieved by acting in concert with others, they will not readily be shoved back into "solitary confinement." If this catalyst or others trigger widespread civil disorder, the businessperson must be poised for a social explosion.

At what point does a rebellion become a revolution? Only the best intelligence can predict that a rebellious movement is gathering enough momentum or forming coalitions with other antisystemic groups to topple a political or social system. Only the most objective analysis of the coordination between capital and villages can indicate whether the central government is decaying and its influence deteriorating. A simple paradigm, comprising the existence of a rebellious organization or coalition, a binding revolutionary ideology, and the delegitimation of the central government might not necessarily reflect a specific reality. External interference and unknowns also can affect the outcome. As we approach the culmination of a revolutionary movement— let us say, well after the theater was set ablaze in Iran in 1978—what at first might have seemed to be a rebellion becomes a more predictably successful revolution. But there is often very little a corporate or bank executive can do about recovering assets from the host country. Indeed, while the existing regime still has a chance, the investor/creditor is inclined to tie his fortunes to the government that welcomed him. After all, many revolts are launched; few succeed. A survey of companies with investments or trade exposures in Iran prior to 1979 indicates that more than 75 percent lost all but a small percentage of their assets in the Iranian revolution.

A national liberation struggle, like the war for black rule in Zimbabwe (formerly Rhodesia), poses a particular problem for the corporate strategist. In revolution-torn Zimbabwe, only a radical would have been so bold as to support Robert Mugabe or pro-Soviet Joshua Nkomo, and only a blind conservative would have identified too closely with Ian Smith or Abel Muzorewa. The pragmatic and conservative businessperson had only one choice:

> to ensure that his losses would not be disastrous and equally that he was positioned to take advantage of opportunities if they occurred. Because of the uncertainty, he would not align himself with any individual or party. But he would recognize that the old order was finished and would carefully but visibly cut any strong existing ties to the associates of Smith and Muzorewa, taking care to do so in a way that would not lead to government reaction in the short run.[2]

If a bank or multinational already has substantial interests at stake as an apparently revolutionary movement unravels, a concerted effort should be made to analyze the character of the movement and consider one's options in the country. On-site operations executives often are politically myopic, or they just don't want to believe that they are witnessing the ground caving in beneath them. Key factors to observe in assessing the denouement of a revolutionary movement as it might affect future business interests are:

1. *The nature of the personality of the revolutionary leaders.* What

is their social background? Are they likely to embrace a populist world view because of their origins?

2. *Factionalism.* Are there cleavages within the revolutionary elite, and can one position oneself appropriately? Is it best to address the impending revolutionary government as a collective entity?

3. *The nature of the ideology.* Does the ideology promise the realization of some apocalyptic vision upon accession to political power? Is it an adaptation of some external ideology, like Marxism-Leninism? Is it being used primarily to hold a broad-based revolutionary organization together? Is there room within its theoretical bounds for the sorts of tactical, or even strategic, flexibility that would permit private investment to continue after the revolution's victory?

4. *The question of external assistance.* In a complex revolution/civil war, as in Zimbabwe or Angola where different revolutionary groups have remained at odds with one another, does the struggle invite external interference from a superpower or a jingoistic regional power? A given faction in any internal war should not be labeled "pro-American," "pro-Soviet," or a "Libyan ally" just for accepting donations. The recipient of aid may repay with rhetorical fealty, but in fact the exploiter may well be the one who is being exploited. In the actual case of Zimbabwe, Robert Mugabe, called "pro-Chinese" and a "Maoist" in the 1960s and 1970s, still shares a cordial relationship with the PRC, but then China's character has changed markedly; Mugabe's ZANU party–dominated government, like the Chinese, now supports a mixed, private-public economy but in no real way is trying to emulate a Chinese model of any sort.

Given the likelihood that revolutionary movements from time to time will ascend to power, a foreign company or bank can roll with the punches. Gulf Oil is still ensconced in Angola ten years after independence and civil war. And Marxist-Leninist revolutions do evolve—a basically foreign ideology that serves a revolutionary movement well as an organizing set of principles may have to be altered to cope with the harsh realities of restoring order in the aftermath of victory.

## Notes

1. See *Christian Science Monitor*, August 28, 1984, 16–17.
2. William H. Overholt, *Political Risk* (London: Euromoney Publications, 1982), p. 20.

*Chapter 2*

# Cultural Factors, the Critical Threats to Foreign Investment, and the Trade Constraints We Impose on Ourselves

### The Political Culture Side of International Business Understanding

One very important facet of international environment analysis is the recognition that every country has its own unique cultural characteristics, the more salient of which can affect political attitudes and behavior and might even constitute constraints against social disorder and upheaval. For this analysis, the political science term "political culture" serves best to describe this dimension. Sidney Verba defines this approach thus: "The political culture of a society consists of the system of empirical beliefs, expressive symbols, and values which defines the situation in which a political action takes place."[1] Defining the term further, Lucian Pye states: "Each generation must receive its politics from the previous one [and] react against that process to find its own politics."[2] In other words, political culture can be a country's subjective orientation to politics that develops psychodynamically over generations.

Often, an appreciation of special characteristics that influence one nation's particular political orientation can have a direct, positive impact on doing business there. The strategic planner or international business development executive can draw on these elements to formulate a marketing approach to that country or to position his or her organization comfortably for a long stay in that particular host country. Let us examine the ways in which a country's political culture might affect the stability of the broader political environment for international business operations.

## Constraints Against Upheavals

Any society has certain values, orientations, and organizational characteristics that lend themselves to top-down manipulation for the purpose of control. Often, these psychological levers of political and social control outweigh the apparent threats to political order, and the analyst should be as attentive to one side of the equation as to the other. Some societies have safety valves, such as a prevalent "minority" of entrepreneurs, against which the government can deflect hostilities that ought to be directed against the system itself.

In societies like Indonesia and Algeria, social control and manipulation by the political leadership seem to coincide with a deep attitude of deference toward authority on the part of the people. In Algeria, the regime will respond to a mass demonstration first by dispatching the military to the scene to knock heads and make arrests and then by taking steps to pacify the interest groups in question. The military barracks are omnipresent throughout Algiers and outlying towns, and create a peculiarly somber atmosphere. In Indonesia, the authoritarian approach of the Suharto government always has been effective; however, ironically, because it has compromised too much in its treatment of the Islamic fundamentalists, it might face tougher problems ahead. Other societies seem inclined to accept the oppressiveness of authoritarian regimes as a preferable alternative to earlier periods of political chaos, gang or guerrilla terrorism, or general social unrest.

Oftentimes, a combination of political culture orientation and social structure work against mass upheavals. For instance, a dense urban population, comprising relatively educated people who are unable to find proper employment, would be a constituency for organized social protest. Yet, though circumstances conform to this paradigm in Algeria, they are offset by the migration of whole extended families to the city at one time. The preservation of the rural family unit ameliorates the psychological trauma of leaving home, and of not finding a "better life in the city."

In Mexico, a plethora of complex social and political conditions exists that in another cultural milieu could portend a political cataclysm. These include the following: an extremely uneven distribution of wealth between the cities and countryside, a high debt burden coupled with near-zero economic growth, an adult work force only 50 percent of which is adequately employed, an acute population growth problem, an inordinate number of politically aware young people entering an overburdened job market, an outmoded land tenure system, extreme rural-to-urban migration, and a frightening density of population in the main cities. Add to these factors severe economic jolts, which stem in part from worldwide conditions, and one can imagine hordes of political risk consultants clamoring at the doors of major corporations like Mexican jumping beans, offering a diagnostic work-up pointing the way to terminal social revolution.

Mexico, however, is in little danger either of social revolution or military takeover for a number of sound political and economic reasons. The facets on which we will focus here are social and political-cultural:

1. Mexico's social structure in general and its political system in particular are characterized by patron-client relationships through which political dissidents are co-opted into the system and which assures top-down control. The people seem to respect power and central authority. Each person in a position of authority is limited by authoritative and paternalistic figures above him. The patron-client relationship is so well developed that in most instances local grievances involving everything from health clinics to sewerage are settled by appeal to the local political authority. More vocal critics of the system at the grass-roots level of the system usually are co-opted into it.

2. An apparently low level of interpersonal trust tends to militate against the formation of collective groupings that might pit themselves against the macrosystem.

3. Family consciousness is strong and normally will take precedence over other social and political obligations—a factor that also works against a person's taking the risk of joining or forming a political organization that is apt to get his family into trouble. Also, as in the case of Algeria, the existence of large, extended families in urban areas tends to dispel feelings of anomie that might otherwise contribute to antisocial behavior expressed through political channels.

### *Image of the World*

A people's image of itself, its memory of events, fundamental attitudes, and unconscious fears can be relayed from one generation to another and can be reflected in its view of the outside world. This perception may be revealed in the speeches and writings of its preeminent personalities—past and present—and in the efforts of political leaders to manipulate certain sentiments among the people. Some insight concerning a country's purpose and how it fits into the outside world can help the foreign businessperson understand how and why she might be perceived a certain way. Can the American operations executive, for example, who is seeking to make headway in a francophone African country, adapt to the prejudices against him and exploit the weaknesses of competitors who are nationals of other countries? Can a businessperson trying to establish an enterprise in Zimbabwe cut through "antiimperialist" allusions and "anti-Zionist" political rhetoric and realize that these are almost ritualistic incantations that have little to do with the realities of negotiating a sound deal?

From the standpoint of risk to foreign business, what is the propensity of a country to xenophobia or to more specifically directed hostility toward a foreign power with nationals at work within its borders? At the outset of sanctions in the 1980s, Libyans taunted expatriates who had remained behind to maintain a foreign company's installations.

Could a national leader, under adverse economic conditions, point a finger at a foreign country or company and evoke a special emotional, popular reaction that would divert attention away from the government in power? Could a Third World nation—at one time wedded to the West in a colonial or neocolonial relationship—have a national compensation neurosis? In China, to cite one possible example, there may be a historical memory, perpetuated by political elites over generations, of the depredations wrought by the Western imperialist countries in the nineteenth century. Are the United States, European countries, and the Japanese now being made to compensate for past misbehavior by difficult negotiating terms and an unusually demanding sort of technology transfer? Or, to go back in history even further, are the barbarians expected to pay tribute to the middle kingdom before resuming their normal commerce? Westerners put themselves at a disadvantage with the Chinese by virtue of standing in awe of China. The above are merely musings—but important musings nonetheless.

### *An Underlying Inclination to Default, Nationalize, or Expropriate Gradually and by Attrition*

Let us consider an issue that is close to political culture considerations but is perhaps best considered in its own separate context.

Expropriation or nationalization without preagreed compensation is a real hazard to foreign investment. Certainly the strength and viability of a political system matter little if there are underlying attitudinal factors that would encourage nationalization or default on debt. A formal guarantee against nationalization without fair compensation is little safeguard against the expropriated investor's sustaining tremendous losses. As we analyze a new society and how its characteristics might influence our bottom line, we should be aware of the importance of historical attitudes, particularly with regard to default on debt or nationalization without reasonable compensation—the gravest risks to international business. The multinational corporation fears the outright expropriation of its equity and assets by a foreign country or the host government's takeover of the local company under the pressure of mounting regulations and restrictions.

Of course, such unfavorable outcomes for multinationals can be influenced by a host of variables:

1. The nature of the industry (for example, is it considered strategic?);
2. The ideology of the ruling political elite (for example, has a certain type of social revolution just taken place?);
3. Economic conditions and domestic and international political issues. (Could a regional political maneuver by a foreign company's home government serve as pretext for threatening the company's local assets?)

Generally speaking, the international sweep of finance and investment has helped considerably to define the parameters for doing business and has been making banditlike expropriation more of an anachronism. It is far more likely now that new enterprises considered by the host country to be of critical strategic importance are established from the start as joint local/foreign companies, with a formula for gradual nationalization built into the agreement in a way that affords the foreign investor a profitable tenure as the business develops.

But the exceptions to this assumption make it important to look at the host country's history of performance with regard to expropriation and default, or more specifically, the attitudes of the host country's differing political groups concerning these matters. Of course, one should be sufficiently flexible to recognize that the positions of certain political groups have evolved—in some cases 180 degrees—with the passage of time and with such changing circumstances as the increased popularity of monetarist theory and the increasing tendency to recognize relatively unfettered foreign investment as a stimulus to economic growth. Venezuela's President Carlos Andres Perez, for example, who in 1974 had nationalized the country's oil industry, had become a champion of the private sector by the time of his second bid for his country's presidency in the late 1980s. Many foreign businesspersons who had witnessed the earlier expropriation of the oil industry or whose perception of Perez's early persona remained frozen in history were slow to grasp the radical shift in Venezuela's foreign investment orientation, but they were wiser to play it safe for a while.

A look at each country's history of intervention in the private sector can provide additional insights and often reassurance about the paradoxical advantage and/or leverage a foreign firm now might enjoy in a specific cultural context.

Many nations, particularly in Latin America, have learned that excess expropriations have led to a monstrous, unproductive public sector that saps the country's reserves. Mexico is in a curious position. In September 1982, because of critical economic circumstances involving a run on the banks, the Lopez Portillo government nationalized the banks and, with them, 45 percent of bank-owned private companies. That administration's realization of the negative effects of government ownership and the memory thereof would tend to prevent nationalization in the future. Any political proclivity henceforth to appease a bellicose domestic left with rhetoric about a greater role for the state in economic operations would have to be offset by this harsh recollection of statism gone awry.

A still more clear-cut case of a country's having developed an aversion to nationalization from its own historical experience is Peru. Between 1968 and 1975, Gen. Juan Velasco's junta redistributed the country's wealth. Several large multinationals were expropriated, and foreign mining companies were forced to expand their investments at contractual disadvantage to themselves. The result was ruination for Peru. From the tenure of President Fernando Belaúnde Terry onward, the economy has become increasingly liberalized. Even if there were another military coup, it is unlikely that the next junta would be as radical as its precursor in the 1970s. It might flex its rhetorical muscle, but it would be unlikely to rape the private sector or toss out foreign interests. On the contrary, foreign enterprises now constitute a critical interest group and can use their position for leverage with the new administration. Not only are they a bulwark of the economy but the message they transmit to the outer world can give credibility to the new regime.

A country also might try to compensate for its historical image with regard to expropriation. The People's Republic of China wants to repatriate both Taiwan and Hong Kong, yet it must show the free world that this is *repatriation without expropriation*. The foreign community wants to feel as politically and socially unrestricted as in colonial Hong Kong. Immediately after the revolution, China granted "autonomous" status to its largest external trading zone of Shanghai; many Shanghainese capitalists stayed behind to manage their enterprises. Within five years, however, Shanghai's enterprises had been integrated into the socialist economy through harassments ranging from punitive taxation to regulations and personal political pressures. But the China of today is much different!

It has begun to recapture its prerevolutionary entrepreneurial spirit, to open up to foreign banks and service industries, and to delineate sectors of the economy in Shanghai, Shenzhen, and perhaps Hainan that seem to be unburdened by socialist strictures. These internal developments bode well for the future of an economically unbridled Hong Kong in 1997 and laissez-faire in Taiwan if it rejoins the mainland in years to come. China's willingness to give the former colony the breathing space it requires in the years following reintegration will be an encouragement to the already active foreign investors and a positive signal to Taiwan concerning the promise of political rapprochement.

Even given the apparently protective cocoon of globalization, we should examine the history of nationalization/expropriation and default as a political act in a given country. These things still can happen. A review of the historical situation should be an integral part of investment planning in a new host country. The review will ascertain the level of expropriation risk for investments and in some cases might well guide the investor to seek risk insurance coverage. We can also learn whether there might be ways to structure a contract in terms of technology transfer as well as joint ownership to put us in the best possible position to control our own outcomes.

Because expropriation "in the nation's interest" is a tradition that has not quite died in some places, and such decisions are always political, we must be certain to investigate the attitudes of the whole spectrum of the political elite, particularly (if relevant) the way they react to their own past history of nationalization or how they have adjusted to the foreign economic presence currently in their midst. Even in Peru where there is an almost overwhelming horror at the economic disaster of the 1970s, some elements of the younger military officer corps might allow their populist leanings to cloud their judgment if they came to power. And in China, if ever old ideologues were to resurface or new ideologues were to emerge to challenge the materialist modernizers, China could regress to an extreme version of "self-reliance" and rejection of Western capitalism, which could lead to repudiation of contract and expropriation, with or without compensation. Indeed xenophobia, or resentment of foreigners, is still a popular sentiment in a number of areas of the developing world. Beware of a desperate political elite that is in a position to manipulate such feelings during difficult economic times in order to scapegoat foreign enterprise.

The above discussion, perhaps contradictory in referring to the predilections of a given host country, only serves to underscore the need to be aware of the relevant variables and possible contingencies for each country and to monitor events from this baseline of knowledge.

Finally, a word about default on debt. A country's decision to default on external debt can reflect a fundamental attitudinal problem in the historical memory of the people. Officials and local businesspeople alike may seem to feel that they should be compensated for injustices suffered at the hand of the powerful nations a century ago. The foreign creditor, big or small, and the trader who expects to be paid are held accountable for their forebears. This resentment is rife in Latin America. A Venezuelan or a Mexican, for example, is not uncommonly disposed to justify not paying his debt by rationalizing that he is being unfairly gouged by a predatory company from the North. Almost at the other extreme, the Chinese government has demonstrated its creditworthiness and aversion to default when it first repaid its loans from the Soviet Union after the Sino-Soviet dispute erupted in 1960. Like an adolescent child seeking to demonstrate its autonomy to its parent, China proved its independence and integrity to its erstwhile benefactor. And since the start of China's modernization program in cooperation with Western investors and commercial and multilateral lending institutions, it has been very judicious about using the credit lines made available to it.

### U.S. Government Constraints Against Doing Business Abroad

Heretofore, we have examined political problems for business undertakings that have derived from the environment of the host country.

Often, the political relations between our government at a given time and that of the host country have a direct influence on opportunities and conditions for doing business there. A company that operates in a country where its own government cannot protect its nationals is taking on an added risk. The corporation should determine first whether opportunity outweighs risk and/or whether it has the leverage on its own to secure its position in the country in question.

A diplomatic reversal can constitute even more of a trauma than the absence of normalized relations in the first place. Whereas the opening or upgrading of diplomatic relations between the home country and country X can lead to an investment treaty, trade initiatives, and even a honeymoon period in bilateral business relations, the deterioration of diplomatic relations can severely impair business with the host country. A U.S. multinational is particularly vulnerable to hostility and abuse, sometimes expressed in violent acts of terrorism against installations because they seem to stand symbolically for the politics and economic policy of the home government. Robert Ebel notes:

> Contracts cannot be equated with diplomatic relations, which can be turned on and off as circumstances dictate. A corporation cannot pull out, leaving behind an "Interests Section" to look after matters. . . . A corporation either attempts to live up to the terms of a contract, or it leaves. Generally, a corporation will do what it can to protect its current and future income and will stay on unless forced out by threat of life.[3]

A corporation can ill afford the damages to its reputation, not to mention the loss of its investments or assets, of withdrawing from the country in question. At the same time, it stands naked in the chill of the host country's political climate and frequently suffers from the related punitive measures taken by its own government (such as the Reagan administration's refusal to grant visas for needed personnel to maintain existing American-owned facilities in Libya).

## Trade Sanctions/Embargoes/East-West Trade

It is easy to understand that the climate of diplomatic relations between two countries might have an indirectly salutary or conversely dissonant impact on the tone and volume of bilateral commerce. But for international businesspersons, the most noisome aspect of international relations concerns the manipulation of trade to augment foreign policy objectives. Indeed, sometimes the political disincentives to doing business overseas derive not from the aspects of instability in the projected host country, but from our own government's manipulation of the flow of trade for political leverage.

The United States, in particular, always has controlled exports for purposes of national security and foreign policy and when certain resources have been in short supply. The United States also is notorious for using embargoes or exercising restrictions on dual technology solely for punctuating a specific political policy message to the government of the country in question. When another country acts in a way that the United States finds threatening, or even takes a stand at counterpoint with our national policy, we frequently resort to trade sanctions against it. Sometimes, as in the case of the Jackson-Vanek Amendment, Congress will have mandated certain courses of action for certain types of abuses (e.g., impeded immigration from socialist bloc countries) and the president must act, but usually a given administration has a great deal of leeway and can forestall or instigate such initiatives. Thus, President Jimmy Carter responded to Russia's incursions against Afghanistan by promulgating sanctions against the export of grain to the former Soviet Union. Conversely, President George Bush resisted strong congressional efforts to mandate binding sanctions against the People's Republic of China for human rights abuses in the wake of the Tiananmen arrests.

Economic sanctions forged from political steel surely send a message to the targeted country, but the U.S. government also deals a blow to interested exporters from Iowa to New York and jeopardizes the financial commitments of corporations that have positioned themselves in that market and hurts others that have invested time and money in imminent commitments. In effect, we attempt to punish a particular foreign government by not permitting it to purchase the goods and services we regard as important to it. Unfortunately, seldom is one country the sole source of supply available to the purchaser, and our corporations often suffer in the process.

Short of actual embargoes but just as harmful to the U.S.-based corporation, export controls imposed for foreign policy purposes can be employed as sanctions over such issues as apartheid, human rights, nuclear nonproliferation, transnational aggression, terrorism and, in earlier days, East-West tensions. Here again the U.S. private sector pays the price! Efforts also to influence the lending policies of the multilaterals in certain countries indirectly make credit and projects less available to the U.S. developer.

The proclivity of large, supplier nations—particularly the United States—to utilize trade controls against other countries makes it necessary for us to look for trends in our own government's foreign policy instead of merely casting our gaze toward the host country in which we contemplate an exposure. In strategic planning, we can do our best to ready ourselves for this sort of foreign policy device and its concomitant loss of business by looking closely at our own administration in power and then examining which countries might be most vulnerable to the administration's prioritized issues and ideological values.

## The U.S. Foreign Corrupt Practices Act

In 1978, in the spirit of continuing to make the United States a standard bearer for the rest of the world, Congress passed the Carter administration's Foreign Corrupt Practices Act, which was designed to prohibit corporate bribery of foreign government officials or involve them in a conflict of interest. Putting aside the philosophical question of whether one nation should impose its values on another, the language of the act puts the American businessperson in jeopardy whenever she attempts to do business in a Third World country where some degree of what we call corruption has become an institutionalized social and political practice. What we regard as corruption often is just "the way things are done" in country X, whether it is "tea money" for a bureaucrat in Hong Kong or payment of a blind commission to an agent in Saudi Arabia with ties to pivotal figures in the royal family. The language of the Foreign Corrupt Practices Act places an undue burden on the U.S. businessperson to become enough of an insider both to understand and, if necessary, reform local business practices.

Let us focus on just one particular aspect of the act. Under the bribery provision, a corporation can be liable in accordance with the "reason to know" standard if an intermediary or agent pays a bribe from his own pocket, even if the company had no knowledge of the agent's actions or intent. Moreover, there are no concrete standards for what constitutes a "reason to know." Suppose a certain corporation is seeking an oil concession in the Persian Gulf area. To accomplish the objective, the corporate representative has no alternative but to hire an agent in the country in question. Through his connections, the agent makes it possible for the representative to meet with the appropriate officials to negotiate a concession. The agent then collects his commission from the outsider. It is known that payoffs are commonplace in this particular country. Does the foreign company representative have "reason to know" that this agent's fee will be shared with government officials? In effect, was he paying the appropriate officials for meeting with him and even determining the outcome, and did he have cause to know that this would be the case? If so, he might be charged with violating the Foreign Corrupt Practices Act and could be subject to fine and imprisonment.

In effect, the Foreign Corrupt Practices Act inhibits the American businessperson from seeking to penetrate certain markets. Many corporations have ignored opportunities in Indonesia or Nigeria for this reason; others have approached new international business too cautiously and inadvertently have yielded ground to their competitors. Should the corporate representative ask for a letter from a host country's local agents or principals in which they disavow the intention of using bribery, or will he be offending and alienating them in the asking?

In general, this act is a real hindrance to American business overseas. Corporations invest in legal counsel to monitor conformance of divisions and subsidiaries with this law. Not only is the language of the law ambiguous, but its purpose is questionable and even self-defeating. What we regard as venality is just a way in many societies of distributing wealth or compensating underpaid bureaucrats and officials.

## Antiboycott Restrictions

In yet another way, the U.S. government obstructs business operations overseas. The Export Administration Act expressly prohibits U.S. entities from doing business with a boycotted firm or in a boycotted country, in cases where that boycott is fostered or imposed by any country against a country that is friendly to the United States. Of course, the allusion is specifically to the Arab boycott of Israel. As Hermann Eilts indicates in his chapter on Saudi Arabia, U.S. businesspersons, like the U.S. government itself, are now often caught on the horns of a dilemma in which Arab countries can yield only so much in order to attract business from the West. As long as the Arab-Israeli dispute persists (perhaps an end is in sight), corporations must adhere to a panoply of statutes in the law that enumerate in exhaustive detail what U.S. firms can and cannot do under the boycott. All of these legal conditions are accompanied by very detailed reporting requirements. As an example, a company may be charged for failing even to report a boycott request, let alone for complying with such a request.

Suffice it to say that the reporting burden alone deters many smaller companies from entering the international marketplace, and for larger firms it means maintaining separate staff to follow boycott-related development in order to ensure compliance.

## *The Act of State Doctrine*

The Act of State Doctrine is largely unique to the United States. Conceived in more gentlemanly times 200 years ago, it affirms in essence that the legality of any action by any foreign state committed within its own territory cannot be challenged in our courts. An aggrieved U.S. company may be offered sympathy but nothing else. The denial of legal resource in situations in which a sovereign government is involved as adversary makes it all the more clear to us why a thorough understanding of a welcoming country's politics and political culture, not to mention its economic and commercial circumstances, is particularly critical in deals to which the government is party. Thus, if a business interest is selling a service like public affairs representation to the executive office of a foreign government, negotiating the architectural and engineering consulting work for a nuclear power plant, or seeking a petroleum exploration and production concession, it should be circumspect about its partner on the other side and recognize its singularly unshielded exposure.

It is ironically noteworthy in the end that the U.S. government can be the private sector's worst enemy in dealing with certain foreign countries. In a sense, in many areas of the world, U.S. business and financial interests might be at counterpoint with our own government policy. The activities of several U.S. oil companies in Angola serve as an example of being somewhat at odds with the U.S. government. And when our government fails to recognize a particular country, it makes operations in that country more unsheltered and frightening for U.S. corporations and personnel. Further, because our government will always assume a neutral position in territorial disputes, certain operations in contested areas will not be protected by the U.S. government. And if a contract is repudiated in the middle of a deal, our own courts will refuse to consider the matter. Finally, if a U.S. administration wants to apply pressure on a given country in which U.S. corporations are doing business, it can implement economic sanctions and withhold the approval of licenses that effectively will disrupt their in-country operations and possibly put them out of business altogether in that market.

## **Notes**

1. Lucian W. Pye and Sidney Verba, eds., *Political Culture and Political Development* (Princeton: Princeton University Press, 1965), p. 513.

2. Ibid., p. 7.

3. Robert E. Ebel, "The Magic of Political Risk Analysis," in Mark B. Winchester, ed., *The International Essays for Business Decision Makers,* Vol. V (Houston: Center for International Business, Amacom, 1980), p. 300.

*Chapter 3*

# Taking a Country's Economic and Commercial Temperature

As has been stated, the risk involved in financial transactions, particularly in developing countries, are at once political and economic. Political and economic development are intertwined, and in reality should not be separated. We often ask the question of how political changes will affect the economy. But fundamental economic restructuring and new exposures to foreign direct investment can have an equal impact on political configurations and attitudes.

Yet when a corporation looks at its exposure and its bottom line, it sometimes seems more convenient to focus on certain indicators that will point to direct and imminent risk to profits rather than seek a more complex picture of the political and social terrain. Good strategic planning should encompass the whole tapestry. We have seen that the more apparent political threats to the financial well-being of an enterprise stem from such government actions as expropriation or the imposition of crippling legal restrictions that will lead to expropriation; freezing a foreign company's assets or insistence on divestment; a government's failure or paralysis that can induce political uncertainty, social confusion, or chaos; and disruptions from various types of civil disorders including strikes, terrorism, and revolution.

## Indicators of General Financial Risk

Sometimes corporate strategic planners and international marketing executives can be satisfied with a "quick fix," something concrete into which they can sink their teeth. Numbers, especially numbers that seem likely to predict specific outcomes affecting profits and currency outflow, are appealing. Financial risks—currency inconvertibility, devaluation of the local currency, delays in payment, default or rescheduling of external debt, and deposit blockages—are easier to predict because the indicators are quantified and are in the public record. Still, one must never forget their interrelatedness with political and social variables, which can buffet them at every turn.

Historically, we know what margins to apply to macroeconomic parameters and can make our comparisons at an early stage when we are first prioritizing new markets for investment. Although the political/social and economic environments should not be regarded as separate, they can be treated as analytically discrete. For our purposes here, we will examine more closely the salient economic indicators that can provide at least a measure of the financial context in which we will be implementing our business deal.

Although it is impossible to foresee what risks are entailed by investment in a particular country, it is possible for the treasurer or finance departments, with the assistance of the political and economic support staff in international strategic planning, to develop an accurate, up-to-the-minute assessment of those factors—foreign exchange fluctuation and control, devaluation, and payment delays—that most closely affect investment and to maintain and update these analyses at short intervals. This part of a country evaluation, if scrupulously researched and carefully organized, can be presented in a concise, comprehensible form that will make sense to all reading it. To demonstrate this approach, Colombia in the early 1980s will be used as a case study. (And afterward perhaps the readers would care to do a bit of research and make their own forecasts for the 1990s.)

When an organization lends foreign exchange to an entity in another country or expects to earn foreign exchange from operations in that country, it must rely on the ability of that nation's economy to generate sufficient foreign exchange not only to carry out its day-to-day operations, but also to repay loans denominated in foreign currencies. Therefore, while it is important to consider the host country's overall economic performance in a longer term, more reflective, and academic analysis, what matters most at the outset of an investment in a foreign country are the international transactions of the economy. These have the most direct bearing on whether a multinational intermediate-size company doing business in that country will be able to realize a return on its outlay. For this reason, our financial evaluation of Colombia a decade ago begins with an "overview" (not unlike the brief executive summary) that sets forth the primacy of this perspective in recent historical context and pinpoints the key factors involved:

> The general long-term deterioration of the current account since 1972 and the large amounts of maturing short-term debt are two of the more pressing problems facing this economy. In general terms, the current account deficit can be attributed to the two-year slump in world commodity prices. Commodities in this country constitute a key source of its revenues. The commodity price slump is a result both of the world recession and the historical overvaluation of this currency relative to the currencies of its major trading partners. Colombia must take corrective measures to improve its current account position. Failure to take positive steps in this direction is apt to affect adversely the country's long-term development plans because of shortages of foreign exchange. Consequently, in the next six months, the government must accelerate its efforts to devalue the currency and will have to maintain or increase foreign exchange restrictions in an effort to improve the economy and avoid payment delays to suppliers.

After presenting this sort of profile of the country's international economic standing, noting the urgent need for a devaluation and the likely effect of such a devaluation on foreign exchange restrictions and the capacity to repay debts, we can then focus on at least six key indicators that justify our analysis of the country's environment for international business. To chart a course of some certainty, we need only check the following signposts:

1. Current Account
2. Debt Service Ratio
3. Reserves-to-Imports Ratio
4. Export Composition
5. Currency Competitiveness
6. Import Incompressibility

These indicators reliably measure a country's ability to generate the foreign exchange necessary to service foreign investment, repatriate capital and profits, and repay international loans because they produce a comprehensive and interrelated picture of the economy. These same indicators also will serve as a concrete basis for assessing the risks and opportunities in one country over another and prioritizing locations for business expansion. It is imperative that the data used in calculating these parameters be current—as up to date as possible. The volatility of developing nations as well as that of the general international marketplace requires that economic developments be followed closely, that the economic reports on these countries at least be updated quarterly or even more often, and that special attention be focused on the semiannual and quarterly trends of the previous two years. Stale data might not only be useless but it might mislead us and distort our image of the economy. Therefore, information from commonly available references such as the *World Bank Debt Tables* and *International Financial Statistics* (IFS) ought to be supplemented by the most current available data gathered from private, independent experts and especially from field representatives of divisions or subsidiaries. Furthermore, this information must be verified by other sources (perhaps two) to ensure that it is reliable and unbiased. Current data are useless if they are not totally objective.

Let's look closely at the definition, implications, and significance of each of our six international economic indicators and see how Colombia measures up to standards in each case.

## *Current Account*

The current account position is the net balance (exports less imports) on all transactions of merchandise, services, and unilateral transfers with all other countries within a specified time period. Consequently, this figure constitutes a measure of the foreign exchange flow in and out of a country. Generally, in developing countries, a current account deficit of 10 to 20 percent is cautionary; above 20 percent, it is alarming. Persistent deficits affect exchange rates and can result in the imposition of currency controls and import restrictions, which could hamper the operations of foreign corporations. Our data show that Colombia's current account position has been undulating at an alarming level since 1981 (see Table 3–1).

## *Debt Service Ratio*

The debt service ratio is the percentage of total export (i.e., debt : exports) required to finance annual interest and principal payments on the country's external debt. It covers the portion of the country's foreign exchange earnings that must go to pay loans. Under such circumstances, foreign exchange that must be used to repay debt becomes unavailable for expenditures in other areas of the economy.

**Table 3—1. Colombia's Current Account (in millions of U.S. dollars)**

| | Exports FOB | Imports FOB | Transfers Net S-T | Curr. Acct. Balance | Curr. Acct. Exports % |
|---|---|---|---|---|---|
| 1977 | 3514.00 | 3133.00 | 59.00 | 440.00 | 12.5213 |
| 1978 | 4130.00 | 3881.00 | 73.00 | 322.00 | 7.7966 |
| 1979 | 4851.00 | 4461.00 | 100.00 | 490.00 | 10.1010 |
| 1980 | 5862.00 | 6186.00 | 165.00 | − 159.00 | − 2.7124 |
| 1981 | 5014.00 | 7152.00 | 243.00 | − 1895.00 | − 37.7942 |
| 1982 1st half | 2571.00 | 3712.00 | 124.00 | − 2034.00 (a) | − 39.5566 |
| 1982 2nd half | 2421.00 | 3795.00 | 124.00 | − 2500.00 (a) | − 51.6316 |
| 1982 | 4992.00 | 7507.00 | 248.00 | − 2267.00 | − 45.4127 |
| 1983 1st quarter | 1204.00 (e) | 1720.00 (e) | 62.50 (e) | − 1814.00 (a) | − 37.6661 |
| 1983 2nd quarter | 1355.00 (e) | 1648.00 (e) | 62.50 (e) | − 922.00 (a) | − 17.0111 |
| 1983 3rd quarter | 1304.00 (e) | 1863.00 (e) | 62.50 (e) | − 1986.00 (a) | − 38.0752 |
| 1983 4th quarter | 1154.00 (e) | 1936.00 (e) | 62.50 (e) | − 2878.00 (a) | − 62.3484 |
| 1983 | 5017.00 (e) | 7167.00 (e) | 250.00 (e) | − 1900.00 (e) | − 37.8712 |

(a) = annualized.
(e) = estimate.
Note: All 1977–82 data from November 1983 IFS.

Different analyses may use different figures for computing the debt service ratio. In general, ratios that are based on both public and private debt are more accurate and reflective of the reality of the economic condition. While short-term debt (less than a year) is not often included in debt service calculations, it must be ascertained that this category of debt per se does not rise too rapidly as a percentage of total borrowing. A debt service ratio of 20 to 30 percent is cautionary; above 30 percent, alarming. All other things being equal, an alarming debt service index indicates a need for a more restrictive foreign exchange policy. Our data demonstrate that Colombia's combined public and private debt service ratio reached a precarious level in 1983 (the culmination of this case study), while its public sector debt service ratio continued to move upward toward a cautionary level (see Table 3–2).

Generally, in looking at the debt service ratio of a country, the corporate strategist or marketing officer should weigh other factors before assuming the worst about a country's impending need for currency controls or limits on the repatriation of a foreign company's profits. Apart from the magnitude of a country's hard-currency reserve (discussed below), one might look for the existence of special sources of inflowing aid or low-interest loans that have political or strategic implications. Examine also the government's political awareness of the

**Table 3–2. Colombia's Debt Service Ratios: Public, and Public and Private**

| | Debt Service Ratio—Public Only (millions US $) | | | | | Debt Service Ratio—Public and Private (millions US $) | | | | |
|---|---|---|---|---|---|---|---|---|---|---|
| | Principal payments | Interest payments | Total debt service | Exports | Debt service ratio | Principal payments | Interest payments | Total debt service | Exports | Debt service ratio |
| 1977 | 175.50 | 137.10 | 312.60 | 3556.00 | 8.79 | 234.10 | 161.00 | 395.10 | 3556.00 | 11.11 |
| 1978 | 224.80 | 168.20 | 393.00 | 4174.00 | 9.42 | 287.30 | 198.80 | 486.10 | 4174.00 | 11.65 |
| 1979 | 430.10 | 227.10 | 657.20 | 4952.00 | 13.27 | 472.20 | 270.10 | 742.30 | 4952.00 | 14.99 |
| 1980 | 263.10 | 282.20 | 545.30 | 5655.00 | 9.64 | 316.20 | 296.70 | 612.90 | 5655.00 | 10.84 |
| 1981 | 308.70 | 416.90 | 725.60 | 4953.00 | 14.65 | 581.70 | 564.10 | 1145.80 | 4953.00 | 23.13 |
| 1982 1st half | 164.55 | 263.20 | 427.75 | 2571.00 | 16.64 | N.A. | N.A. | 674.50 | 2571.00 | 26.23 |
| 1982 2nd half | 164.55 | 263.20 | 427.75 | 2421.00 | 17.67 | N.A. | N.A. | 674.50 | 2421.00 | 27.86 |
| 1982 | 329.10 | 526.40 | 855.50 | 4992.00 | 17.14 | N.A. | N.A. | 1349.00 | 4992.00 | 27.02 |
| 1983 1st quarter | 101.15 | 140.05 | 241.20 | 1204.00 (e) | 20.03 | N.A. | N.A. | 477.00 | 1204.00 (e) | 39.62 |
| 1983 2nd quarter | 101.15 | 140.05 | 241.20 | 1355.00 (e) | 17.80 | N.A. | N.A. | 477.00 | 1355.00 (e) | 35.20 |
| 1983 3rd quarter | 101.15 | 140.05 | 241.20 | 1304.00 (e) | 18.50 | N.A. | N.A. | 477.00 | 1304.00 (e) | 36.58 |
| 1983 4th quarter | 101.15 | 140.05 | 241.20 | 1154.00 (e) | 20.90 | N.A. | N.A. | 477.00 | 1154.00 (e) | 41.33 |
| 1983 | 404.60 | 560.20 | 964.80 | 5017.00 (e) | 19.23 | N.A. | N.A. | 1908.00 | 5017.00 (e) | 38.03 |

N.A. = not available.
(e) = estimate.
*Note:* 1977–81 total debt service and exports from World Bank Debt Tables.
1982 and 1983 public debt service figures are World Bank Debt Table projections.
1982 and 1983 public and private debt service figures are Morgan Guaranty projections adjusted for short-term rollover debt. Without this adjustment the debt service figures would be 95% for 1982 and 98% for 1983.
1982 exports are from IFS.

need to take corrective action without scaring off foreign direct investment and the political climate (i.e., consensus among the active political constituencies) in the host country for such remediation as mea-
sured devaluations that will limit purchasing power and the outflow of
currency.

### Reserves-to-Import Ratio

International reserves consist of a country's holdings of gold, its
special drawing rights (SDRs), and its foreign exchange and reserve
position in the International Monetary Fund. The reserves are used to
protect a country from fluctuations in foreign exchange earnings.
International reserves divided by the imports of goods and services
produce what we call the reserves-to-imports ratio. From a different
perspective, this percentage can be expressed in terms of the number
of months for which the reserves can cover the current influx of
imports. A ratio of two to three months is considered cautionary; less
than two months is considered alarming. This ratio measures a country's ability to endure temporary balance-of-payments difficulties. A
country's foreign exchange reserves can be used to finance imports
and debt payments during periods of reduced export earnings or high
import demand. In general, an indicator that falls in the "alarming"
range reflects a country's loss of flexibility to cope with foreign
exchange fluctuations and a need for immediate action if conditions of
cross-border flow continue to deteriorate. Because the diversity of
export and import baskets affect the need for reserves, this factor must
be considered when interpreting this ratio.

In other words, a worst case might be an economy whose exports
are limited primarily to one or just a few agriculturally derived commodities. (We will look at this question as a separate indicator below.)
Such a country would be particularly vulnerable to fluctuations in the
price of international commodities; and if it were in the position of still
being a net importer of food for its people, its hard-currency reserves
could be depleted in an unstable and frequently soft international
market. Our data show that Colombia's reserves-to-imports ratio remained at the satisfactory level by the last year of our study, still
representing a relative decline from the last years of the 1970s (see
Table 3–3).

### Export Composition

Export composition is the degree of concentration of each commodity in the overall export picture of the country. We look for vulnerabil-

**Table 3—3. Colombia's Reserves/Imports (in millions of U.S. dollars, end of period, except imports)**

| | Reserves less gold | Gold—million troy ounces | Gold—market price edp London | Gold reserves | Total reserves incl. gold | Imports | Reserves as % of imports | Reserves in months of imports |
|---|---|---|---|---|---|---|---|---|
| 1977 | 1747.00 | 1.7310 | 160.60 | 278.00 | 2025.00 | 3133.00 | 64.63 | 7.76 |
| 1978 | 2366.00 | 1.9610 | 208.20 | 408.28 | 2774.28 | 3881.00 | 71.48 | 6.58 |
| 1979 | 3844.00 | 2.3170 | 455.20 | 1054.70 | 4898.70 | 4461.00 | 109.81 | 13.18 |
| 1980 | 4831.00 | 2.7870 | 595.20 | 1658.82 | 6489.82 | 6186.00 | 104.91 | 12.59 |
| 1981 | 4801.00 | 3.3550 | 410.70 | 1377.90 | 6178.90 | 7152.00 | 86.39 | 10.37 |
| 1982 1st half | 4301.00 | 3.5790 | 314.90 | 1127.03 | 5428.03 | 7424.00 (a) | 73.11 | 8.77 |
| 1982 2nd half | 3861.00 | 3.8170 | 444.00 | 1694.75 | 5555.75 | 7590.00 (a) | 73.20 | 8.78 |
| 1982 | 3861.00 | 3.8170 | 444.00 | 1694.75 | 5555.75 | 7507.00 | 74.01 | 8.88 |
| 1983 1st quarter | 3157.00 | 3.9230 | 419.90 | 1651.05 | 4808.05 | 6880.00 (a) | 69.88 | 8.39 |
| 1983 2nd quarter | 2774.00 | 4.0250 | 413.00 | 1662.33 | 4436.33 | 6592.00 (a) | 67.30 | 8.08 |
| 1983 3rd quarter | 2015.00 | 4.1450 | 405.30 | 1679.97 | 3694.97 | 7542.00 (a) | 49.58 | 5.95 |
| 1983 4th quarter | 2000.00 (e) | 4.2000 (e) | 385.00 (e) | 1617.00 | 3617.00 | 7744.00 (a) | 46.71 | 5.60 |
| 1983 | 2000.00 (e) | 4.2000 (e) | 385.00 (e) | 1617.00 | 3617.00 | 7167.00 (e) | 50.47 | 6.06 |

(a) = annualized.
(e) = estimate.
*Note:* All reserve data from November 1983 IFS.

ity due to dependence on one commodity or a narrow range of commodities. The export composition factor measures what percentage of a nation's export revenue is accounted for by the commodity(ies) and how dependent those items are per se on the commodities market in general. Reliance in one narrow commodity group for 30 to 50 percent of the economy's foreign exchange earnings would be cautionary, while more than 50 percent would be alarming.

### Currency Competitiveness

Currency competitiveness measures the extent to which local inflation has been offset by the exchange rate movements. It is computed by dividing the inflation index by the exchange index.

A high domestic exchange rate, reflected in the Consumer Price Index, eventually will render a country's exports noncompetitive in the world market. And imports will damage local industry by being less costly than domestic goods. This situation augurs ill for the survival of domestic producers and causes large current account deficits. The customary remedy is to devalue the local currency and thereby reverse the trend. Politically unpopular with local populations, devaluations have become the thrust of the IMF's economic restructuring recommendations to Third World countries and the former nonmarket economies of Europe.

The theoretical extent of devaluation needed to achieve currency competitiveness tentatively can be projected. An index of 1.3 to 1.5 is cautionary; if it exceeds 1.5, it is alarming. However, it really is difficult to project a completely reliable range for this factor. In the case of Colombia about ten years ago, our data show that the country's currency competitiveness hovered at the cautionary level during the four years preceding our study (see Table 3–4).

### Import Incompressibility

When a country is not self-sufficient in food and fuel, these commodities necessarily constitute its essential imports. They are the country's lifeblood and vital to the functioning of the economy. From our perspective, the ratio of food and fuel to the total import of goods and services should determine what we call the *import incompressibility* of a country's economy. The ability of a country to discourage imports by manipulating the exchange rate depends in large part on the composition of its whole import package. Comparatively high dependency

**Table 3—4.   Colombia's Currency Competitiveness: Change in
             Inflation/Exchange Rate**

|  | Consumer Price Index—Colombia 1975 = 100 | Exchange rate in pesos | Consumer Price Index—USA 1975 = 100 | Ratio |
|---|---|---|---|---|
| 1977 | 159.40 | 37.86 | 115.40 | 1.20 |
| 1978 | 189.40 | 41.00 | 125.90 | 1.21 |
| 1979 | 258.50 | 44.00 | 142.60 | 1.36 |
| 1980 | 327.70 | 50.92 | 160.30 | 1.32 |
| 1981 | 413.50 | 59.07 | 174.60 | 1.32 |
| 1982 1st half | 473.90 | 63.84 | 180.30 | 1.36 |
| 1982 2nd half | 512.96 | 70.29 | 181.42 | 1.33 |
| 1982 | 512.96 | 70.29 | 181.42 | 1.33 |
| 1983 1st quarter | 536.38 | 74.19 | 182.04 | 1.31 |
| 1983 2nd quarter | 570.87 | 78.51 | 184.94 | 1.30 |
| 1983 3rd quarter | 607.97 (e) | 83.40 | 188.22 (e) | 1.28 |
| 1983 4th quarter | 647.49 (e) | 89.27 (e) | 190.49 (e) | 1.26 |
| 1983 | 647.49 (e) | 89.27 (e) | 190.49 (e) | 1.26 |

(e) = estimate.

*Note:* All data except estimates from IFS.
       1975 CPI (US and Colombia) = 100.
       1975 exchange rate: 32.96P/dollar.
       CPI and exchange rate are end of period figures.

on essential imports reduces the feasibility of the devaluation option
as a mean of cutting down total imports to more manageable levels;
the end result might be as desperate as the resort to foreign exchange
controls. Further, external dependency in an area so critical to the
operation of the economy is subject to the vagaries of international
politics. The cutting of a pipeline by terrorists from a port country
inland or a war in the Persian Gulf to punish Saddam Hussein could
throw this sort of vulnerable economy into a state of paralysis. An
indicator between 25 and 35 percent suggests that the situation is
cautionary; a ratio of above 35 percent should be considered precarious. Our data show that Colombia's import incompressibility rose
steadily from a satisfactory level in 1970 to a possibly stable but
cautionary level by 1983, the last year of our study (see Table 3–5).

The data used in calculating the above six indicators and the trends
that the indicators suggest can be aggregated simply, allowing us to
determine the soundness of our footing purely from a macroeconomic
standpoint (political considerations, of course, always can intervene)
in any country in which we might contemplate an exposure. In an

**Table 3—5.  Colombia's Import Incompressibility**

| | Fuel imports | | Food imports | | Food and fuel |
|---|---|---|---|---|---|
| | *% of imports* | *US $ millions* | *% of imports* | *US $ millions* | *as % of total imports* |
| 1977 | 6.80 | 213.04 | 9.70 | 303.90 | 16.50 |
| 1978 | 7.30 | 283.31 | 8.50 | 329.89 | 15.80 |
| 1979 | 10.10 | 450.56 | 7.10 | 316.73 | 17.20 |
| 1980 | 12.20 | 754.69 | 9.30 | 575.30 | 21.50 |
| 1981 | 13.00 | 929.76 | 10.00 | 715.20 | 23.00 (e) |
| 1982 1st half | 14.00 (a) | 1039.36 | 11.00 (a) | 816.64 | 25.00 (a) |
| 1982 2nd half | 14.00 (a) | 1062.60 | 11.00 (a) | 834.90 | 25.00 (a) |
| 1982 | 14.00 (e) | 1050.98 | 11.00 (e) | 825.77 | 25.00 (e) |
| 1983 1st quarter | 15.00 (a) | 1032.00 | 12.00 (a) | 825.60 | 27.00 (a) |
| 1983 2nd quarter | 15.00 (a) | 988.80 | 12.00 (a) | 791.04 | 27.00 (a) |
| 1983 3rd quarter | 15.00 (a) | 1117.80 | 12.00 (a) | 894.24 | 27.00 (a) |
| 1983 4th quarter | 15.00 (a) | 1161.60 | 12.00 (a) | 929.28 | 27.00 (a) |
| 1983 | 15.00 (e) | 1075.05 | 12.00 (e) | 860.04 | 27.00 (e) |

(e) = estimate.
(a) = annualized.
*Note:* All data except estimates from IMF Supplement on Trade Statistics.

integrated approach designed to convey a thorough conception of the financial risks that bear on investment in a particular country, the user is encouraged to dig into the data base, the tables and graphs, as well as the discursive assessments and judgments made from the statistical and analytical substructure of the report. Understanding as fully as possible the basis for our interpretation should instill confidence and increase the user's sensitivity to the need to monitor longitudinally the data for certain critical indicators. In the case of Colombia in the early 1980s, the user has been naturally pointed in the direction of such negative possible outcomes as sudden maxidevaluations; foreign exchange controls; and problems with debt repayment as consequences of a worst-case downward spiral in current account position, debt service, currency competitiveness, and import incompressibility. The financial risk picture in a given country becomes clarified but not oversimplified. In the case of Colombia, for example, incontext analysis of the data interpretation of the trends based on six key indicators lead to a detailed but succinct assessment of what we might expect.

This kind of analysis—focusing on the problems themselves—is very useful to strategic planners and regional marketing executives as they order their priorities. However murky the economic situation of a country, it is important, indeed essential, that the delineation of its pivotal problems be as unambiguous and direct as possible. The commitment to a persistent analytical clarity should not produce simplistically blanket descriptions of a country's general economic situation, but an eyes-open and tough-minded interpretation of the current facts and the recent historical trends. No financial risk assessment is foolproof or capable of pointing a sure finger to actual outcomes, but in its precision it can instill confidence in the likelihood of certain scenarios. Correct numerical data and solid interpretation can deter even the most zealous marketing officer, who is anxious about meeting short-term pressures to deliver at the bottom line and who thinks that he is staring at what he thinks is a jewel of a business deal, from walking into a minefield.

The advantage of the financial/macroeconomic overview for countries under consideration either for foreign direct investment or long-term trade is that they permit the user at different levels to approach individual transactions in the context of a clearly defined topography of a less developed economy's critical financial characteristics and with a personal understanding that is supported by up-to-the-minute and reliable data.

For multinationals or smaller companies ensconced in an economically troubled country, panic is supplanted by the assurance of a foreknowledge of trends. The information based on an ongoing tracking of a country's economy facilitates certain expectations of problems associated with operations like the year-end translation of funds. Major devaluations, currency controls, significant debt rescheduling, and delays in payment all can be anticipated.

In addition, this use of risk indicators can provide the basis for a compromise between centralized and decentralized control of foreign exchange transfers in the case of multinationals. It provides the local manager with the leeway to borrow and lend as well as to cover exposed positions at corporate rates. At the same time, the central treasury of the corporation is able to assay the net local position of its subsidiaries in order to decide if it needs to obtain a forward exchange contract from a commercial bank. This system is particularly beneficial to the nonbank multinational because it encourages local initiative while leaving the management of foreign exchange controls to the centralized treasury. Service companies, which depend on the foreign exchange earnings of the country for their funding, will derive special benefits from this approach.

Our suggested analysis of financial risk and planning for certain types of outcomes finally is meant to be particularly helpful to corporations whose local projects have longer gestation periods (e.g., nuclear power plants or coal mines) and those multinationals whose project financing depends on future local earnings either to repay a loan involved or to compensate the parent multinational company.

## Commercial Conditions and Disincentives

Politics aside and in plain business terms, the macroeconomic environment should be only the second criterion for deciding whether to invest in a given overseas (particularly a Third World or Russian/Eastern European) market. In considering the underpinnings of a good business deal overseas, the paramount priority is the desirability of the undertaking itself: its contractual terms and capital, reliability of partners, credit arrangements, return of invested capital, time frame, and profitability.

But the merits of the deal and the soundness of the broader economic environment are not sufficient. Still another problematic facet of doing business overseas consists of the market conditions in a host country. We do not refer here to the marketability of specific products or services. Rather, we are concerned with the procedural and circumstantial context of doing business in a particular country, particularly where economic development is at a different stage from our own and where cultural behavior can vary so widely. For example, when we identify a problem of a shortage of skilled labor in a given country, we are not throwing up a red flag and advising a certain type of investor to stay away. We are simply educating ourselves properly about the commercial environment. Indeed, skilled-labor shortages need not be a drawback for some types of business operations, and even can serve as leverage at the negotiation table.

Similarly, when we prepare ourselves before negotiations in many countries to expect the host country to demand that the foreign enterprise provide certain types of peripherally related infrastructure, we already will have been able to estimate additional costs relative to profits. We then can decide judiciously what options, if any, would make the job feasible and approach the table properly informed.

A corporation should familiarize itself with the host country's business regulations. The U.S. Department of Commerce or the U.S. International Chamber of Commerce will provide a list of local legal firms. Punitive taxation is a critical factor to consider. For example, if we already are aware that taxation on foreign enterprise and expatriates is excessive, we can weigh this fact against the other variables and may choose to go elsewhere. As Rensselaer W. Lee's case study of Colombia later points out, harsh taxes seem to be keeping companies away, particularly in the petroleum industry where taxes are discriminatory; the foreign oil companies now producing in Colombia are getting increasingly uncomfortable as taxes rise and whispers about nationalization can be heard in the distance.

If the financial variables that we have discussed in this chapter must be examined in terms of *risks*, then commercial conditions must be regarded critically as *disincentives*. Although the commercial features of a host country are more like disincentives than risks, they do have the capacity to erode a business deal after it is underway.

An interrelationship also exists between the commercial environment and the political and social dimensions. Spain is an example. To appease the left wing of its socialist party (PSOE) and secure its support for joining NATO shortly after it was voted into office, the Felipe González administration canceled contracts for five of ten U.S. Export-Import Bank–financed nuclear power facilities. In this case, political considerations clearly determined commercial circumstances. Similarly, commercial factors have influenced political moods. In Venezuela in the late 1970s, just as political attitudes were softening toward foreign intervention, an American construction company—with more than the usually-permitted share of equity ownership—advertised its enterprise as its own, reactivated Venezuelan nationalism, and, in turn, reinforced the formalized restraints on foreign ownership.

### A Hall of Mirrors: Never Lose Sight of the Analytical Interface Between Categories

It is important to recognize the interdependence of macroeconomic/financial, political/social, and commercial criteria as part of the necessary education to gain a business footing in a strange country. If the business planner and marketing officers do not do the proper homework, they are apt to trip themselves up! International marketing executives certainly are capable of developing their own "feel" for the local terrain and certainly can handle the "nuts and bolts" detailed analysis themselves. But it is important to enumerate here the broader aspects of commercial disincentives: drawbacks that can virtually be taken as risks and, under certain circumstances, could subvert a business operation. These include *restrictions on capital flows*, such as import controls and deliberately engineered problems in currency transfer in both directions through the central bank; *limitations on foreign investment*, including prescribed limits and guidelines for equity ownership, expansion, and divestment (these conditions might vary with a change in the host government's administration or with a modification of political atmosphere); *limits on the employment of expatriate personnel at varying levels* (a real impediment when a project requires skilled labor that is not readily available in the host country); *limits on the local availability of skilled or unskilled labor* (in some countries, like Tunisia or Pakistan, even the less-skilled workers customarily might migrate to other countries in the region for more lucrative jobs); *bureaucratic inefficiency and corruption*, which in some cases can bog down business deals and ongoing operations to such an extent that they make the Ethiopian government's management of the distribution of food and aid to the starving seem smooth; *contract repudiation*, for which even the best safeguards—personal political contacts—in a country like Indonesia do not always come through on your side; in the case of construction and infrastructure projects, a pattern of *arbitrary actions against performance guarantee bonds* by a state agency; the aforementioned *punitive corporate or personal income taxation* (in Tunisia, expatriates are taxed so highly that a company's use of its own managerial personnel is de facto restricted); *the official attitude toward contract arbitration*; and in the not-to-be minimized drawbacks of confronting a weak and inadequate physical infrastructure to provide access to and from, and to support, the project at hand.

(Often the local government will try to entice the investor to establish a presence in outlying areas by offering tax holidays and other incentives. The businessperson must weight the infrastructural costs, as well as skilled-labor needs, against these inducements. In Guinea, with less than 1,000 miles of paved roads, any undertaking necessarily would incur a heavy front-end cost just to create the proper environment, transportation, and communications to get underway. And in remote parts of China, onshore oil is so waxy and viscous that it would be unfeasible for a potential foreign joint-venture partner to construct a heated pipeline to transport the petroleum in liquid state to the coastline or any major urban center.)

Although analytical distinctions must be made, it takes little imagination to suppose that politics, political culture, macroeconomic circumstances, and commercial conditions all are interrelated. Nevertheless, how often do we hear, both in the home office and in the field, that because there is little one can do to control the vagaries of a nation's politics, one ought to focus on financial variables alone. Yet to position itself for a long-term stay in a country a company must not only know what is going on politically but perhaps become a player— an unobtrusive one—in the game. And to operate effectively, it must adapt to, as well as from time to time manipulate, the mechanics of the commercial system.

On the economic side, politics is often a critical consideration. Many a decision not to introduce a maxidevaluation, when financial variables might have warranted such a radical step, was either deferred or implemented in dribbles for political reasons. The memory of riots in the streets and coups elicited either by populist inclinations of a segment of the military or the draconian suppression of the chaos can deter a government from performing much-needed radical surgery.

The commercial environment too is intertwined with political considerations. Political influence from above can cut through the red tape and conflicting regulations of an obdurate commercial bureaucracy. Governments can be lobbied to streamline existing regulations and take further steps toward eliminating parastatal companies as well as rationalizing the public's oversight role in the commercial arena. Many governments, like Egypt's and Gabon's, muddy the business environment by dumping political friends into the commercial bureaucracy. Where public sector companies play an important role in the economic process, their utilization as receptacles for political patronage appointees does little to increase the efficiency of carrying on business.

## A Word Before Proceeding

The reader now should have a certain grasp of the analytical variables that make an investment in Siberia more complex than one in Alaska, a trade agreement with an agency of the government of China more arcane and difficult to negotiate than with a major company in San Francisco's Chinatown. It is not just a question of strange faces and strange places—although that is indeed a psychological facet of the process. In spite of the fact that foreign environments increasingly are becoming part of the international legal and business mainstream, the differences that remain can determine the successful outcome of both the business deal in the making and the seminal operation at a stage when it wants to secure and improve its position in a host country.

As much as we might continue to expect modernity to homogenize phenomena throughout the world, we will be startled from time to time

by the reenactment of pre–World War I ethnic fights several generations after they had supposedly receded into the annals of history. We
will continue to witness the undermining of the legitimacy of seemingly
well-anchored governments, terrorism against foreign businesspeople,
and in all likelihood, nearly all the factors that we have attempted to
present in this core section of the book as a prism for the businessper-
son-adventurer to gain her or his bearings in a host country.

Whether or not a knowledge of these variables will help the businessperson of the 1990s in concrete ways to navigate new markets and avoid
all the pitfalls, the section's perspective (replete with illustrative examples
from over thirty countries) at least will sensitize the businessperson to the
need for proceeding with a wide-angle lens at all times.

The country case studies to follow, all contributed by area specialists, and framed according to the variables outlined in our preceding
discussion, will go a step farther. The writers, each in their creative
way, have emphasized those variables from the book's method and
approach that most seem to apply to circumstances in the specific
country under discussion. We hope that they will illuminate in greater
detail some of the key points that we have made, perhaps even
providing the reader with some of the practical information that can be
used in the here and now in actual work in one of the important
countries under discussion.

Finally, if the reader identifies critical environmental difficulties that
may jeopardize assets and personnel, and still cannot resist the promised profits of the investment, the corporation always can resort to
political risk insurance. Such coverage is offered by the government-
linked Overseas Private Investment Corporation or, for exports, the
FDIC. In some cases, private insurers will cover those countries that
do not yet qualify for U.S. government backing in diversified portfolios
for several countries. We have included a section on this practical
information because it is a conservative way to shield your investment
once you have identified serious vulnerabilities in your project and in
the political and economic environment of a given host country.

*Part Two*

# COUNTRY CASE STUDIES

*Chapter 4*

# The Broader Areas of Uncertainty for Foreign Business in the People's Republic of China

## Guocang Huan

### Examining the Business Environment in China

China's political uncertainties have always been a difficult subject for
government and corporate executives to explore. Over the past four
decades, scholars in the field of Chinese studies have also tried to
study this set of problems. Yet most of them have failed because of the
following major reasons:

1. There are no sufficient data about China's political and economic
development available;
2. The perspectives and methodologies that these scholars use to
conduct their research do not fit China's fast-paced, changing reality;
3. Risk studies must be a multidisciplinary undertaking;
4. China's activities in the international market have expanded
rapidly over the past fourteen years and studies of political risk must
be placed in a global economic context; and
5. Most of these scholars do not know how the business community
works, nor are they attentive to individual industries both in China and

overseas. Therefore, they cannot know adequately how to draw implications from their studies for the practical business process.

A typical example was the predictions about China's political and
economic development since the Tiananmen crisis of June 1989. There
were basically two major schools of thought. One, which represents
the majority of China specialists' view, believed that the crackdown on
student demonstrations was the end of China's reform and open-door
policy. According to this view, the hard-liners in Beijing would bring
the nation back to the prereform period; indeed the Tiananmen phenomenon meant that reform had already failed. In addition, they
believed that due to the country's internal instability and its troubled
ties with most OECD nations, the risk of investing in China would
exceed the potential gains. After the collapse of the Communist system
in the former Soviet Union and Eastern Europe, this school believed
that the political system in China also would fall eventually.

The second school believed that business would go on as usual: the
central government in Beijing had no intention of reversing the reform
process; it was capable of getting the country in order; the majority of
the population wanted stability and prosperity and they did not care
about democracy, which might result in chaos; China would likely
follow the authoritarian or neo-authoritarian model adopted in many
Asian newly industrialized nations (NICs) to transform its system
smoothly; as a result, they believed the political risk for foreign
investors in China was low and would remain low in the years to come.

Nevertheless, both schools failed to explain what has really happened in China over the past four years. The system in China did not
fall and will not fall in the foreseeable future. The reform in China did
not come to an end, but rather continues to advance, especially on the
Chinese coast. Yet there is no question that the hard-liners in Beijing
did try their best to reverse the reform process, especially during the
second half of 1989 and the first half of 1990. Only because of the
strong resentment and resistance from broad sectors in Chinese society, including local authorities, did their efforts fail. Meanwhile, fundamental political and economic problems remain unsolved, although
the country's rapid economic growth, its continued economic reform,
and the post–Cold War international environment have partially
changed the nature of issues with which China must deal.

To provide business executives with a framework to analyze China's
political risk, this chapter first reviews the country's recent political
and economic changes, then discusses its future trends, analyzes

China's position in the international system, and finally outlines basic implications of these trends for the international community.

## The Chinese Economy in Rapid Transition

The Chinese economy is in transition. Over the past four years, the central government has been heavily dependent on macroeconomic instruments (fiscal policy, investment strategy, interest rates, money supply, taxation, and import and export controls) to guide economic growth and bring down the inflation rate. Its efforts to reform the existing economic system were inconsistent between the summer of 1989 and the end of 1991. In 1990 the central government, for instance, launched a campaign to attack the private sector and recentralize fiscal power from local authorities. It also substantially reduced bank credit to rural industries and other non-state-owned enterprises while increasing taxes on them. Its development strategy shifted back to support for large-sized state-owned enterprises by providing them fiscal subsidies and low-interest loan rates. These policies, in turn drove the economy into a deep recession in 1990.

By the middle of 1990, the inflation rate dropped to about 2 percent, while the growth rate fell to 1.7 percent, the lowest since 1978. The total number of unemployed surged sharply to 70 million because of the government's recessionary policies and its campaign against the private sector and rural industries. The living standard of urban residents remained stagnant. The recession also significantly reduced the government's tax revenue and drove up its fiscal deficits. At the same time, the state sector's efficiency continued to decline while its debts rose sharply.

The only major improvement was in fact the foreign trade sector. In both 1989 and 1990, because of the central government's tough control over imports, China's balance of trade turned to surplus as its foreign exchange reserves began to rise. Between summer 1989 and summer 1990, when the Japanese government announced its decision to resume its yen loans to Beijing, most OECD nations imposed economic sanctions against Beijing. International financial organizations such as the World Bank and Asian Development Bank (ADB) stopped their lending to China, and most multinational banks temporarily cut off their business ties with their Chinese clients. Beginning in fall 1989, however, Hong Kong, Taiwanese, and South Korean investors substantially increased their investment in China.

The summer of 1990 was a turning point. Under strong pressure from local authorities and the society at large, the central government began to give up its recessionary economic policies, which created social instability, especially in those areas where the nonstate sector declined sharply and unemployment was severe. It once again endorsed its support for the expansion of non-state-sector and rural industries. Having increased money supply and credit for industries, the government granted more autonomy to local authorities, especially those along the Chinese coast, to decide their own economic, development, and foreign economic policies. In addition to establishing securities and foreign exchange markets, the government also provided new tax incentives to foreign investors. As a result, the economy quickly recovered. In 1991, real GDP rose to 7.2 percent. In particular, the nonstate sector, rural industries, and foreign-involved enterprises grew rapidly, while the efficiency of the state sector remained poor. Due partially to China's cheap labor and huge market potential, companies from Asian NICs, which have been under strong pressure to upgrade their labor-intensive manufacturing operations to higher technology and capital-intensive industries, significantly increased their investment in China. In 1991, the amount of foreign contracted investment surged by 50 percent to U.S. $18 billion. These developments supported China's exports, resulting in a trade surplus of U.S. $9.5 billion in 1991.

Since Deng Xiaoping's meaningful trip to the South in early 1992, the government has resumed most reform programs that were delayed and canceled soon after Tiananmen. It once again initiated a price reform, lifting 90 percent of its control over prices and cutting most of its subsidies to agricultural and other products. It has expanded securities markets and foreign exchange markets and established real estate markets. In October 1992, the government formed new national organizations to regulate and supervise financial markets. Having further encouraged the development of non-state-sector and rural industries, which now produce about one-third of the country's total GDP, the government converted more than 30,000 state-owned enterprises into more rationalized corporations. State-owned enterprises increasingly have received management autonomy with regard to finance and foreign trade. In these enterprises, managers now enjoy the power to determine wages, salaries, and bonuses. They can fire workers without government interference.

The government has substantially increased money supply, bank credits, and its own investment in infrastructure and industrial projects. For the first eight months of 1992, total state investment increased 36.5 percent from the previous year. The amount of credit supply was 150 percent higher than the government's previous plan. In addition to granting greater decision-making power to local authorities, which now control about 70 percent of the total state budget, the central government has granted foreign investors more favorable conditions, including tax vacations, greater market shares, exemptions from import and export duties, the right to form 100 percent foreign-owned enterprises, and the right of converting profits in yuan that foreign investors made in China into hard currencies through the Bank of China.

These policies have resulted in an economic boom: during the first eight months of 1992, the real GDP surged about 10 percent while industrial production increased 19 percent. The total number of proved foreign investments reached 30,000, bringing about contracted investment of about U.S. $5 billion. The degree of China's dependence on the international market has thus increased sharply. More important, local authorities have become more independent than ever while the nonstate sector has expanded rapidly. As the role that the State Planning Commission plays has declined, the market mechanism has become an increasingly important factor in determining the behavior of individuals, enterprises, and even governmental institutions.

Fast economic growth has also brought about a number of new challenges. First, it was an investment-led growth. The rapidly increased investment has pushed up inflation. In particular, prices of capital goods, raw materials, and energy increased sharply. According to the Chinese government, by the end of summer 1992, thirty-five large cities had already returned to double-digit inflation rates. If the government fails to reduce money and credit supplies and if the economy remains at the current growth rate, inflation will become a major threat to the country's economic and political stability sometime in the spring of 1993.

Second, there has been a lack of coordination between the government's macroeconomic management on the one side and its institutional reform programs on the other. Its policy of expanding securities markets, for instance, was not supported by its monetary and interest-rate policies. Nor was there much coordination between its policies governing the new real estate market, securities markets, and other macroeconomic policies. As a result, while personal savings rose to 1,000 billion yuan, deposit interest rates remained at least 200 base points lower than the real inflation rate. There are, however, only limited investment instruments available to Chinese residents and the size of the stock market does not meet the demand. The stock market is not linked to the bond market (which does not have much secondary trading) or the money market. Moreover, the newly established stock market has been strongly influenced by the government's frequently changing policies. Consequently, the stock market has been highly volatile.

Third, most investment has gone to various industries and real estate development. Only a small portion has been put into infrastructure. As a result, the gap between the strong growth in industrial production and poor infrastructure has widened. During the first half of 1992, industrial output increased by 18 percent, while the production of electric power only grew 1.8 percent and the transportation and communication sector increased 5.6 percent. According to the government, the country's railway system only meets about 60 percent of the demand.

Fourth, the state sector's efficiency remains low, its profits have fallen sharply, and its inventories of industrial goods continue to rise. As a result, the government's tax revenue has declined. Its efforts to clean up "triangular debts" within the state sector have only had limited success. In the first half of 1992, the state sector's total losses exceeded its total profits, while 70 percent of state-owned enterprises posted losses in profits. The state sector's growth was only 1.7 percent vis-à-vis the nonstate sector's 34 percent. There was also a 15 percent increase in inventories. In the next few years, China's real GDP growth rate is likely to swing between 3 percent and 13 percent, while the pressure of inflation and fiscal deficit and debt will remain high. Development between the state sector and nonstate sector is likely to remain unbalanced. Politically, the growth of the nonstate sector has rapidly changed the relationship between the state and society and created new interest groups, which could eventually become the new industrial middle class in the future.

Fifth, the Chinese economy is now a mixed economy. While the competition for capital, market shares, and raw materials between the state sector and nonstate sector has heightened, the conflicts between a free market and a government-controlled market have continued to rise. And with the government's decentralization program between 1978 and 1988, local authorities have gained strong decision-making and fiscal power. They have become increasingly independent from the central government, pursuing their own reform programs, development strategy, and open door policy. This development in turn has protected local economies, especially on the Chinese coast, from the central government's frequent intervention. It has also increased local authorities' ability to expand their business ties abroad. At the same time, however, it has increased China's internal trade barriers and monopolistic competition among various provinces.

Sixth, there have been some major challenges to China's rapidly expanded foreign economic relations as well. China's trade surplus with the United States has grown rapidly over the past few years. In 1991, it reached more than U.S. $10 billion. For 1992, it reached around U.S. $18 billion. The rise occurred partially because Taiwanese and Hong Kong manufacturers have transferred their export-oriented operations to China, thereby strengthening China's export ability in general and increasing its sales to the United States in particular. Nevertheless, given the U.S. domestic recession and human rights-related complaints against China, tensions over trade issues have increased in Sino-American relations. At the same time, the process of integration of Europe, the formation of the North American Trade Zone, and other Asian countries' international competitiveness have challenged China's position in the international market of labor-intensive manufactured goods.

## Domestic Politics and Society: Leadership Succession and Legitimacy

A primary problem in Chinese politics is that of political succession. China's highly uncertain succession arrangement, great political tensions between the state and society, and economic instability (corrected at least for the moment) indicate that domestic politics are likely to be unpredictable when the succession approaches. Although senior leaders, who are in their eighties, remain at the power center, a large number of younger leaders have been promoted within the party, government, and military institutions. Unfortunately, there have only been limited changes in the central government's decision-making process. A few top senior leaders, including Deng Xiaoping, continue to enjoy the power of making final decisions on crucial policy issues. The current power structure has failed to transfer much real authority to the younger leaders, who will have to earn popularity and legitimacy by improving the country's living standard and furthering the political and economic reform programs. Nevertheless, the secondary generation of leadership is also highly divided ideologically and politically.

Such a division is apt to produce another round of bloody power struggles within the establishment soon after Deng Xiaoping's departure.

High tensions within the leadership have eroded the government's ability to maintain control. More important, several key mechanisms that the government has used previously are no longer effective. For example, it is no longer capable of organizing and launching effective mass campaigns. Nor is the official ideology appealing to the majority of population. Former legitimating symbols for the Communist government have become hollow. The heightening power struggle within the top leadership and continued political uncertainties have discouraged bureaucrats, especially those at local levels, from committing themselves to the current central government's policies. The recent collapse of Communism in the former Soviet Union and Eastern Europe has presented a tremendous challenge to the legitimacy and stability of China's political system. It has shocked many party cadres in China and further undermined the legitimacy of the current Chinese political system. At the same time, minority groups in Tibet, Xinjiang, and Inner Mongolia have become more active in their demands for independence and autonomy from the central government.

It is more difficult than ever for the government to rely on heavily corrupt party organizations or discredited official ideology to control Chinese society. Instead, the government has become increasingly dependent on the security and military forces as the sole means of retaining power. Despite the recent restructuring of the military leadership, hard-liners' efforts to strengthen their political control over the more modernized and professional army has achieved only limited success. All 103 military academies still operate according to the principles defined before summer 1989. More than 400 internally circulated military publications continue to focus on topics about military technology, strategies, tactics, and new development in foreign armies rather than party ideology. Promotions are made mainly according to officers' professional performance rather than their loyalty to the conservative leadership. It is questionable whether the military will support the highly unpopular and ineffective hard-line leaders in the forthcoming succession crisis. Rather, it may choose to back the future reformers if they can mobilize strong popular support.

### Center/Local Tensions and the Strengthening of Interest Groups

While the central government's authority has declined significantly, local governments, especially those at the provincial level, have strengthened their powers. At present, the central government merely controls about 30 percent of the total state budget whereas local governments share about 70 percent. Given the wide-existing regional gap in development, reform progress, and access to the international market, this trend will further weaken the central government's power and widen the gap in economic and political development among various provinces, especially those on the coast and those in inner parts of China.

The continuing political tensions and economic problems have heightened the antagonism between the state and society. Many people, especially urban residents, have distanced themselves from the government, refusing to participate in political campaigns. Others have lost all their interest in official ideology and politics. In both rural and urban areas, the government has failed to reorganize effective mass organizations for the purpose of controlling the Chinese people. During the past fourteen years, the agricultural reform has already only neutralized the People's Commune system and the party organization in rural areas. It has created new interest groups, which now begin to pursue their own increasingly independent political and economic interests.

The government also faces increasingly determined defiance from ethnic minorities, who have been strongly encouraged by the recent development in the former Soviet Union. In Tibet, ethnic tensions and protests have continued. The Dalai Lama has received increasing international support from the OECD nations. In Xinjiang, under the leadership of an exile Islamic fundamentalist government located in Turkey, which is partially financed by Saudi Arabia and Turkey, the ethnic dissent movement has continued to expand its organizational network and to smuggle weapons into Xinjiang in preparation for armed struggle in the future. The victory of the Afghan resistance movement and the collapse of the Soviet empire could develop into a strong Islamic fundamentalist movement that may undermine the stability of China's northeast region.

In Inner Mongolia, having been encouraged by the progress of democratic transition in the People's Republic of Mongolia, activists of the independence movement have increased their demand for greater autonomy and independence. In the next few years, ethnic tensions in these regions are likely to increase. Over 15 million Muslims in China wish to practice their religion and eventually become part of the central Asian Muslim empire. If there is a serious political crisis in Beijing over the political succession or a revival of confrontation between Taiwan and China, ethnic tensions could soon develop into large-scale bloodshed and possible civil war.

Chinese politics will remain tense in the next few years. The forth-coming succession may provoke another power struggle within the central leadership. The country is unlikely to produce another "strong man." Rather, some sort of collective leadership will most likely be formed during the transitional period. More important, lacking a strong central authority, local governments, especially those in the south and on the coast, are likely to play a more independent and significant role in restructuring their relations with Beijing as well as in local politics. It is also possible that they may work together in forcing the central government toward further reforms and "open-door" policies. The Chinese people, including various new interest groups created by the reform process, will play a more active and independent role, pressing the government for further reform and implementing open-door poli-cies.

### China's Global Relations and the Foreign Businessperson's Responsibility to Track Developments

Both to understand China better and for general regional planning purposes, it behooves the international business to consider its own place and objectives internationally and in the region and appreciate the dynamics of interaction among countries. The end of the Cold War has significantly changed the contemporary international scene and strongly affected China's foreign policy and security strategy. In particular, the collapse of the Soviet empire and recent progress made in arms control and disarmament have significantly reduced China's strategic importance to OECD nations, especially the United States. This development has begun to shift Washington's perspective on its ties with Beijing. The two countries are currently in sharp disagree-ment over many policy issues such as human rights, trade, and weap-ons (both conventional and nonconventional) proliferation. Over the past few years, U.S. domestic politics has become an increasingly important factor in reshaping United States policy toward China. During the 1992 presidential campaign, President Bush made a decision to sell 150 F-16 jet fighters to Taiwan. This move in turn violated the Sino-American joint communiqué of August 17, 1972, which an-nounced that U.S. arms sales to Taiwan should not exceed quantita-tively and qualitatively the level of the early 1970s. More important, this decision has already had a strong impact on Taipei's policy toward China as well as on Taiwan's internal politics.

Nevertheless, political tensions between China and the United States have not yet reached the point where the countries view each other as threats to each other's national security. They still share some common political and security interests in Northeast Asia, South Asia, and Southeast Asia. The future development of their relations will hinge on the dynamics in the former Soviet Union, China's internal development, interactions between Washington and Beijing, and other OECD and Asian nations' policies toward China. In addition, whether or not the current China-Taiwan relations can be managed rationally is another key factor that will determine China's overall foreign relations.

Over the year and a half, Beijing has gradually ceased its criticism of domestic politics in the former Soviet Union. Rather, it has taken a more realistic approach to improve ties with Russia and other republics. Despite the fact that the military balance between the two countries has only changed slightly, Beijing succeeded in convincing both Moscow and Alma-Ata (Kazakhstan) to respect agreements signed between China and the former Soviet Union regarding the reduction of troops deployed along the Chinese border and the resolution of their territorial disputes. Beijing has also purchased a large quantity of advanced weapons from Moscow and Kiev (Ukraine) and recruited hundreds of scientists and military engineers from the former Soviet Union. Meanwhile, trade among China and most of the republics has expanded rapidly.

Beijing has been worried about the influence of collapse of the former Soviet Union on the stability of its own Inner Mongolia, Xinjiang, and Tibet, where ethnic tensions have been high. To counter Taipei's flexible diplomacy, a policy designed to compete against Beijing in the international community, Beijing quickly established diplomatic relations with most former Soviet republics, the only exception being Latvia, which recognized Taiwan. The collapse of the Soviet empire has removed the principal threat to China's national security. In the international community, having increased its political and economic support for North Korea, Beijing has further normalized its ties with Hanoi and India, the two countries that no longer challenge China's security interests.

In other parts of the Asia-Pacific region, however, rapid changes in the former Soviet Union's domestic politics and foreign policy have had limited influence on the structure of international system. This is largely due to the great uncertainty in the former Soviet Union and its significantly weakened influence and presence in the region. Having decided to provide some "technical assistance" and emergency relief aid to the former Soviet Union, Tokyo has pursued a cautious approach toward Moscow of "wait and see"; it has continued to increase aid and loans to Beijing. This development in turn has increased the latter's dependence on Tokyo and its leverage in dealing with other OECD nations. Nevertheless, Beijing has been alarmed by the progress of Tokyo's rearmament program and its decision to send troops overseas. Beijing has been particularly concerned that Tokyo might transform its economic power into political influence and military power, becoming a leading country in the Far East.

On the Korean peninsula, both Pyongyang and Seoul have made efforts to reduce tensions between themselves. They are still at an early stage of reassessing the changes in the former Soviet republics. Both countries have joined the United Nations. Beijing and Seoul established diplomatic relations despite Pyongyang's strong reservations. If the internal politics of the former Soviet republics remain highly unstable in the near future, both Seoul and Pyongyang are likely to move closer to Beijing. Beijing's fundamental interest should be to maintain stability and peace on the peninsula. Therefore, it has been encouraging Pyongyang to give up its nuclear program, further reduce tensions with Seoul, increase its international participation, and reform its economic system. In addition, Beijing has tried to maintain the balance of military power.

Similarly, at least in the near future, the diminution of Soviet influence and presence in Southeast Asia and South Asia will increase Beijing's leverage there, pushing India, the ASEAN states, and Vietnam closer to China. Over the past three years, China has taken initiatives to reduce tensions and improve ties with both India and Vietnam. It has received the Indian defense minister in Beijing and has held talks with Hanoi over the territorial disputes between them. While Sino-Vietnamese border trade has expanded quickly, Chinese businesspersons have begun to invest in Vietnam. China has also improved relations with most ASEAN nations. Nevertheless, the unresolved, oil-related territorial disputes over the South China Sea among China and most ASEAN nations and Vietnam may become a source of new international conflict in the next few years, risking pressure on businesses in the petroleum field (especially those already doing business offshore China).

Outside the Asia-Pacific region, the collapse of the Soviet system may provide Beijing with some new opportunities to increase its influence. To fill Moscow's role, Beijing could possibly increase its economic aid and political support to Third World countries that previously were backed by Moscow. Nevertheless, it is highly unlikely that Beijing will alter its foreign policy priorities from building a relatively stable international environment in the region and improving ties with the West to one of becoming leader of the Third World again. Nor will it have substantial resources to do so.

More important, as a permanent member of the U.N. Security Council, Beijing has been increasingly active in the international community. During the recent Gulf war and imposition of sanctions against Libya, it used the leverage of its veto power at the Security Council as a trade-off for better relations with the Western powers. Because of recent Sino-U.S. political tensions, however, China has already withdrawn from the "big five" (i.e., the United States, France, Russia, China, and Britain) negotiations on the banning and destruction of chemical and biological weapons. Washington's decision to sell F-16 jet fighters to Taiwan is likely to provoke Beijing to increase its own arms sales, not to mention the possibility that China may no longer be as cooperative with Western countries at the U.N. Security Council.

The rapid changes in the former Soviet Union and Eastern Europe have already heightened the competition between Beijing and Taipei in the international community. Within the past two years, Taipei has made strong efforts to expand its ties with most East European countries and the former Soviet republics. It followed Washington in recognizing all former Soviet republics and promised to provide economic aid to them. Its trade with most East European countries and the former Soviet republics has increased. On the other hand, Beijing's relations with a number of East European countries has been constrained by the gap in politics and ideology between them as well as the desire of these countries to obtain economic resources from Taipei. Although it is unlikely that East European countries and most former Soviet republics will shift their diplomatic recognition from Beijing to Taipei, China is in a very weak position to prevent them from developing semiofficial relations with Taiwan.

China's overall foreign policy has been influenced by its relations with Taiwan. Over the past few years, Beijing has made strong efforts to reduce tensions and increase contacts with Taipei. It has offered many favorable investment incentives such as tax holidays, internal market shares, and cheap labor and raw materials to Taiwanese companies. Such companies in Taiwan are under strong pressure to upgrade their labor-intensive manufacturing operations (Taiwan has faced difficulties from the rise in labor costs and land prices as well as heightened international competition). In addition to improving the living standard of those citizens who have close relatives in Taiwan, the Chinese government has also encouraged Chinese academic and cultural institutions to develop exchange programs with their Taiwanese counterparts. Consequently, business ties between the two sides of the Taiwan Strait have expanded rapidly. By the middle of 1992, Taiwanese investment in China had risen to U.S. $4.8 billion. The China-Taiwan trade will have reached U.S. $8 billion in 1992. Each year there are a few million Taiwan Chinese citizens visiting China. Under strong social pressure, the government in Taipei has loosened its restrictions on cultural exchanges and business interactions between the two sides of the Taiwan Strait.

Nevertheless, Taiwan's rapid progress of democratization has generated an increasingly strong demand for independence. Over the past three years, native Taiwanese, who constitute 83 percent of the island's total population, have significantly increased their power and influence within various government institutions and the parliament. In the next few years, native Taiwanese will become the dominant force on the political scene, demanding to move further away from China politically.

In the international community, due partly to the Tiananmen issue and partly to a recognition of Taiwan's successful political and economic development over the past twenty years, more and more Western countries have gradually and quietly readjusted and even upgraded their relations with Taiwan. Under the name of "China, Taipei," or "Chinese Taipei," Taiwan has returned to or joined more than 700 international organizations during the past ten years. With its huge amount of international reserves and strong export capacity, the role that Taiwan plays in the international community must be respected. While Beijing has succeeded in convincing all Asian countries to give up Taiwan and recognize the Beijing government instead, competition between the two sides for international recognition and support has heightened.

By and large, tensions between Beijing and Taiwan have declined substantially over the past ten years. Hostility between them, however, has not yet ceased. While the military balance has continued to tilt toward China, Taiwan has developed a credible deterrence capability with Western aid. At the same time, massive Taiwanese investment in the Chinese coast has already created a "buffer zone" between Taiwan and the central government in Beijing.

More important, the expansion of business activities across the

Taiwan Strait has created new areas in which the two sides may share common interests. In short, economically Taiwan and China have moved closer and will continue to do so. Politically the two parties have moved apart, and their competition for influence and support in the international community has intensified. The central questions for the future are whether both parties can deal with their complex relationship rationally and whether other nations, especially those of OECD and those in Asia, can play a constructive and stabilizing role in this relationship.

The Tiananmen flare-up in June 1989 was certainly a major setback to Beijing's policy toward Hong Kong. It severely damaged Beijing's credibility among Hong Kong residents. Nevertheless, over the past three years Beijing has shown great commitment and flexibility in dealing with Hong Kong. Its policy can be summarized as follows: First, Beijing has significantly increased its investment and other types of presence in Hong Kong. It is now Hong Kong's primary investor with more than U.S. $15 billion in assets. The Bank of China now holds about one-fourth of the colony's total retail deposits. Backed by Beijing, Chinese investors have been aggressively purchasing properties in Hong Kong. These policies have stabilized Hong Kong's economy. In 1991, Hong Kong's GDP grew 3.9 percent and in 1992 was expected to surge by more than 5 percent.

Second, Beijing has strengthened its ties with most powerful local businesspersons by offering them favorable business opportunities. Increasingly these businesspersons share more common interests with Beijing, although most of them have already obtained foreign passports or resident rights and have channeled their own money overseas. Many of these businesspersons have lobbied for the Chinese government in London, Washington, and even Hong Kong. These developments have not only contributed to Hong Kong's stability but have also reduced Hong Kong residents' political pressure on the Chinese government.

Third, in addition to China's ties with the West, the best support for Hong Kong's prosperity and stability has been indeed China's own growth, economic reform, and open-door policy. Since summer 1990, and especially since early 1992, the Chinese economy has been booming, and the Chinese government has made strong efforts to continue its reform program and open-door policy. This is particularly true in Guangdong, Fujian, and other southern coastal province locations, where Hong Kong companies invest most. Consequently, Hong Kong businesspersons have found not only more business opportunities in China but also a narrowing institutional gap between the two economies.

Fourth, politically the Chinese government has tried its best to reduce the influence of local democrats and promote its own supporters in Hong Kong. Over the past three years, the Chinese government has kept the British authorities in check concerning the development of a local process of democratization in Hong Kong. Economically, Beijing has tried to make compromises with London. In addition, the Chinese government has not only provided more financial and political support for those local politicians on its own side but has applied direct political pressure on local democrats. To date, these efforts have only had limited success. During the legislative elections in September 1991, all Chinese government-backed candidates lost while local democrats won all but one seat at the Legislative Council. Since then, tensions between British authorities and the Chinese government have remained high, although neither can afford to jeopardize their relationship.

Over the next few years, Hong Kong's transition will be critical. The issue is not whether the Chinese government wants Hong Kong in its present state, but whether it can sustain the entity. The Chinese government has overwhelming interests in Hong Kong: it has huge investment in Hong Kong; through the colony, China now conducts about 60 percent of its total foreign trade; Hong Kong remains China's number-one investor; Hong Kong's prosperity and stability will have a strong impact on China's relations with OECD nations and with Taiwan; and last, but not least, if Beijing fails to implement a smooth transition in Hong Kong, China's own stability and economic growth, especially in the South, will be jeopardized.

Five major challenges confront China's Hong Kong policy. First, Hong Kong's transition to 1997 might occur in conjunction with China's political succession. Such a prospect would likely increase the degree of political uncertainty in the colony. The uncertainty will increase a few years prior to the final turnover of jurisdiction. By that time, the business community itself will have made its decision about whether to stay or leave.

Second, if in the next few years China's economic reform or growth experiences some serious difficulties or even crisis, Hong Kong's growth and stability immediately will be challenged. This is because of the high degree of interdependence between the two economies. Third, if some crisis were to occur in the relations between China and a major Western power or Taiwan, Hong Kong's stability would be undermined. The confidence of the Hong Kong business community and residents at large about the transition to 1997 might be shaken. Fourth, Beijing might have serious difficulties in pursuing the transfer of power.

Conflicts with local democrats will escalate further, tensions between Chinese and British authorities may also rise, and the Chinese government might simply lack the technocrats and civil bureaucrats to manage Hong Kong after the transition. Finally, how the "one country, two systems" model works will be viewed largely as a function of China's overall economy, politics, foreign policy, and dynamics of the international environment.

For the foreign businessperson, especially the investor with stakes in one or more of these areas, the key to the continued stability and growth of business operations might be the proper monitoring of the dynamic of change within the China–Taiwan–Hong Kong triangle. United States politics and policies under a new administration could also affect business with China. Finally, as China increases its strength and integrative role in Asia, the foreign investor, with intentions of transnational expansion and smoother coordination, stands to benefit logistically.

## Assessing the Environment in China for the Next Few Years

How should one predict or measure China's political and social stability and attractiveness to the foreign investor? In my opinion, the first thing to do is to define the levels of risk. China's political, economic, and foreign relations developments may affect risk to foreign business in the broader sense and at the microlevel. One can differentiate between risk at the macrolevel and the microlevel. The macrolevel of risk reflects the way changes in China and in China's ties with other parts of the world affect China's overall business environment. The microlevel of risk describes how these changes would affect a specific company's business operations, from hotel services to pharmaceutical manufacturing, in China.

It is easier for the outside analyst to focus on the macrolevel. The in-house analyst or field marketing executive can use this assessment as a springboard for focusing on industry-specific concerns. To measure the degree of risk at the macrolevel, one has to study China's political and economic fundamentals as well as its overall foreign relations. In this regard, the following factors are essential:

*1. Open Door.* During the past twelve years, the reform and open-door policy has already changed the basic foundation of China's political, economic, social, and cultural structure.

*2. Mixed or Centrally Planned Economy.* Economically, the system has already become a mixed one (i.e., the nonstate sector produces about 65 percent of the total industrial output and more than 80 percent of the total agricultural output). There are two markets as well: the state market, which continues to decline, and the nonstate market, which is growing quickly. The key factor is that after fourteen years of reform, the government does not have much incentive and conceivably could restore the previous central planning system based on state ownership. The competition between the market forces and the state will surely continue, and sometimes could be tense. Nevertheless, no matter what happens politically, the state is unlikely to be the owner, although no one would expect the state sector to disappear soon. This is because the nonstate sector has already become too big to be taken over without a massive political campaign, which would wreck the national economy. Another reason is that the government has failed and will probably continue to fail to improve the state sector's efficiency. In the foreseeable future, it is likely that the government will choose to reform the state sector further, especially by changing the current state ownership to the corporate structure. However, the government may not pursue a massive and aggressive privatization program. Nevertheless, the government will encourage a further expansion of the nonstate sector and continue to reform the macroeconomic system, focusing on price mechanisms, the banking system, securities markets, the managerial system of state-owned enterprises, and so on.

*3. Central/Local Conflict of Interests.* The central government will continue to compete against local authorities and confuse the foreign businessperson about the locus of decision making. But it is unlikely that China will produce a strong central government in the near future. This is because it is not apt to produce a strong, charismatic leader who is capable of carrying out the mass political campaigns that would be necessary to recentralize political and economic power. Various local authorities enjoy differing access to the international market and the whole economy has already been localized. The key issue here is whether the government will be able to establish an effective monetary and fiscal authority to manage the national economy.

*4. Growth and Fiscal Policy.* The country is likely to continue its high economic growth. Its labor-intensive and export-oriented manufacturing industries will grow particularly rapidly. Nevertheless, the growth in real GDP is likely to be unstable, swinging between annual rates of 2 percent and 12 percent. This is because the economy will continue to be influenced by the government's weak abilities in macroeconomic management, which is increasingly complicated by the mixed nature of the economic system and the country's rapidly increasing participation in international competition. In particular, the government will face a challenge of how to formulate and implement effective and stable growth, monetary, and fiscal policies. In addition, the economic reform process itself will create some instability, as it will change the mechanisms of economic management at both macro- and microlevels and redistribute resources among various regions, industries, interest groups, and individuals. The growth also is likely to be handicapped by low development in infrastructure unless the economic system changes the incentive mechanism to make the infrastructure sector profitable. Moreover, economic growth may be interrupted by the unbalanced location of resources and distribution of income. The fast population growth may also drive unemployment up, even causing social instability in a leadership succession struggle at the central level of government.

5. *Closing the Gaps in Development.* China's economic structure will further change. Rural industries will continue to expand while the service sector will grow strongly. Gaps in development and growth among different regions will continue to enlarge because the regions enjoy different opportunities and access to resources and the international market. The defense industry will decrease somewhat, while light industries will expand rapidly. In addition, the real estate sector will grow strongly, especially in urban and suburban areas. This development may gradually force the government to change the current state ownership of land and massively sell state-owned housing to private individuals.

6. *Place in the International Market.* China's dependency on the international market will continue to grow. This is because investment from other Asian countries—especially Japan, South Korea, Taiwan, Hong Kong, and Singapore—which are under pressure to upgrade their industrial base, will continue to rise. These investments will continue to contribute to China's fast economic growth and strengthen its competitiveness in the international market. They will also increase the country's foreign exchange earnings. Nevertheless, this trend makes it imperative that China maintain a relatively stable economic growth and make further efforts to narrow the gaps within the economic and legal systems and with market economies overseas. It also requires that China maintain its advantages and incentives, especially in the areas of labor cost, taxation, land prices, infrastructure, prices

of raw materials and energy, and the general investment environment. China must also institute an effective government management to compete against other Asian economies such as Indonesia, Malaysia, Thailand, and Vietnam, which have also worked hard to attract foreign direct investment in manufactured goods. Further, China has to build a relatively stable relationship with the major OECD nations. In this regard, it is particularly important to analyze possible changes in U.S. policy toward China after the presidential election in November 1992.

The progress of European integration, the formation of a North American trade zone, and increased international protectionism will create new difficulties for specific Chinese goods entering these countries and will force China to open its own markets further. The global business circle will have a stronger effect on the Chinese economy than reliance on an upswing in the international market. In addition, without a relatively peaceful and stable international environment, especially in the Asia-Pacific region, foreign investment in China will fall. Finally, peaceful, rational, mutually beneficial ties between China and Taiwan and stable relations between China and Hong Kong are the key to China's efforts to increase its participation in the international market.

*7. Leadership Succession.* Politically, the key issue is the process and outcome of the forthcoming succession to Deng Xiaoping. In addition to the ten years of the "Cultural Revolution," fourteen years of reform and the open-door policy, the prodemocracy movement in 1989, and the shock of collapse of the Communist system in the former Soviet Union and Eastern Europe, the ongoing economic progress has further changed the existing political system. The government no longer enjoys some key mechanisms that it used to rule China since 1949: a charismatic leader, an effective bureaucracy, an attractive official ideology, its strong ability to use mass terror and the launching of mass political campaigns, effective party and other social and political organizations, and a highly centralized planned economy. In short, the government is no longer able to use the old methods and instruments to rule China, yet it may be unable to create a new and effective system in the near future.

*8. Generational Cleavage.* China is experiencing a fundamental generational change at almost all levels. Younger generations have been increasingly alienated and independent from the government. There is no coherent ideological framework that the government can use to appeal to them and consolidate them. They have become increasingly individualistic and materialistic, and their expectations for higher living standards and individual freedom have risen faster than the pace of government reform and actual economic progress. For the young, the fundamental problem is no longer one of whether some reform leader can "fix" the existing system, but a growing conviction that the system simply does not work. They are looking for alternatives.

9. *Freedoms, the Quest for New Leadership, and the Potential for Disorder.* No matter who is in charge after Deng Xiaoping's departure, at the minimum he will have to deal with the following four issues domestically: rehabilitating the victims of Tiananmen and reducing tensions between the state and society, reducing corruption, improving the living standard, and increasing individual freedom and the society's political rights. In fact, these are society's basic current demands. The succession process will have to be short and decisive. Otherwise the country, at least in its northern parts, may experience chaos and civil disorder. This is because a long process (say six months to one year) of intensive power struggle at the top could provoke the rise of a mass movement, which, facilitated by the large amount of unemployed population, would pose a threat to the country's political stability. If disorder develops, whether or not it spreads to the whole country or to what degree it affects local politics and economic development will depend largely on the ability of local authorities to distance themselves from the politics at the center.

From the experience of local authorities who dealt with the Tiananmen crisis, it is safe to say that local authorities' ability to differentiate their own policies and protect their own interests from those of the central government is strong. After the political succession, local authorities will become even stronger and more independent than they are now. This trend is likely to reduce the degree of destruction or chaos caused by the possible dramatic political changes of the succession. This is because in the south and the coastal regions, where economic reform and open-door policies have been most successful and the nonstate sector has boomed, local authorities and most entrepreneurs share common economic and political interests. Consequently, they may well cooperate in resisting pressure from the central government. This in turn should create stability at the local level and prevent the spread of possible chaos and civil unrest.

Although disorder in Beijing might cause some degree of confrontation among various political and interest groups, the probability of a long and large-scale civil war is low. This is because the structure of today's military in China is different from the one during the 1910s and 1920s. Today, military commanders retain strong ties with local civil authorities, but their relations with the local business community are not strong enough to receive sufficient support to gain financing for a warlord-style civil war that would wreak havoc with the economy. Commanders do not raise money locally but depend on the central government for their budget. More important, not only have commanders been rotated to different geographic locations, but the rank-and-file soldiers usually are drawn deliberately from different parts of the country. Thus, it is difficult for a military commander to mobilize his troops to fight a war that could be directed against his soldiers' hometowns or home provinces.

*10. International Positioning.* Internationally, the possibility that China would engage a large-scale military confrontation with its neighboring countries in the foreseeable future in rather low. The fundamental interests of China and these countries cannot be served by engaging in such confrontations. Nevertheless, either because of temporary political chaos and disorder caused by the succession process, or because of the rising pressure from society on the government, Beijing might initiate international conflicts in order to defuse its internal problems and strengthen its power base by invoking symbols of Chinese nationalism. In this regard, the key areas of tension would include China-Taiwan relations, Sino-American ties, and the territorial disputes among China and some Southeast Asian countries over the South China Sea. A factor determining the degree of potential volatility in these areas, however, is the ongoing communication and diplomacy between China and the international community, especially the United States. This is because the United States is the only country that has the means to deter a large-scale military confrontation in Asia, and the U.S. influence on Taiwan and other Asian countries regarding their policies toward China remains strong.

To what extent are these macrodevelopments apt to affect any individual industries or even a multinational corporation's business activities in China? In my opinion, this depends on the following factors:

1. The degree and nature of these macrodevelopments in an either positive or negative direction;

2. The relationship between China and the specific country of a foreign company's origin;

3. The degree of a specific industry's importance to China's economic survival and growth both at the national level and at local levels;

4. The ability of a specific local government or other social forces to resist influence from the center or its neighboring provinces or regions;

5. The working relationship between individual foreign investors and their Chinese counterparts including local authorities;

6. The international competitiveness of a specific industry in which a foreign investor seeks to collaborate in business activities in China;

7. The degree of a foreign country's dependency on the Chinese market and its flexibility to shift to other markets.

In short, in the next few years, China will experience a succession to Deng Xiaoping. The final outcome of the succession will affect China's investment environment and its business ties with other parts of the world. The key to reducing the degree of risk is to analyze carefully the macrofundamentals and their implications for specific regions in China as well as for individual industries. Finally, given the great room in which local authorities, managers, and even individuals in China can maneuver today, to handle well your working relationship with your Chinese counterparts can significantly reduce your risk under abnormal social and political circumstances. Management, after all, is the art of dealing with problems.

*Chapter 5*

# Investing in the Russian Oil Industry: A Case for Examining Political Conditions

## Robert E. Ebel

I recall an early meeting between a group of American oil companies and their Russian counterparts, held in Moscow in July 1991. The Russian side simply was not prepared to accept any linkage between political risk and rate of return to the investor. They could grasp the importance of economic factors and our concerns about infrastructure, but the connection between doing business and domestic political stability was a mystery to them. Had the American companies returned to Moscow as planned in September 1991, in the wake of the aborted coup, it might have been easier to describe to the Russians what political risk was all about, particularly for the long-term commitment involved in petroleum production.

Let's return to a still earlier time and shift our attention to the Soviet petroleum industry.

### I  Decline in Oil Production: Mismanagement of a Valuable Resource

The first oil delegation from the United States to visit the Soviet Union in the postwar years traveled to that country in August 1960. Members of the delegation were not impressed with what they saw. They saw an industry lagging fifteen years or so behind the West in terms of technology. They saw a labor force poorly paid, poorly housed, and poorly fed. But the delegation left with an awareness of the obvious potential of the country to become a major oil producer and exporter. And, given the government control over natural resources, there was fear that the rich oil fields represented a very real threat to the world oil market and in turn to those multinational oil companies operating in that market.

Indeed, an interview given to the *Saturday Evening Post* by a member of the delegation following our return to the United States reflected the concerns of the U.S. oil industry. The headline of the story read "Drowning in a Sea of Red Oil."

His fear was never realized. While the Soviet Union did enter the world market, and eventually became a major player, it conducted itself in a fashion no different from its competitors. It sought the greatest return on what it had for sale. Contracts were strictly honored; politics rarely intruded.

What if another delegation were to visit those oil fields today? What would it find? Unfortunately, it would find a growing technological gap, a decaying infrastructure, a high labor turnover, and idle oil wells exceeding 27,000 in number.

In the years following the visit of this first oil delegation, the former Soviet Union had made the most of its oil potential, becoming the world's leader in oil and gas production, a major player in oil exports, and the world leader in the export of natural gas.

In 1988, the peak year, the Soviet Union produced 12.5 million barrels of oil per day (b/d) and exported around 4.1 million b/d. Then, the bottom fell out. A decline set in around mid-1988 and continues today, on an accelerating scale. This decline is without precedent in world history, in that it was brought about not by war nor by the workings of the market, but rather by the mismanagement of a superior resource.

Did this collapse catch the Russians and the West by surprise? Let us reach back in history to April of 1977. The setting is this. Jimmy Carter had not been president long, but already he was seeking ways to reduce the growing dependence of the United States on foreign oil.

In his gloomy assessment of future world oil supply and demand, President Carter relied heavily on two reports on the world oil status, both prepared by the CIA. The first was entitled *The International Energy Situation: Outlook to 1985*, released in April 1977. That particular report foresaw world oil demand substantially exceeding supply by 1985. Prices would rise sharply, to allocate available supplies. All this would take place if energy conservation were not greatly increased, which of course was what Carter was advocating.

Much of the pessimism regarding the state of the world oil market derived from a companion study of the Soviet Union, issued under the title *The Impending Soviet Oil Crisis*. This report on Soviet oil concluded that Soviet oil production would soon peak, possibly as early as 1978 and certainly not later than the early 1980s. Output would reach a maximum of between 11 and 12 million b/d; then the decline would set in. By 1985, just a short eight years away, production would be no more than 8 to 10 million b/d. For comparison, oil production had averaged 10.4 million b/d in 1976. In the decade following, the report continued, the Soviet Union might well find itself not only unable to supply oil to Eastern Europe and the West on the then present scale (about 3 million b/d), but also forced to compete for OPEC oil for its own use.

Other than for the audacity of its projections, the report became infamous for two reasons. Almost no one agreed with the findings. Moreover, charges of politicizing intelligence estimates followed. This prediction of an impending collapse of Soviet oil, some observers charged, was but part of the campaign to justify then-President Jimmy Carter's efforts to encourage Americans to conserve energy.

There was no collapse in 1978, nor even in the early 1980s. Production continued to show strong growth through 1983, reaching 12.33 million b/d. A decline did set in during 1984 and 1985, of some 300,000 b/d, but former Soviet leader Mikhail Gorbachev's personal exhortations, plus more investment, more equipment, and more drilling crews, got the industry back on track.

It was in the year 1988 that the CIA prediction of a dramatic decline, made more than a decade earlier, began to come true. By the latter part of 1988 it was clear that the industry was in serious trouble. This time, however, there would be no personal intervention by Gorbachev, no additional funds or stepped-up equipment deliveries, or crews flown in from other oil regions. The country was exhausted economically; it could do nothing more to help.

The factual evidence behind the 1977 analysis is not disputed. How then did Soviet authorities manage to prolong the oil industry for another ten years? Was the CIA report itself helpful in providing an early warning that a decline was not far away if remedial steps were not taken? Or was the allure of high oil prices and high hard-currency earnings during the latter 1970s and the first half of the 1980s so strong that the industry was sacrificed for these short-term gains? Apparently so, on both counts.

What had gone wrong with the CIA estimates, first for world oil supply and demand, and then for Soviet oil production?

For the world, the impact of higher prices—which both depressed demand and expanded supply—was missed by analysts everywhere. For the USSR, the willingness to direct increasingly larger amounts of investment capital toward expanding oil supply was also missed.

What was the rationale in 1977 behind the prospect of declining Soviet oil production? It was much the same then as it is now: a failure to find and develop new oil fields to replace falling production in mature areas, emphasis on developmental drilling at the expense of exploration drilling, and water incursion (encroachment) of the producing wells. It was concluded that the initial falloff, when it came, would almost certainly be sharp and might continue to drop rapidly.

All have now come to pass.

## II   For Want of Know-How, Reopening to Foreign Investors

At the beginning of this century, Russia was the world's leading oil producer, accounting for more than half of the world total. But a decline set in, beginning in 1904, and by 1921 production had fallen to just 30 percent of the peak reached in 1901. Much of that decline was triggered by labor disputes and armed uprisings in the Baku area in 1905. A similar situation exists in the Caucasus today, but now triggered by ethnic conflict, with disruptions centering more on oil equipment supply than on oil production itself.

Prior to the Communist Revolution in 1917, Western oil interests and investments in Russia were considerable. On June 1, 1918, the oil industry was nationalized and all of the Western interests were expropriated. But history was not yet complete. Baku fell into the hands of Turkey in September 1918. Two months later the English took command, and reinstated the former property owners. Some eighteen months later, in May 1920, the Bolshevik forces, victorious in the civil war, came into control of Baku and once again the oil properties were nationalized.

Some seventy years later the country has been reopened to foreign investment. Why? If your own means are limited, as they are for members of the Commonwealth of Independent States (C.I.S.),[1] then the natural recourse is to look abroad for help. Thus the rationale for joint ventures. Joint ventures offered to date generally involve the development of a known but complex oil deposit, beyond local financial, technical, and managerial know-how. Or a joint venture may involve the rehabilitation of a producing field, available for the same reasons.

To date, however, there are only four joint ventures actually producing oil, and their volumes are totally insignificant nationally. Political and economic uncertainties, the absence of an appropriate body of laws, under which an investment could be made and protected, the absence of a banking system, the lack of a convertible currency, and the inability or unwillingness to accept the concepts of risk and return on investment—all combine to delay investment decisions.

Western Siberia is the center of oil production in the Russian Federation, accounting for 6.5 million b/d or 63 percent of the 1991 total, while Russia in turn provides some 89.5 percent of crude oil production in the C.I.S. Western Siberia is composed of two political subdivisions: Tyumen Oblast and Tomsk Oblast. Of these two, Tyumen is by far the dominant producer, providing some 95 percent of Western Siberia output or around 6.2 million b/d in 1991.

To put Tyumen Oblast in proper perspective, it produces more oil than any area in the world other than the United States and Saudi Arabia. But it has absolutely nothing to show for this wealth. The oil has been sold to Moscow on the cheap—until recently, most went at a rate of around 50 cents per barrel. Nothing was returned to the locals. Life in Tyumen is life in the developing world. In terms of adequate housing, schools, hospitals, and telephones, Tyumen ranks near the bottom in the country. And its people resent their poor status very much.

In what could be viewed as a most humiliating experience, two C-141 military transport aircraft arrived in midsummer 1992 at Tyumen from the U.S. Air Force base in Frankfurt, carrying out a humanitarian gesture organized by a U.S. company, Western Atlas. A cargo of medical equipment and supplies, valued at some U.S. $32 million, was destined for a children's intensive care unit at a hospital under construction, and also for a sanitorium that was to open soon.

Reports in the Russian-language press viewed this humanitarian aid through somewhat conspiratorial eyes. Some local politicians regarded the aid as a form of bribery, offered in the hopes of receiving certain concessions in future oil field development. The press offered its own rationale, that the aid, coming in as it did on USAF military aircraft, could also be regarded as a cover for electronic intelligence gathering.

But not all shared these cynical opinions, and others saw the aid simply for what it was—nothing more than a humanitarian gesture from one people to another.

## III   Center versus Locality in the Decision-Making Process

Local producers' resentment over past inattention by Moscow in turn is reflected in the desire to gain control over as much of their oil as possible, which has placed the local oil-producing associations in direct conflict with the Center.

Perhaps the most telling example of the struggle for control over oil—or, in this instance, who makes the final decision regarding the selection of a foreign joint-venture partner to develop the oil in question—is that offered by the Sakhalin Shelf project.

In May 1991 the director-general of the Sakhalin State Oil and Gas Company announced that a joint venture with an international partner would be established, first to conduct a feasibility study relating to the development of two fields offshore Sakhalin Island: the Lunskoye gas field and the Piltun-Astokhskoye oil field. Development of these fields, whose existence has been known for a considerable time, was beyond Russia's technical and financial capability.

While a number of companies had indicated their interest in becoming involved, the Sakhalin Oil Development Company (Sodeco), together with Exxon and the Mitsui group, were labeled as early favorites. Two American companies, McDermott International and Marathon Oil, were included in the Mitsui group, which soon came to be known as the 3M group. The deadline for bids was August 10, and the tender review committee that had been formed to review the individual bids announced in early October that 3M was the winner.

Sakhalin Oblast officials were furious, and declared the decision null and void. Moreover, in seeking to obtain maximum local benefit from the award, these authorities requested that all bidders make additional commitments for improvement of Sakhalin's infrastructure. Obviously, they were looking to these potential investors to resolve all the problems that the island faced—asking for, among other things, the reconstruction of a 500-mile highway, expansion of the electric power grid, reconstruction of its airports, the development of a coal export industry, the building of a number of medical facilities, the rebuilding of the three major ports, and the like. It was separately estimated that if this wish list was fulfilled completely, it could cost as much as $15 billion.

President Boris Yeltsin acquiesced to the continuing pressures from Sakhalin, the award to 3M was annulled, and a new bidding process instituted. In the interim, the war of words between Moscow and Sakhalin continued unabated, leaving the bidders considerably confused as to where the decision-making authority actually lay. In early December 1991 a committee of experts was convened by President Yeltsin to resolve the issue. At the end of January 1992 3M was again named the winner by this committee of experts.

This decision did not sit at all well with the governor of Sakhalin Oblast, who continued to protest long and loudly against the concept of separate firms developing separate fields. His approach was built around the idea of giving one group (Exxon was his choice) the right to develop all the proven fields offshore Sakhalin—five in number— reasoning that this approach would make it more likely that the infrastructure projects he was seeking from the foreign investor would actually be built in return for the larger award.

Once again Moscow yielded, and a special Russian parliamentary commission was set up in early March 1992 to look into the decision-making process. The commission at the conclusion of its work disagreed with the actions of the Russian government. Nevertheless, the government confirmed its original decision, and on March 30 the right for 3M to prepare a feasibility study relating to development of the Piltun-Astokhskoye and Lunskoye fields was finally formalized.

Yet, in this battle for control over oil resources, the regional and local authorities are not without power, and Moscow has come to recognize that. As a beginning, the Russian government has exempted Tatarstan, an autonomous republic and a major oil producer in the Urals-Volga region, from paying export and import tariffs on crude oil, petroleum products, and consumer goods. Tatarstan is the first to be granted such an exemption, and others most assuredly will press their case as well. Not having to pay an export tax on crude oil and petroleum products signifies a considerable financial loss for Moscow, and the prospect of considerable financial gain for Tatarstan.

## IV   Introduction of the Western Criteria of Country Environmental or Political Risk

Questions over the economic future of the country have made the potential Western investor ever more mindful of the uncertainties to be faced. However, perhaps care should be taken not to make too much of Russia and political risk. After all, there is a good measure of political risk taken on by our oil industry as it attempts to do business within the borders of the United States. Is Kazakhstan any riskier than California? Ask Chevron.

Chevron several years ago made a major discovery offshore southern California but has been unable to date to reach an environmentally and politically acceptable agreement with local authorities to bring the oil onshore. In the interim, much of the production remains shut in. At the same time Chevron has taken on considerable risk with its agreement to develop the giant Tengiz oil field in the republic of Kazakhstan. But do the risks here carry any more potential damage than the risks of trying to do business in California?

Political and economic stability are desirable elements for any investment, wherever that investment might be made. U.S. companies and the U.S. government have worked hard to bring that message to Russia. In the early days it was apparent that this message was not understood, nor was it accepted in the way that had been hoped.

It was not understood because we are separated by different languages. First, we are separated by the language of daily communication. One side speaks English, the other side Russian, although that obstacle can be overcome by the professional interpreter or translator. But there is another language that separates us, and that is the language of business, the language of a market economy. This difference is not so easily overcome, because Russia has no experience in working in an open market. Its tradition has been one of a planned economy, where decisions were centralized and where the influences of supply and demand really did not matter. The ability to think, to operate in a free market, is not going to emerge overnight. This absence of experience translates into a resentment of the foreign investor, and to a reluctance to make a decision, for fear of being accused of giving away the national heritage to foreign interests.

We may think we are communicating in our decisions, but in reality we often are not. The separation is great, and continues.

In July 1991, at the initiative of the Department of State, a number of major U.S. energy companies met in Moscow with their counterparts in the first of a series of Energy Roundtable meetings. The purpose of the roundtable was to define and help resolve those obstacles confronting the prospective American investor in the Russian oil and gas industry. The Moscow meeting centered around discussion of what was described as the "Ten Keys to Start-Ups." These ten keys set out what constituted, in the judgment of the participating energy companies, major impediments to investment:

1. The rate of return should be commensurate with the risks and difficulties, and competitive with other opportunities elsewhere in the world.
2. There should be greater certainty in the terms and access to the Soviet pipeline system. Swaps are an important tool and should be encouraged.
3. There should be more certainty in customs fees. Customs regulations and procedures should be simplified.
4. The export tax should be eliminated.
5. Taxes are too high and complicated. The excess-profits tax should be reduced. The calculation of distributable profits should be based on cash flow instead of taxable income. The Soviet Union and Republics and the U.S. petroleum industry should establish a tax task force to discuss ideas to simplify and establish certainty with regard to taxes.
6. Multiple forms of business structures—joint ventures, licensing of concessions, and production-sharing contracts—are desirable, as each investor and each project has a different need. Soviet and Republic laws, and administration of those laws, should permit and encourage all forms of business structure.
7. The right to export freely at market prices and retain proceeds of sales abroad is critical.
8. Internal sales should be made at international market prices, with remuneration in convertible currency.
9. Visa and travel restrictions that hinder effective business operations should be reduced, including the requirement for a formal invitation from a Soviet host. International arrival and immigration clearance at more major cities should be allowed. Visa procedures should be simplified and travel within the then-USSR unrestricted, except in those areas closed for specific reasons.
10. It is critical to existing investors that neither the Union nor Republics subsequently enact legislation or adopt regulations or practices that impose a new burden.

During the course of the two-day Energy Roundtable meeting, it soon became evident that the Russian side was not able to understand the American linkage of political risk and rate of return. While they professed to understand technical risk and even economic risk, the concept of political risk eluded them.

The participating oil companies might have had more success in advancing this concept had they returned to Moscow in September 1991, in the wake of the failed coup. Or even in early January, following the break-up of the Soviet Union the preceding month. The companies could have then cited these events as examples of what political risk was all about.

U.S. Deputy Secretary of State Lawrence Eagleburger, in his remarks before the annual meeting of the Trade and Economic Council at the Palaces of Congresses in Moscow on May 27, 1992, listed what he believed to be the most frequently cited impediments to investment:

> . . . constant changes and lack of transparency of laws and regulations,
> . . . constant changes and prohibitive increases in taxation, and
> . . . uncertain ownership, particularly of natural resources, and overlapping jurisdiction among various levels of government.

Deputy Secretary Eagleburger's concerns were shared by many potential investors, notwithstanding the fact that several major projects were moving forward, and a number of other, mostly smaller projects in Northwest Russia and in Western Siberia were in various stages of development.

In late spring of 1992, the Department of State had taken the initiative for a second roundtable, this time to be held in Washington. Almost a year had passed since the first roundtable, and some progress in facilitating investment was visible. Unfortunately, however, most of those obstacles outlined at the Moscow meeting still remained, and others had been added in the interim. In the end, a second roundtable session did not occur, having been set aside because of President Yeltsin's visit to Washington in mid-June 1992.

Had the interested oil companies been given the opportunity to meet collectively once again with Russian authorities, they probably would have presented the following comprehensive listing of just what then was deterring the industry from a more aggressive response to those investment opportunities being offered.

1. Various taxes that together eliminate the possibility of achieving an adequate and acceptable return on investment. Of these taxes, the most important is the oil export tax;

2. Continuing uncertainties as to where decision-making authority to conclude oil and gas deals rests, particularly the division of authority among the local, regional, and national governments;

3. Uncertainty as to ownership rights to oil and gas reserves and the authority to enter into binding negotiations and contracts;

4. The absence of a clear and comprehensive legal framework that would provide investor confidence;

5. Excessive taxation of expatriate salary and benefits;

6. Arbitrary contract renegotiation, such as that faced by the American firm Phibro Energy and its joint venture known as White Knights;

7. Discriminatory treatment favoring domestic firms in contract terms, taxes, and other critical factors;

8. The arbitrary seizure by Vneshekonombank of hard-currency revenues generated by the sale and export of joint-venture oil; and

9. A continuing unwillingness by Russian negotiators to relate return on investment to risks of such investment.

It is likely that investors would be attracted to Russia if solutions to all these issues could be reached reasonably soon. If the United States and Russia are to secure the benefits of their newly developing relationship, there is no better place to begin than with the creation of an environment that will encourage investment by American companies in the Russian oil and gas industry.

The failure of the West to respond to prospective investment opportunities in Russia has been particularly frustrating for the authorities. Valeriy Churilov, the chairman of the Khanty-Mansiysk Autonomous Okrug, which is the core of the West Siberian oil industry and which produces some 3.6 million b/d, reflected the depth of this frustration in a recent interview in the *Russian Petroleum Investor*: "Please, come to Khanty-Mansiysk, sit down and talk with us. I will tolerate discussions for a little more time, but frankly speaking, I am tired of all this talk. Regrettably, there is too much talk and too little business."[2]

The preceding listing of obstacles to investment by no means is exhaustive. The U.S. Department of Commerce released in March 1992 the results of a comprehensive survey of impediments to trade and investment in the former Soviet Union, as seen by the general U.S. business community.[3] While there was a considerable comparability with those obstacles noted by the oil companies, other, equally significant barriers appeared in the Department of Commerce listing:

. . . Severe lack of commercial, legal, and market information.

. . . High cost and difficulty of establishing offices; serious visa restrictions and internal travel difficulties.

... Lack of a normal bilateral commercial relationship between the United States and the C.I.S. republics.

... Shortcomings in U.S. financial and commercial support; absence of a comprehensive U.S. business-government partnership.

## V   Easing the Way for the Potential U.S. Investor

If risks cannot be avoided, and that is possible only if the investment itself is avoided, then steps must be taken to share existing risks. For U.S. companies, among other approaches this means utilization of the Export-Import Bank loan, guarantee and insurance programs, and the Overseas Private Investment Corporation (OPIC) insurance programs.

In the aftermath of President Yeltsin's visit to the United States in mid-June 1992, a number of agreements and joint declarations on economic and trade matters were announced, which hopefully would help ease the way for the potential U.S. investor. Among the more pertinent agreements were the following:

• A U.S.–Russian trade agreement provided for reciprocal Most Favored Nation tariff treatment to the products of each country.

• A Bilateral Investment Treaty was signed (see also Table 5–1). This treaty guarantees nondiscriminatory treatment for U.S. investments in

**Table 5–1.   Status of Bilateral Investment Treaties Between the United States and the Newly Independent States***

| Republic | Status |
|----------|--------|
| Armenia | No** |
| Azerbaijan | No |
| Belarus | No |
| Georgia | No |
| Kazakhstan | Yes*** |
| Kyrgyzstan | No** |
| Moldova | No** |
| Russia | Yes*** |
| Tajikistan | No |
| Turkmenistan | No |
| Ukraine | No |
| Uzbekistan | No |

*As of July 18, 1992.
**Negotiations in progress.
***Awaiting ratification by country's parliament.

Source: *Biznis Bulletin*, September 1992, p. 4.

their admission to Russia and their operations there; guarantees the right to repatriate into hard currency those profits earned in rubles; guarantees prompt, adequate, and effective compensation in the event of expropriation; and provides for third-party international arbitration in the event of a dispute between a U.S. investor and the Russian government.

• On April 1, the U.S. Congress repealed legislative restraints on Export-Import Bank activity in Russia, lifting the $300 million ceiling on financing of oil and gas transactions. Medium-term loans and guarantees and short- and medium-term insurance programs are now available.

• The bilateral OPIC Investment Incentive Agreement entered into force on June 17. This agreement will allow OPIC to make investment insurance, finance, and promotion programs available to U.S. companies considering investing in Russia.

• A Treaty for the Avoidance of Double Taxation was signed. Among other things, this treaty will provide relief from double taxation, assurances of nondiscriminatory tax treatment, and will allow cooperation between tax officials of the two countries to resolve potential problems of double taxation.

• Steps were taken that, if successful, will allow Russians and others significantly wider access to advanced Western goods and technology.

In addition, a new U.S.–Russian Agreement on Scientific and Technical Cooperation in the Field of Fuels and Energy provides for cooperation in the fields of energy data exchange, energy and ecology, fossil energy sources, electric power, energy conservation and end-use efficiency, and renewable energy sources. For the status of agreements with the separate republics, see Tables 5–2 and 5–3.

While individual companies can seek protection against various risks through political risk insurance, what can governments do when for example, they are concerned that their growing dependence on a foreign supplier of oil or gas may jeopardize national security? (See Table 5–4.) Western Europe has found itself notably dependent upon natural gas supplies from the former Soviet Union, although that dependence has been held in check because of U.S. concerns in the early 1980s, when our government viewed the former Soviet Union as an unreliable supplier and pressured importing governments to hold imports at the 30 percent level.

The importance of stimulating the energy sectors of the Eastern Europe and the former Soviet Union and their integration into the

**Table 5–2. Fact Sheet on U.S. Commercial Relations with the Republics of the Former Soviet Union**

| Republic | TDP* | Business Development Committee | Business Councils | International Monetary Fund | GATT** |
|---|---|---|---|---|---|
| Russia | Yes | Yes | TEC+ | Yes | Observer |
| Ukraine | Yes | Yes | Ukraine-American Business Council | + + | No |
| Belarus | Yes | No | + | + + | No |
| Georgia | Yes | No | + | Yes | No |
| Moldova | Yes | No | + | No | No |
| Armenia | Yes | No | + | Yes | No |
| Azerbaijan | Yes | No | + | Yes | No |
| Uzbekistan | Yes | No | + | + + | No |
| Turkmenistan | Yes | No | + | + + | No |
| Tajikistan | Yes | No | + | + + | No |
| Kazakhstan | Yes | No | US-Kazakh Trade Council | + + | No |
| Kyrgyzstan | Yes | No | + | Yes | No |

*Trade and Development Program, U.S. Department of State.

**General Agreement on Tariffs and Trade. Russia has full observer status in the GATT; the United States suports full observer status for all the independent states.

+ The (then) Trade and Economic Council, or TEC, works in all former Soviet republics.

+ + Approved for membership.

Source: Based on a compilation by the U.S. Department of Commerce, International Trade Administration (current as of 6/6/92).

**Table 5—3.  Status of Agreements Between the United States and the Newly Independent States (as of July 28, 1992)**

| Republic | Trade Agrmt. | MFN | GSP | OPIC | Eximbank |
|---|---|---|---|---|---|
| Armenia | Yes | Yes | No | Yes | No |
| Azerbaijan | Pending* | No | No | Pending* | No |
| Belarus | Pending* | No | No | Yes | Yes |
| Georgia | Pending* | No | No | Yes | No |
| Kazakhstan | Pending** | No | No | Yes | Yes |
| Kyrgyzstan | Pending** | No | No | Yes | No |
| Moldova | Yes | Yes | No | Pending** | No |
| Russia | Yes | Yes | No | Yes | Yes |
| Tajikistan | Pending* | No | No | Yes | No |
| Turkmenistan | Pending* | No | No | Pending* | No |
| Ukraine | Yes | Yes | No | Yes | Yes |
| Uzbekistan | Pending* | No | No | Pending* | Yes |

*Negotiations in progress (for OPIC, signing expected shortly; companies are encouraged to register projects with OPIC now).

**Awaiting ratification by country's parliament.

MFN—Most-Favored-Nation status; GSP—Generalized System of Preferences; OPIC—Overseas Private Investment Corporation; Eximbank—Export-Import Bank of the United States.

Source: *Bisnis Bulletin*, July/August 1992, p. 3

global energy market was recognized early on. In part, if the proper stimulation were to come forward, much would have to be provided by Western investors. That in turn means that adequate protection of these investors and the creation of an attractive investment climate would have to be provided.

In addition, Western Europe has been and will continue to be a major importer of oil and natural gas from the former Soviet Union. As noted, the reliance upon natural gas from Russia in particular is quite high, and carries a certain political risk with it. That risk had to be minimized to the extent possible.

The organizing meeting of European Energy Charter, hopeful of providing the above desired results, was held in July 1991. Negotiations during the fall of 1991 led to the signing of the charter in December 1991.

Signatories to the charter included the United States, the Baltic States, ten republics of the C.I.S. (importantly, Russia, Ukraine, and Belarus), and Japan, plus the European Community.

The charter itself is more a political document, setting out political principles, and lacks substance. But with the signing of the charter,

**Table 5—4.  Western and Eastern Europe Dependence on Natural Gas from the Former USSR, 1990**

| | Imports | |
|---|---|---|
| *Importing Country* | *(Billion Cubic Meters)* | *As Percent of Consumption* |
| Germany* | 26.6 | 33 |
| Czechoslovakia | 14.2 | 90 |
| Italy | 13.6 | 28 |
| France | 10.6 | 31 |
| Poland | 8.2 | 60 |
| Romania | 7.4 | 21 |
| Bulgaria | 6.9 | 100 |
| Hungary | 6.4 | 50 |
| Austria | 5.1 | 75 |
| Yugoslavia | 4.5 | 65 |
| Turkey | 3.3 | 6 |
| Finland | 2.7 | 100 |
| Switzerland | 0.3 | — |
| Total | 109.8 | |

*Includes East Germany.

Source: *Stroitelstvo truboprovodov*, no. 2, February 1992, p. 12.

work would begin on the so-called Basic Agreement, which would provide the necessary legal framework surrounding the charter, and a series of protocols to this agreement. The concept behind the charter is a very simple one: to develop global energy markets on the principles of nondiscrimination and economic pricing.

Securing signatories to the charter was the easy part. A number of working groups have been established to prepare the detailed guidelines necessary for the charter to have the proper substance. But on a number of issues—nondiscriminatory or national treatment for investors, transit rights, a commitment to roll back all restrictive legislation—while easy to identify, it will be difficult to secure agreement from all the parties concerned. Thus, it is probable that the Basic Agreement to the charter is not likely to be signed by the consenting nations until 1993.

The European Energy Charter is designed to safeguard Western investments in the C.I.S. and hopefully will provide the confidence necessary for such investments to be made. But the charter is a two-way street; it not only imposes Western rules on the C.I.S. but also provides safeguards for Russians (and others) who may want to invest in Texas or the North Sea.

Certain Western signatories will find it difficult to relinquish the degree of sovereignty required by the Basic Agreement.

## VI  Weighing Risk and Opportunity Against the Decline of the Energy Sector

The oil industry of the former Soviet Union is in desperate shape, brought about by poor management practices, the exploitation of the industry without regard for its future, and the inability or unwillingness to allocate investment funds sufficient to ensure that there was a future.

What does the industry look like today?

• More than 27,000 wells are shut in, not because of the market but because of the lack of equipment, spare parts, and the like.

• Water is overwhelming the producing fields. Today, on average, every barrel of crude brought to the surface is accompanied by about four barrels of water.

• New oil discoveries are small in size and fall far short of replenishing produced oil.

• Oil refineries are badly outmoded by Western standards, with light product yields averaging barely 63 percent.

• Only 14 percent of the production equipment in the oil industry meets world standards.

• More than 70 percent of the equipment in the oil-refining industry is obsolete and requires replacement.

• Only 10 percent of the productive assets of the gas industry can be said to meet world standards, and about 15 percent await replacement.

• Corruption is widespread, led by the allure of hard currency and the huge gap between domestic oil prices and world market prices. Not long ago, acting Prime Minister Yegor Gaidar described the oil and gas industry of Russia as a breeding ground for crime.

• Oil pipelines are in a sorry state of repair, and leaks are an everyday occurrence. The volume of oil spilled last year because of these breaks works out to the equivalent of a Valdez-size tanker accident every month.

• Natural gas pipelines are in no better shape. About 10 percent of the production of natural gas in the former Soviet Union reportedly is lost during movement through the transmission gas pipeline network. More than 2 billion cubic meters of the transported gas escapes during pipeline repair operations.

Most of the publicity surrounding the energy posture of the Commonwealth centers on the crash in oil production, and on the opening up of the republics to foreign investment, particularly joint ventures. Oil is always a high-profile commodity, it seems, no matter what the country. No one is immune to the allure of oil. Control over oil means political power and economic wealth, wherever that oil is produced. And Russia, Kazakhstan, and Azerbaijan, the key oil republics of the Commonwealth, are certainly no exception.

Oil production in the United States has been declining in recent years, as our production has been replaced by cheaper foreign oil. Our decline can be traced to the workings of the market: consumers will always buy the cheaper product, if it is of comparable quality. U.S. oil is more expensive than foreign, in part because ours is a more mature industry, which means that all the easy—and cheap—oil has already been found and in part because access to prospective unexplored areas is being denied for environmental protection reasons.

While our oil decline is worrisome, it has not been nearly as dramatic as what has been happening in the former Soviet Union. Oil production here has fallen from a peak of 12.5 million b/d in 1988 to 10.3 million b/d in 1991. A further drop of some 1.3 million b/d during 1992, to 9 million b/d, is considered likely.

From a broader perspective, the decline has been the result of disastrous policies pushing for overproduction, faulty management, poor technology, and bad maintenance, all against a general back-

**Table 5—5.  Oil Exports\* from the Former Soviet Union, Selected Years, 1975—92**

| Year | Million Barrels/Day\*\* |
|------|------------------------|
| 1975 | 2.6 |
| 1980 | 3.2 |
| 1985 | 3.3 |
| 1986 | 3.7 |
| 1987 | 3.9 |
| 1988 | 4.1 |
| 1989 | 3.7 |
| 1990 | 3.2 |
| 1991 | 2.1 |
| 1992 (est.) | 1.4 |

\*Includes both crude oil and petroleum products.
\*\*Excerpt for 1975 and 1992, from CIA, *International Energy Statistical Review*, 28 July 1992, p. 13. Data for 1975 from *Soviet Energy Data Resource Handbook*, May 1990, p. 21.

ground of shortages of capital and lack of motivation. Yet the Commonwealth is still an oil exporter of substance, having sold about 2.1 million b/d of oil in 1991 to buyers outside its borders (Table 5–5).

This might be a good time to ask, can we believe their statistics? There really is no alternative, but one must wonder from time to time. To illustrate:

The secretary of the local Communist Party—when there was a Communist Party—makes his annual visit to a nearby state farm, to meet with its manager.

"Tell me, Misha," he asks, "how are things going?"

"Comrade Secretary," says Misha, "things are going very well. Why, if we were to pile our potatoes one on top of the other, they would reach all the way to God."

"Now, Misha," the Secretary admonishes, "you are a good Communist, and all good Communists know there is no God."

"Well, yes, I know that, I know there is no God," answered Misha. "And by the way, there are no potatoes either."

Generally when the status of a particular oil industry is reviewed and production levels evaluated, we usually relate to national averages, expressed in barrels per day. That approach is particularly dangerous for the former Soviet Union, because it masks the deterioration in the latter half of the year.

Oil production in the Commonwealth in 1992 has been placed at around 9 million b/d. This represents a very substantial drop of some 1.3 million b/d since 1991, but still supplies would appear more than adequate to meet domestic requirements, if the proper volumes are so allocated.

However, the situation changes very dramatically when production is examined month by month. By December of 1992 oil production in the Commonwealth will have fallen to possibly as low as 8.4 million b/d, and oil production in Russia itself might be no more than 7.3 million b/d. If these circumstances arise, then a variety of difficulties will emerge. They spell trouble for Russia's ability to earn hard currency through oil exports and in turn put its creditworthiness in doubt; they spell trouble for the harvest season and for consumers in general; and they spell trouble for the other Commonwealth republics and for Eastern Europe, whose contracted oil deliveries from Russia could be in jeopardy.

Can the decline in indigenous oil supply be offset through increased availability of other fuels? A brief look at other forms of energy offers no solace.

**Table 5—6.  Production of Crude Oil in the Former Soviet Union,
Selected Years, 1975—92**

| Year | Million Barrels/Day* |
|------|----------------------|
| 1975 | 9.82 |
| 1980 | 12.03 |
| 1985 | 11.91 |
| 1986 | 12.30 |
| 1987 | 12.48 |
| 1988 | 12.45 |
| 1989 | 12.14 |
| 1990 | 11.40 |
| 1991 | 10.30 |
| 1992 (est.) | 9.0 |

*Includes natural gas liquids.

Source: *International Energy Statistical Review.*

• After a number of years during which the annual increments in natural gas supply averaged 1.4 to 1.6 trillion cubic feet, gas extraction actually fell in 1991. Output during 1992 will not match last year's level.

• Coal has fallen from a peak of 772 million tons in 1988 to 629 million tons in 1991. Further, possibly significant, losses must be anticipated.

• The electric power industry has not yet recovered from the explosion at the Chernobyl nuclear power plant in April 1986. Public rejection of nuclear power followed quickly in the wake of the accident. Operating plants have been shut down, construction of new reactors halted, and plans for new reactors torn up. In sum, it would appear that around 109 million kilowatt hours of nuclear power have been taken off the books—roughly triple the current nuclear generating capacity.

The nuclear power problem, however, is one which governments will have to address, and now. The problem is this: the prospect of another Chernobyl-like explosion is a clear and present danger.

In all, a total of seventeen Chernobyl-like reactors have been built in the former Soviet Union—eleven in the Russian Federation, four in Ukraine, and two in Lithuania. Of these, fifteen are currently operating. Two have been shut down in Ukraine: reactor #4 following the explosion and reactor #2 following a fire in late 1991. Chernobyl is to be completely shut down by the close of 1993.

The Chernobyl-type reactor is distinguished by the absence of a containment structure that would act as a barrier to the release of radioactive elements in the event of an accident. There is a broad-based call in the West to shut down, immediately, these fifteen Chernobyl-type reactors, because the risks inherent in continued operation are too great. Their operators, however, are adamant that these reactors cannot be shut down. They are too important, nationally and locally, in terms of power supply. In Russia, about 6 percent of the power supply would be lost, but 58 percent would be lost in Lithuania.

Western governments, including the United States, will have to work out some way to shut these reactors down, yet ensure that the local power supply remains adequate.

The generation in Russia of all forms of electric power in 1991 actually declined from the previous year. That decline, while only slight, should continue. Russia, if only because of its sheer size and natural resource base, dominated the Soviet Union, just as it dominates the Commonwealth. It produces two-thirds of all electric power in the Commonwealth, about 90 percent of the crude oil, 79 percent of the natural gas, and 56 percent of the coal.

Outside Russia, the only other republics that count, in terms of energy production, are Kazakhstan, which has good coal, oil, and gas prospects; Turkmenistan, which supplies a bit more than 10 percent of total gas production; and Ukraine with its coal resource base. Azerbaijan has an aging oil industry, but Western firms believe that there are good prospects in the deep water of the adjacent Caspian Sea.

Ukraine is vulnerable in terms of energy supply, simply because of the tremendous volumes of oil and gas it must import to meet demand. The Baltic states are vulnerable, too, in that they have little or no oil and gas of their own.

But both Ukraine and the Baltics are in a position to offset these vulnerabilities. The Baltics offer ports of export to the West for Russia. Ukraine not only is a major supplier of grain to Russia, but the pipelines through which Russia exports oil and gas to Eastern and Western Europe pass through the republic.

Ukraine and the Baltics can be expected to use their geography to the best advantage.

The republics of Central Asia are perhaps in the poorest position. Their geography isolates them from sources of supply of oil and gas from countries other than Russia, except for Iran.

What can the United States do in the way of foreign assistance to help revitalize the energy sector of the former Soviet Union? Throwing money at their problem, even if such were politically acceptable, will not accomplish much.

**Table 5–7.  C.I.S.: Production of Electric Power and Extraction of Basic Fuels, by Member State, 1991**

| Republic | Electric power | | Crude oil* | | Gas | | Coal | |
|---|---|---|---|---|---|---|---|---|
| | Billion kwh | % of 1990 | Million tons | % of 1990 | Billion m³ | % of 1990 | Million tons | % of 1990 |
| Azerbaijan | 23.3 | 101 | 11.7 | 94 | 8.6 | 87 | — | — |
| Armenia | 9.5 | 92 | — | — | — | — | — | — |
| Belarus | 38.7 | 98 | 2.1 | 100.3 | 0.3 | 99 | — | — |
| Kazakhstan | 79.1 | 98 | 26.6 | 103 | 7.9 | 111 | 130 | 99.3 |
| Kyrgyzstan | 14.0 | 106 | 0.1 | 92 | 0.1 | 87 | 3.5 | 93 |
| Moldova | 13.0 | 84 | — | — | — | — | — | — |
| Russia | 1,046 | 99 | 461 | 89 | 643 | 100.4 | 353 | 89 |
| Tajikistan | 17.5 | 97 | 0.1 | 75 | 0.1 | 83 | 0.3 | 66 |
| Turkmenistan | 14.9 | 102 | 5.4 | 97 | 84.3 | 96 | — | — |
| Uzbekistan | 54.1 | 96 | 2.8 | 100.8 | 41.9 | 103 | 5.9 | 92 |
| Ukraine | 275.8 | 93 | 4.9 | 94 | 24.4 | 87 | 136 | 82 |
| Total for C.I.S. | 1,586 | 98 | 515 | 90 | 810 | 99.5 | 629 | 90 |

*Including gas condensate.

Source: *Ekonomicheskaya Gazeta (Ekonomika i Zhizn)*, No. 6, February 1992, p. 15. Data provided by the State Statistical Committee.

We can visualize the former Soviet Union as an automobile with an empty gas tank and an engine that doesn't work. We can supply financial aid (that is like putting gasoline in the tank), but until the engine is fixed (and that will come only with the proper political and economic reform), the car still can't run.

First, the United States should weigh in, where it can, to assure that U.S. companies have a level playing field when it comes to doing business in the former Soviet Union. And that means the availability of a trade treaty, a bilateral tax treaty, a bilateral investment treaty, risk insurance coverage from the Overseas Private Investment Corporation, and ample Export-Import Bank funding—all pieces of paper quite important to the potential investor. Further, the United States can assist in helping the C.I.S. develop a body of tax laws in the energy sector comparable to those in place elsewhere.

But beyond that, it will be up to individual oil companies to decide whether to invest, and their decisions will be pragmatic ones. Will the rate of return equate to risk? If not, the investment dollars will be taken elsewhere.

## VII   Other Domestic Obstacles

Within the list of obstacles facing the foreign investor who would like to make a commitment in the former Soviet Union, there are four major issues that, in themselves alone, serve as powerful and sometimes final deterrents.

- Instability of the legal and tax framework;
- The reality that taxes imposed are more confiscatory in nature, rather than signaling encouragement to the potential investor;
- The struggle between Moscow (the center) and local authorities over control over oil;
- Corruption; and
- Prospects of civil war.

### *Legal Framework*

Partial progress has been made in trying to bring some stability to the legal and tax framework. That came about in May 1992 with the passage by the Russian Parliament of the Law on Mineral Resources (or, more correctly translated, the Law of the Subsoil). While this law does little to clarify matters with regard to resource control, while it may not be responsive to all the concerns that Western legal counsel might raise, and while it does not provide for international arbitration or direct negotiations between the investor and the local responsible organization, it is generally regarded as a positive initial step. The investor now awaits the passage of an acceptable oil and gas tax law.

While U.S. companies in particular continue to press for a precise and all-inclusive oil and gas tax law, Russian authorities are not so certain that detailed regulations would be appropriate. Instead, as one official suggested, let specific regulations be established through presidential decrees and parliamentary orders. It is highly unlikely that the foreign investor would be supportive of such an approach, however, reckoning that it would only add to the uncertainties of doing business; that presidential decrees would come and go with presidents.

The Russian side has countered the justifiably cautious stance of the foreign investor with the encouragement of "just come on in. We can work it all out during the negotiations." But, as the Russian side has learned, words of encouragement are not nearly enough to offset perceived risk.

### *Taxes*

The prospective investor in Russia is immediately confronted with an imposing array of taxes and tariffs: an oil export tariff, corporate income taxes, and value-added taxes, plus a variety of local and regional taxes. It has been calculated that, for some ventures, the sum of the taxes imposed would exceed gross revenues.

The uncertainties of the tax system can be completely unnerving for the foreign manager. Take, for example, the statement in January 1992 by current acting Prime Minister Gaidar that 40 percent of all hard-currency earnings from the export of energy would be subject to compulsory conversion into rubles. Protests by the foreign community quickly followed and, as a result, any joint venture or subsidiary having more than 30 percent foreign capital was freed from this requirement.

Another example: It was announced that all expatriates would have to pay an income tax based on 60 percent of their *worldwide* income. Again, protests followed, and the levy was reduced to 30 percent.

One particular tax, out of the many imposed at the local, regional, and national levels, and a tax that directly threatened the economic viability of foreign investment, was the oil export tax, imposed at the rate of $5 per barrel and which stood, at the exchange rate prevailing in August 1992, at $7 per barrel. One could not argue with the original premise behind the tax—to capture a portion of the difference between domestic price for crude oil, and the prevailing world market price. As August 1992 came to a close, the exchange value of the ruble stood at 210 rubles/U.S. $1. Which meant that a barrel of crude oil was then selling internally in Russia for the equivalent of $1.17 to $1.44 per barrel. With a barrel of crude oil selling on the world market for, say $18, and given the desperate need for hard currency, oil exports to hard-currency buyers would be maximized to the extent possible. At the same time, this gap is an invitation to corruption on a massive scale, and we discuss that particular element of risk in some detail elsewhere in this chapter.

Those Russian organizations—or entrepreneurs—who could acquire an oil export license stand to make unconscionable profits per barrel, in part because the low internal price falls well short of covering the true costs of production.

Foreign investors complained bitterly. Of the four joint ventures that were producing successfully when the export tax was announced in December 1991, one, the White Knights project, literally brought its operations to a halt, explaining that with this tax in place, it was not economically feasible to continue.

The prospect of eventual relief emerged when it was later announced that two new projects, one involving Gulf Canada and British Gas as the foreign partners, and another in which Conoco was the foreign partner, had been granted exemptions from the oil export tax. Efforts then began to secure exemptions for those joint ventures initiated prior to January 1, 1992, and these efforts are proving successful. But then, only four joint ventures actually met those criteria.

Qualifications for exemption from the oil export tax unfortunately does not mean that the matter has been fully resolved. There was a caveat attached to the exemption that in turn almost equally complicates the future for the investor. That caveat stipulates that the export tax will not come into play until the foreign partner's initial investment has been recovered. While removal of the tax supports short-term profit margins, the prospect of it being reimposed at a later date is somewhat worrisome. Who has the final say as to when the investment has been recovered, and who defines that initial investment? Perhaps by that time, domestic oil prices will have been freed, and the question of an export tax will have become moot.

Then, not long after these exemptions from the export tax had been granted, along came another tax.

President Yeltsin signed a decree in August 1992 for a new mineral resource tax that would be levied on enterprises exploiting the country's richest oil and gas fields, ostensibly to prevent superficial development and waste of resources. No other details were provided at that time, such as, are joint ventures liable, and equally important, the size of the tax.

## *Corruption*

The huge gap between the domestic price for crude oil and the price an exporter could expect to receive if that oil were sold on the world market has been the *raison d'être* for growing corruption within the industry. This gap, which stood at around $16 per barrel near the close of August 1992, has been too attractive to ignore. A. Rutskoy, vice president of the Russian Federation, has estimated that the illegal export of raw materials reaches some $30 million every day, and the illegal export of oil is thought to be a major part of this drain on the economy. In July 1992 alone, so it has been reported, a total of 1,317 criminal cases were instituted in Russia involving infringement of rules governing the exportation of raw material resources.

An aide to acting Prime Minister Gaidar stated that at least 5 million tons of oil (the equivalent of 100,000 b/d) had been sold illegally in 1991 by speculators, representing a profit potential of roughly half a billion dollars, but as well a loss in hard-currency earnings to Moscow. In the judgment of Alexander Shokhin, Russian Deputy Prime Minister for Foreign Economic Relations, the government had lost control over state-owned oil exporters, and the only way to regain control was to recentralize purchases.

In response, the government has established a special commission—the Commission on Financial and Legal Control and for Fighting Corruption—to look into the matter. Joint ventures will not be immune.

How can illegal trading in oil occur? For example, an oil tanker declares for the Batumi oil refinery but unloads instead at ports in Turkey, where the oil, which had been purchased at the equivalent of $37.50 per metric ton, is sold for $120 per metric ton. Other investigators have found evidence that illegal oil has been hidden in oil pipelines and in secret storage facilities, later to be sold or bartered with the proceeds going to the locals.

A license to export oil has become a very valuable piece of paper, and Russian anticorruption authorities have found that these licenses have been changing hands for the equivalent of about $2 per ton (or around 30 cents per barrel). Such practices, which could affect about 10 percent of Russian oil exports, were particularly rampant in Tyumen Oblast. Rosnefteproduct, the largest state oil-refining operation, was under investigation for irregular sales to former Soviet republics, which resulted in parts of Russia being starved for oil supplies. Managers at Nizhnevartovsk, one of the largest oil-producing organizations in Western Siberia, were under investigation after it was found that around 11 million barrels of oil had been put aside in hidden storage for unofficial sales.

Borders between the individual republics are like a sieve, and oil frequently is shipped across to the Baltic republics, and then reexported for hard currency. A high-ranking Russian official observed in late August 1992 that two-thirds of the crude oil exported during the first half of 1992 had crossed the border duty free, implying that exporters either had simply refused to pay the duty or had found some way to circumvent it.

Corruption is not limited just to the export of oil. Reports also point to the rather wide-scale bootlegging of geological data, involving the copying of data held in the files of various geological institutes, then selling this information to oil companies that may have an interest in exploration in a particular area. Although several rationales have been offered to explain away these illegal sales, the root cause still is the desire for hard currency.

## Civil War

Political humor often provides a valuable insight into what concerns the average citizen of a particular country. Some time ago, a joke was making the rounds of Moscow that gauged the then-current fears of its people. The joke went something like this:

A Russian *optimist* is one who still teaches his children how to read and write in their native language. A *pessimist* is one who teaches his children to read and write in English and Chinese. But a *realist* is one who teaches his children to fire a Kalashnikov rifle for the coming civil war.

Unfortunately, civil war has arrived, although fortunately it has been confined to the southern reaches of the former Soviet Union. There is fighting between Azerbaijan and Armenia, and within the republic of Georgia itself. In the republic of Moldova there is fear that conflict between the ethnic Romanian majority and the Russian-speaking minority will escalate to full-scale war. And for most of the summer of 1992 there had been fighting between the forces loyal to the president of the republic of Tajikistan and a broad opposition coalition that was determined to remove him from office. Meanwhile, the not-so-subtle tensions between Ukraine and the Russian Federation remain for all to ponder.

The fear that these civil wars will break out of their present geographic confines is very real, and this possibility must be considered as one of the political risks to be accepted when making an investment in the former Soviet Union.

### VIII   Achieving Acceptable Involvement in the Republics

From the foreign-investor side, what will make for an acceptable involvement in Russia or in any of the other republics of the former Soviet Union?

First, it you are risk averse, exposure to Russia and to the other republics should be avoided at this time. If a decision is made, however, to at least "test the waters," senior management must be fully committed in its support of that decision. If that commitment is not there, or if it is perceived as somewhat weak, do not move forward. Third, the investor must be willing to walk away at any time, and to absorb whatever financial losses might be incurred.

For the investor who does decide to proceed, a number of guidelines are in order.

• Do your homework. That means risk identification in its fullest extent, and the parallel working out of approaches as to how to minimize these risks.

• Minimize initial financial exposure.

• Recognize that while the political and economic uncertainties may appear unresolvable at the present, there is no investment opportunity anywhere of prospective profit that is without such uncertainties, and that clearly includes the United States.

• The standard "p's" of investment—patience, perseverance, and persuasion—explicitly apply to the former Soviet Union, but with the addition of a fourth "p": presence. Just showing up, as a demonstration of continued interest, is important in building understanding and mutual trust.

• Any venture must recognize and protect the integrity of the Russian work force, including equipment and supplies, to the extent possible.

• Any venture should be driven by consideration for investment return over the long run. Short-term results likely will be disappointing, and this disappointment, against the background of continuing change, of progress and reverses in political and economic reforms, likely will cause some to question their commitment.

• Do not link your commitment to the political fortunes of any one person or any one event. To do so will be counterproductive over the longer term.

• Be prepared to play the role of benefactor, within reason. You may be asked to provide schools, social facilities, housing, hospitals, and recreation outlets, as part of your investment obligations. After all, so the reasoning goes, Moscow did, so then should you.

A comment on political linkages is in order. Business negotiations and agreements with heads of government, as was noted earlier in this book, can be fragile indeed if these individuals leave office for whatever reason. If the business arrangement is then seen as not to the benefit of the republic, that the arrangement instead smacked of favoritism and possibly corruption, at best renegotiation will be in order or, at worst, full dismissal.

In early September 1992 the president of Tajikistan was forced to resign by those opposed to his rule, a carryover from the old Communist apparatus days. As such he was the third elected president of a former Soviet republic forced to leave office since the beginning of 1992 and following the dismantling of the Soviet Union. The president of Azerbaijan had fled Baku in May after the opposition stormed the parliament building, and in early January the president of Georgia was removed after continued fighting in his republic.

All this underscores the risk inherent in any agreement based upon an agreement with a single political actor. The prospective investor would do well to keep this in mind, and to recognize it is essential that the venture be negotiated at all levels, so that its validity can be protected in the event of planned or unplanned changes at the top.

## Notes

1. Membership in the Commonwealth of Independent States (C.I.S.) embraces eleven of the fifteen republics that originally made up the former Soviet

Union. The Baltic republics of Estonia, Latvia, and Lithuania chose not to join in the Commonwealth, and neither did Georgia. These four republics, however, have no oil or gas production of their own.

2. *Russian Petroleum Investor*, August 1992, p. 23.

3. *Obstacles to Trade and Investment in the New Republics of the Former Soviet Union*, International Trade Administration, U.S. Department of Commerce, March 1992.

*Chapter 6*

# Saudi Arabia

## Hermann Frederick Eilts

### Background

Of the Arab states of the Arabian/Persian Gulf littoral, the kingdom of Saudi Arabia is the largest. Its land equivalent is about one-quarter of the United States. It is bordered by Jordan, Iraq, Kuwait, Qatar, Bahrain (with which it is connected by a twenty-one-kilometer causeway), the United Arab Emirates, and the recently united Republic of Yemen. Across the Gulf is the Iranian Islamic Republic. Its major cities—Jidda in the west, Riyadh (the capital) in the center, and the Dammam-Khobar complex in the east—have grown into huge megopoli. Well-paved roads now crisscross the country, and Saudi Arabian Airlines offers rapid transportation to virtually all parts of the kingdom.

Saudi Arabia claims a territorial sea of twelve nautical miles and a contiguous zone of eighteen nautical miles. It has also concluded median-line agreements in the Gulf with Iran and Bahrain. Most of its land boundaries are settled, but border disputes still exist with the United Arab Emirates (Abu Dhabi) and the Republic of Yemen. (A border dispute with Oman was resolved in 1991.) An agreement to divide the Saudi Arabian-Iraqi Neutral Zone was signed in 1989, but has not yet been ratified.

147

The Saudi Arabian government claims a population of some 17 million people, including expatriates, but many observers consider this figure heavily inflated. Although the Saudi Arabian population growth rate is high (over 4 percent), half the above figure is probably a more accurate estimate. This is even more so since the expulsion during the U.N. coalition conflict with Iraq in 1990–91 of some 800,000 Yemenis (including Hadhramis) and other unwanted Arab expatriate workers. The national literacy rate, as claimed by the Saudi Arabian government, is 50 percent and is growing with the continuing emphasis placed on primary and secondary education. Some 60 percent of the Saudi Arabian population is thirty years of age or less. Arabic is the spoken language, though many younger Saudis and Saudi businessmen also speak English.

The kingdom is a conservative monarchy rooted in the orthodox Hanbali school of Sunni Islam. It regards the Koran (*Qur'an*) as its constitution, though a basic law was promulgated in February 1992, spelling out the rights of citizens (see below). The *shari'a*, or Islamic law, governs the legal system, supplemented by a series of *nizam* (royal ordinances) for technical matters not covered by canonical law and to handle disputes involving foreign businessmen or firms. Foreign firms that wish to do business with Saudi Arabia or with Saudi firms often also insist on contractually stipulated commercial arbitration in the event of disputes.

King Fahd ibn 'Abd al-'Aziz Al Saud has ruled the country since 1982. A son of the legendary founder of the present (third) Saudi Arabian state, Fahd is now seventy-two years old and prefers to be known as the Custodian of the Holy Places (of Islam). The heir apparent is Prince 'Abdullah ibn 'Abd al-'Aziz, a half brother and commander of the National Guard. The king is assisted by a Council of Ministers (cabinet) in which he holds the Prime Minister's portfolio. A *majliss al-shura*, or Consultative Council, was recently decreed to advise the monarch and was to be established in October 1992 (see below).

Two aspects of Saudi Arabia give the state special importance: first, its function as the spiritual center of the entire Islamic world; and second, its major role in global petroleum matters.

Mecca and Medina, the two most sacred cities of Islam, are located in the Western Province, more commonly known as al-Hijaz. In fulfillment of one of the five principal religious obligations for every Muslim, some two million Muslims from all over the world make the *haj*, or pilgrimage, to Mecca and its environs each year. Since most

Muslim pilgrims now arrive and leave by air, the annual *haj* is today compressed into a two-month time frame. From a logistical point of view, it is an extraordinarily well-conducted example of religiously motivated mass tourism. The Saudi Arabian government deserves much credit for the enormous improvements it has made over the years in facilitating the pilgrimage.

Apart from being the spiritual focus of Muslims everywhere, the kingdom has the good fortune to contain the largest petroleum reserves in the Middle East. At last count, its reserves were estimated at 252 billion barrels, with new finds still being made. As such, it is second only to the C.I.S. (former Soviet Union) and the United States in recoverable oil reserves. It currently produces about 8 million barrels of oil per day and is expanding its production capacity for future contingency purposes. It is one of the leading members of the Organization of Petroleum Exporting Countries (OPEC) and, while largely dependent on oil-derived income, it has generally sought to keep global oil prices within reasonable bounds. It also belongs to the Organization of Arab Petroleum Exporting Countries (OAPEC) and to the Petroleum Committee of the Gulf Cooperation Council (GCC).

Petroleum was first discovered in Saudi Arabia in the mid-1930s, and commercial production began after World War II. Largely utilizing oil-derived income, the kingdom since 1970 has undertaken a massive economic development effort, through a series of Five-Year Development Plans, each progressively focusing on the short- and longer-term needs of the country and refining these in the light of the experiences gained. Gradually, in the process, the emphasis has shifted from creating major public infrastructure to encouraging the private sector to assume more responsibilities previously borne by government. Other goals have been to increase the standard of living for the Saudi populace, to diversify the nation's productive base from oil and petrochemicals so as to include industry and agriculture, to develop indigenous manpower, and to provide and maintain services for already completed infrastructure. A fifth Five-Year Development Plan is now being inaugurated, with generally similar objectives.

The kingdom's estimated gross domestic product (GDP) for 1990 was approximately $73 billion, a sharp reduction over previous years. This translates into a per capita income of close to $10,000 per native Saudi, exclusive of foreigners. Of its GDP, petroleum accounts for about 80 percent of the total; services, 10 percent; and agriculture, 10 percent. The country's real growth rate is about 3.5 percent, but over the past decade there have been substantial fluctuations in the country's growth rate due to global oil price changes, unexpected expenses associated with the protracted Iraq-Iran war, and the U.N. military coalition effort to expel Iraq from Kuwait.

Exports, mainly in the form of petroleum and petroleum products, go mainly to Japan and the United States, with considerably smaller volumes to France and Bahrain. Imports consist mainly of construction materials, manufactured goods, processed foods, luxury items, and arms, the United States, Japan, the United Kingdom, and Italy being the principal suppliers.

## Domestic Saudi Arabian Politics

For a variety of reasons, Saudi Arabia has sporadically received criticism from elements of the American press and public. For well over a decade, soothsayers of doom, all too many of them uninformed, have predicted the collapse of the Saudi state. In the immediate aftermath of the Iranian Revolution of 1979, which overthrew the Shah of Iran, some observers sought to analogize the Iranian and Saudi Arabian situations and wrongly concluded that the Saud family would follow the way of the Pahlavis. The Islamic fundamentalist attack on the Grand Mosque in Mecca in November 1979, even though it was quickly aborted, was seen by some as evidence of serious internal fissures. None of these predictions materialized, but the few scattered events that took place in Riyadh during the 1990–91 U.N. coalition conflict with Iraq, especially one involving a score or more of Saudi women who dismissed their chauffeurs in the middle of the city and in defiance of the law insisted upon driving themselves, were again exaggerated by impressionable and essentially uninformed observers into presumed evidence that the regime was tottering.

As the paragraphs that follow will seek to show, Saudi Arabia, in its modernization process, has had its problems, but anyone who troubles to look seriously at the dynamics of the country is likely to conclude that such problems as exist are manageable, so long as wise leadership prevails. In fact, Saudi Arabia, in a decade or more of considerable political turbulence in the Middle East as a whole, has demonstrated commendable stability and is likely to continue to do so in the foreseeable future.

### *Leadership Succession and Governance*

King Fahd, before assuming the throne of Saudi Arabia in 1982, had acquired a reputation for progressivism. Since ascending the throne, however, he has been cautious, indeed slow, in implementing promised political liberalization. He has established a leadership style of his own, which is now less dependent than in the past upon Saud family consensus.

Although he and his half brother, Prince Abdullah, the heir apparent, often hold differing points of view, they have worked well together and have cooperated in the affairs of government. The Saud family has had a past history of fractiousness, but it is noteworthy that the last four successions were implemented peacefully and smoothly, despite the fact that one required a monarch to be deposed for incompetence and another followed the assassination of a king by a disaffected cousin. There is a basic recognition on the part of the senior princes of the House of Saud that, whatever their personal differences, they share an interest in uniting and keeping their differences out of the public eye in order to preserve the family's status and for the sake of stability in the country. Most senior members of the Saud family have a high sense of responsibility of their duties toward the nation and its people.

Until early in 1992, the critical succession issue, in terms of procedure, was admittedly somewhat uncertain. The successor to the reigning monarch was informally selected by a consensus of the senior members of the Saud family, whose decision was then formalized in a religious *fatwa*, or advisory opinion, issued by the principal *'ulama*, or religious leaders. Subsequently, the major tribal and other lay leaders of the country would tender the oath of allegiance to the newly designated monarch. The uncertainty in the system arose from the fact that, while in the last several successions the next putative monarch and the heir apparent were generally long recognized by virtue of their seniority based on age, a situation had developed in the Saud family where sons of previous kings and surviving half brothers of the founder of the kingdom were in many instances assumed to have competing ambitions to the throne.

In order to dispel this uncertainty, King Fahd issued a royal decree on February 29, 1992, stipulating that henceforth the reigning monarch would designate his successor and that eligibility for the throne included surviving brothers and half brothers, their sons, and their nephews. The decree likewise stipulates that the monarch is also *ipso facto* prime minister. Immediately after issuing that decree, the king reaffirmed Prince Abdullah in the positions of heir apparent and deputy prime minister. While the new decree remains to be tested, it should be assumed that the reigning monarch will still take into account seniority in the princely ranks as at least one criterion in making his decision on a successor. The new decree, while not addressing the subject, does not dispense with the requisite confirmatory religious *fatwa*, and it may be expected that the traditional system of Saudi lay and tribal leaders subsequently tendering the oath of allegiance to a new monarch, when he ascends the throne, will continue.

As already indicated, under the Saudi system, the monarch and the heir apparent are also prime minister and deputy prime minister, respectively. As such, they preside over the cabinet, which is usually composed of members of the royal family and commoners. Royal family members largely hold defense and security portfolios; commoners tend to hold technical and/or development portfolios (e.g., the minister of petroleum, minister of development, minister of finance). The day-to-day business of the kingdom is conducted through the cabinet and the bureaucracy, subject to the king's approval, and is generally carried on in praiseworthy fashion. Sensitive security issues are handled within the confines of the royal family and by trusted subordinate security officials. The aforementioned massive and impressive development programs of the kingdom, while executed in large part by expatriate labor, are nonetheless indicative of the purposefulness and efficacy of cabinet government.

Based as it is upon Islamic precepts, the economic philosophy of the kingdom is one of private enterprise. The Saudi Arabian government, as the direct recipient of the nation's substantial petroleum income, has been the contracting element for virtually all private enterprise activities, especially those connected with the successive Five-Year Development Plan projects. Nevertheless, the nation is awash with private entrepreneurs of all types and, as already indicated, vigorous efforts are being made by the Saudi Arabian government to persuade the private sector to assume more project activities previously handled by government. There is keen competition among private Saudi businessmen to maximize their individual firms' projects.

Generally speaking, the Saudi Arabian government places great emphasis on honoring contracts. In the mid-1980s, because of financial stringencies brought about by lower global oil prices, the Saudi Arabian government was for a period of time in significant arrears in payments due to Saudi private contractors. In turn, some such Saudi entrepreneurs, who had contracted with foreign firms, sought to evade their payment obligations to the latter by resorting to local *shari'a* courts and contending that such contracts, sometimes calling for interest payments, were invalid according to Islamic law. Although some Saudi contractors succeeded in their efforts, the practice stopped when a distinguished Saudi jurist rendered a decision in one such case, emphasizing that the *shari'a* should not be invoked by Saudi entrepreneurs as a means of evading their contractual obligations. With exceptions, Saudi government officials and private entrepreneurs have since then honored their contractual engagements.

There is no history in Saudi Arabia of the type of nationalization of foreign enterprises that has characterized so many other Middle East states. Indeed, nationalization is contrary to Saudi Arabian and Islamic practice. In the case of the petroleum industry, because of the kingdom's total dependence upon it, the Saudi Arabian government has in effect bought out—through the medium of increasing equity participation—the Arabian Oil Company (Aramco), which had first discovered and thereafter developed the oil fields until the mid-1970s. Renamed Saudi Arabian Aramco, but now subject to the orders of the minister of petroleum and his colleagues, instead of under the direction of former "stateside" companies, the organization continues to function as the primary oil-producing organ of the state.

## The Middle Class

A substantial middle class, made up largely of businessmen, teachers, and bureaucrats, has developed in Saudi Arabia during the past thirty years. Much of the bureaucratic, commercial, and educational activities of the country is in its hands. To date, however, the middle class has been largely passive politically. It exercises influence in the administrative areas, but it has not thus far played a major role in national decision making in the kingdom. Social mobility exists for members of the middle class, in terms of improving their well-being and that of their families, although many would like a greater opening of the political process and a larger voice in national decision making. Some believe that their high-sounding titles in the ministries are incommensurate with their limited decision-making authority. Alongside the desire for greater public participation in the political system, there is a view held by some that the country is too much of a single family preserve, yet there is no evidence to date that this feeling has created any serious wave of disaffection toward the monarchy. The fact of the matter is that Saudis of all classes and ranks share a vested interest in maintaining the political independence and territorial integrity of their nation from perceived covetous regional neighbors, even as they aspire to a greater opening of the political process.

### *The Islamic Factor—A Potential Threat?*

All native Saudis are Muslims. While many have been trained in Western universities, most readily accept the strictures of Islam, even when they return after extended absences. As already indicated, the conservative Hanbali school of Islam predominates in the government of the nation, and in its legal system, but there are also adherents of the Hanafi and the Shafi'a schools of Islam, especially in the Western Province.

Two Islamic factors are sometimes suggested as potential internal threats. The first of these are the Shi'is of the Eastern Province and in the Medina area (i.e., about 300,000 and 50,000, respectively). In the Eastern Province, the Shi'is are Twelvers, similar to those in Iran, southern Iraq, and southern Lebanon. There is a history of discord between the rigidly orthodox Hanbali Sunnis (sometimes known as Wahhabis) and the Shi'is of the Eastern Province. In 1979 and 1980, as a result of Iranian instigation, there were significant Shi'i antigovernment demonstrations in the Eastern Province, which had to be put down by the National Guard. While Shi'is have long been regarded by conservative Hanbalites as heretical, the Saudi Arabian government has sought to work out a modus vivendi with that section of the populace. A son of the reigning monarch is governor of the Eastern Province and has tried to ease tensions with that section of the community. Although Saudi Arabia's Shi'is remain restive because of limitations placed on publicly conducting certain Shi'i religious rites, the governor's efforts have met with some success.

The importance of the Shi'i community in Saudi Arabia does not lie in its overall numbers, which are less than 2 percent of the total population, but rather in its strategic location in the area of the kingdom's petroleum facilities. At the same time, the Shi'is clearly recognize that whatever their residual differences with the Saudi Arabian government, their continued well-being depends upon ensuring no disruption in the production, refining, and exporting of oil. Thus, the 1979–80 Shi'i riots were not in any way directed at petroleum installations.

Paradoxically, a second Islamic factor that needs to be identified is a rise in fundamentalism in the country. In a sense, Hanbalites (Wahhabis) are by definition Sunni fundamentalists. The attack on the Grand Mosque in Mecca in 1979 by Hanbali zealots reflected misgivings on their part at what they considered to be growing derelictions of religious duties by much of the population. That uneasiness persists among the more conservative Hanbali *'ulama*, including the younger ones. It came to the fore again in 1991 in the immediate wake of the massive American troop deployment to the Eastern Province of Saudi Arabia during the conflict with Iraq, when the appearance of such large numbers of non-Muslims, many of them American women in uniform, in the "holy land of Islam" deeply troubled many Saudi religious leaders. King Fahd's decision to invite the United States and others to deploy troops to Saudi Arabia was indeed canonically sanctioned by the principal religious leader of Saudi Arabia, in the form of a *fatwa*, but a great many younger Saudi *'ulama* remained decidedly disturbed about that deployment. They frankly feared the presence of such foreign troops would somehow "taint" the Saudi population and erode traditional Saudi and Islamic cultural values.

In the immediate aftermath of the conflict with Iraq, there was considerable evidence of increased Islamic fundamentalism on the part of many Saudi *'ulama*, the so-called Committees for Public Morality, or religious police, and others. Some Western women encountered unpleasant incidents at the hands of such officials. It eventually required a public warning by the king to the Saudi religious establishment to desist from such harassment, and even now it has not been entirely discontinued. In a time in which much of the Middle East is experiencing Islamic fundamentalist militancy, Saudis at all levels are bound to be affected by this renewed phenomenon of religious zealotry.

While both of the aforementioned religious phenomena could be troublesome, there is no reason to believe that they represent any serious security threat to the stability of the kingdom. The regime has co-opted the principal Hanbali *'ulama* and has taken restraining action against recalcitrant members of the religious police. For foreigners living in Saudi Arabia, especially non-Muslims, such Islamic fundamentalist zealots sometimes represent more than a nuisance. That is not likely to change in the foreseeable future. It is a situation that is manageable, however, if expatriates in Saudi Arabia, including Americans, recognize they are living in a different culture that has its own set of values and that deserves to be respected.

## Labor Situation

The Saudi Arabian work force was estimated in 1990 to be about 4 million, of which 60 percent were expatriates. Unemployment does not exist in the country. Native Saudis largely fill clerical and administrative positions. Some also drive taxis and operate heavy equipment.

Relatively few are involved in what might be called hard, manual labor. Instead, expatriates from all over the world have been brought to Saudi Arabia to handle heavy construction work, road building, maintenance work, and various menial functions. The importation of such expatriate labor requires a Saudi Arabian sponsor, such as a contractor, head of household, etc. The last two Five-Year Development Plans have sought to train more native Saudis for skilled, manual positions, but success has been limited. Traditional Saudi culture looks down on such work.

Labor unions do not exist in Saudi Arabia and are in fact banned. The Saudi theory is that labor, like other elements of Saudi society, benefits from the welfare-state concept that characterizes the kingdom's sociopolitical approach. In years past there have been one or two strikes at the petroleum facilities, but these were instigated largely by expatriate labor. In theory, expatriate labor has the potential for labor agitation. The Saudi authorities watch carefully and utilize preemptive techniques, including arrests and deportations, when dealing with occasional expatriate labor agitators. They also carefully control expatriate labor groups by putting them in camps and other segregated areas.

### The Question of Civil Disorder

Apart from the 1979 attack on the Grand Mosque in Mecca by a group of some 200 Saudi and expatriate Muslim fundamentalists, which was a traumatic shock for the Saudi authorities, and the two aforementioned Shi'i demonstrations in the Eastern Province in 1979–80, there has been no serious civil disorder in the kingdom in recent years. During the June 1967 war, there were demonstrations against Aramco, the American Consulate General in Dhahran, and the offices of the U.S. Military Training Mission in Dhahran, but these were prompted by spontaneous Saudi public outrage over perceived U.S. support for Israel and alleged American responsibility for the defeat of the Arabs. They were put down by the Saudi Arabian National Guard, but not without damage to property at the hands of the mob. Such spontaneous demonstrations could, of course, recur in the event of a new, major Arab-Israeli war.

In the mid-1980s, there were also Iranian-inspired demonstrations against the Saudi Arabian government, the United States, and Israel during the annual *haj*. They had to be forcibly suppressed by the Saudi police authorities, and they subsequently prompted the Saudi Arabian government to take the extraordinary step of limiting the number of

Iranian pilgrims who were allowed to make the *haj*. With the death of the Ayatollah Khomeini and the gradual strengthening of the government of President Hashemi Rafsanjani in Tehran, an easing of Saudi Arabian-Iranian tensions is gradually taking place. The last pilgrimage (1992), in which Iranian pilgrims again participated, took place without incident.

## The Political Process

The Saudi Arabian government is authoritarian. Unlike so many of its neighbors, however, it is generally benevolent. While it maintains police and intelligence organizations, it has not oppressed its public. Despite protests from Saudi exiles about alleged abuses in the kingdom, there are very few political prisoners. Its punitive procedures flow from Islamic court decisions and include flogging or jailing for drinking, stoning for adultery, amputation of limbs for stealing, decapitation for murder, etc. These, it should be emphasized, are not capriciously authorized and only after the most careful review by an Islamic court.

Saudi Arabia has often been criticized for a lack of democratic institutions. While the courts are scrupulously fair, public participation in the political process has been sharply limited. To be sure, the heir apparent and the provincial governors of the country conduct a daily or weekly *majliss* (public audience) at which any Saudi may freely present a petition for redress of a perceived wrong. The effectiveness of this process clearly depends upon the sense of responsibility of the particular senior recipient of the petition. It should be noted that most take their responsibilities in this regard very seriously, and numerous minor issues are handled that way.

For years there has been talk in Saudi Arabia about the possible establishment of a *majliss al-shura* (consultative council). Such an institution, traditional in Islamic polities, existed in the Hijaz when it was conquered by the Sauds and incorporated into their state. It subsequently fell into disuse. During the reign of King Faisal (1964–75), he promised to reinstitute such a body. Not until February of 1992, however, did King Fahd decree the establishment of a sixty-member *majliss al-shura*, with an additional member as chairman, to go into effect in October 1992. Its members are to be royally appointed "from those with knowledge, expertise and competence," cannot be government officials or corporate managers, and may not be reappointed once their four-year terms have expired. While this newly reestablished consultative council is not strictly speaking a parliament, it will have the right—always subject to royal veto—to summon ministers for evidence, recommend possible enactments by ministries, debate and suggest changes to proposed legislature and, in general, to advise the king on policy matters. The monarch is not, however, bound by their advice. It remains to be seen how the system will work and whether its royally appointed members are in any way representative of the Saudi public.

## *The Armed Forces*

The Saudi Arabian Armed Forces consist of three component elements. The Army, Air Force, and Navy are under the direction of a full brother of the king, Prince Sultan ibn 'Abd al-'Aziz, as minister of defense and civil aviation. All three services have benefited from modern weapons acquisitions, training programs, excellent cantonments, and other perquisites. Members of the royal family are strategically placed in various military command positions and are thus able to monitor the loyalty of the military. A U.S. military training mission has been in Saudi Arabia since 1949 to train the Saudi military in the use of weapons systems bought from the United States. While most Saudi military equipment has been bought from the United States, frequent difficulties in obtaining congressional approval for arms sales has prompted the Saudi Arabian government to diversify its arms sources. Other arms suppliers now include Great Britain, France and, in at least once case, the People's Republic of China.

The second component is the Saudi Arabian National Guard, made up largely of regular tribal formations and tribal reserves under the direction of the king's half brother and heir apparent, Prince Abdullah. Equipment for the National Guard has been bought from the United States, Great Britain, and other sources, and training has been provided by British and American military advisers.

The mission of the Saudi Arabian Armed Forces is the protection of the kingdom's 4,000-mile-long border and the maintenance of internal security. Saudi Army, Navy, and Air Force units that participated in the Desert Storm campaign of 1991 to expel Iraq from Kuwait generally acquitted themselves well. Terrorism has not been a problem in Saudi Arabia. The Saudi security authorities are generally quite good and regularly monitor potential dissidents, including expatriates, resident in the country. The expulsion of the greater part of the Yemeni community residents in Saudi Arabia during the 1990–91 conflict with

Iraq has sharply reduced any potential for Yemeni-inspired subversion in Saudi Arabia.

## External Threats

Since the creation of the Saudi Arabian state, its leaders have viewed the kingdom as potentially "encircled." The nature of the encirclers has changed over the years, but putative external threats remain a constant concern. Four such external threats are cited: Saddam Hussein's Ba'athist and expansionist Iraq; the Iranian Islamic Republic, which is viewed by many Saudis and other Gulf Arabs as having hegemonic designs in the Gulf area; the irredentist Republic of Yemen; and Israel.

While the Saudi Arabian Armed Forces have made great strides in developing their defensive capability, the Saudi regime recognizes a continuing need for external security assistance in the event of an attack on its borders. In the already mentioned GCC context, a Peninsula Shield Force, consisting largely of Saudi Arabian troops with smaller elements from other Arab states of the Gulf, exists, but is of limited security value. Hence Saudi Arabia has relied heavily upon the United States to assist it militarily in times of need.

While the Saudis are always reluctant to accept any long-term deployment of an American or other combat force on their soil, King Fahd did request such an American troop deployment following the Iraqi invasion of Kuwait in August 1990. That deployment, which ultimately numbered over a half million Americans, was made easier to accept by the concurrent deployments of British, French, and especially Egyptian, Syrian, and other Muslim troops—all under a U.N.-sponsored coalition. Once the Iraqis were expelled from Kuwait, the Saudi regime quickly requested that the foreign troops on its soil, Americans included, leave. It has since that time been reluctant to conclude a written security agreement with the United States for future contingencies, largely because of the sensitivities of the Hanbalite (Wahhabi) religious leaders, but has not objected to such agreements being concluded with the United States by neighboring Kuwait, Bahrain, Qatar, and (still to be concluded) the United Arab Emirates.

Saudi Arabia has permitted its air facilities to be used by the American, British, and French Air Forces in connection with the August 1992 quadripartite declaration of an exclusionary zone over southern Iraq to prevent Iraqi aircraft from attacking dissident Shi'is in that area. While no Saudi aircraft have participated directly in flying over southern Iraq, they have participated in support missions, such as refueling and AWAC surveillance. Iraq, with its strong conventional military forces, continues to be seen as a potential future threat.

A second potential external threat is Iran, whose hegemonic ambitions in the Gulf area worry many Saudis. Because Iran is the largest state in the Gulf area, with the longest coastline in the Gulf and a population of 55 million, Saudi Arabia and its Arab neighbors view it as a "colossus." The fact that Iran is Twelver Shi'i–dominated adds an Islamic sectarian bitterness to the equation. Although political relations between Iran and Saudi Arabia have improved since the death of the Ayatollah Khomeini, Iran has publicly indicated its displeasure with the Saudi security link with the United States and has emphasized its own proper role in any future security arrangements for the Gulf area. Saudi Arabia and Iran also have differing views on optimal oil policies. While there is an obvious reluctance publicly to cite Iran as a security threat, many Saudis are worried about putative future Iranian aggression in the Gulf area.

The Republic of Yemen, as it has been called since the union of North and South Yemen in 1990, also worries the Saudi regime. There has long been a Yemeni irredentist problem with Yemeni governments wanting the return of Jizan and Najran, two border towns in 'Asir, taken by Saudi Arabia after a successful war with Yemen in 1934. An unresolved border dispute in the area east of the Yemeni mountains also exists between the two countries and has been exacerbated by oil concessions given by the Yemeni government in the disputed areas. Still another factor in the animosity was Yemen's siding with Iraq in the 1990–91 conflict with Saddam Hussein and the consequent Saudi expulsion of almost a million Yemeni expatriates, who have caused major economic burdens for the republic. Finally, the fact that the population of the newly united Yemen (13 million) is greater than the native Saudi population gives it a greater potential military manpower base with which to attempt at some time in the future to recover its lost territories.

Saudi concern about a potential Israeli threat is perennial. Exaggerated though it may be, some Saudis view sometime "Eretz Israel" talk in Israel as likewise applying to formerly Jewish-populated areas of the Hijaz, like Medina, Khaibar, etc. Frequent Israeli surveillance overflights of Tabuk and northern Saudi Arabia are also viewed as provocative. And Israel's nuclear capability is seen by Saudis as a threat not only to them, but to the entire region. Finally, the Jerusalem issue divides the two states, even as Saudi Arabia has become disillusioned with Palestinians. As custodian of the holy places of Islam in Mecca and Medina, successive Saudi rulers have felt they also have a responsibility for the Muslim holy places in East Jerusalem and have insisted on a voice in their ultimate disposition.

## *Traditional Religion and the Fear of Modernity from the West: A Deterrent to Foreigners Living in Saudi Arabia*

The massive economic development that has taken place in the kingdom during the past three decades, the increasing number of expatriate laborers brought in for construction and other purposes, and the massive foreign troop deployment to Saudi Arabia during the conflict with Iraq have all combined to create growing uneasiness among the conservative *'ulama*, or religious leaders, that traditional Saudi and Islamic socioreligious values, upon which the state was built, may be threatened. An element of xenophobia exists in the country, especially among rigid Hanbali Muslims. This has caused foreign expatriates to be viewed in orthodox Muslim circles as potential polluters of traditional Islamic values. Along separate but parallel lines, a certain arrogance on the part of many wealthy Saudi businessmen and others, brought about by constant wooing by foreign firms anxious to do business with Saudi Arabia, also exists.

Western expatriates, especially Christians, often are segregated either in compounds or in largely foreign quarters of urban centers. There is little social contact between them and Saudi nationals, except in the work place. Strict dress codes are enjoined, especially for women, who are also not allowed to drive. Expatriates in Saudi Arabia, men and women alike, Muslim and non-Muslim, are expected to adhere to rigid Islamic behavioral codes. The importation and drinking of alcoholic beverages is forbidden, with violators subject to jailing or flogging. Christian worship services are prohibited. Life in Saudi Arabia for Western expatriates, while bearable and profitable, is closely circumscribed.

## *Regional Relations with the Capital*

Geographically, the present Saudi kingdom consists of five major regions: Al Hijaz in the West, Najd in the center, Al Hasa in the West, Jabal Shammar in the North, and 'Asir in the Southwest. Administratively, Saudi Arabia is divided into fourteen smaller emirates, each with a royally appointed governor. These fourteen emirates are Bahah, Hudud as Shamaliyah, Jawf, Medina, Qasim, Qurayyat, Riyad, Shar- qiyah (Eastern Province), 'Asir, Ha'il, Jizan, Mecca, Najran, and Tabuk. In February of 1992, King Fahd decreed the establishment of provincial councils for each of the fourteen emirates. They are to consist of persons nominated by the governor and approved by the monarch. Their purpose is to advise the governor in the performance of his functions and to permit greater local public participation in provincial governance. Their effectiveness remains to be tested.

A royally appointed member of the Saudi family is governor of the principal provinces of the kingdom. This has been helpful in affording easier entrée for the provinces to the resources of the central govern- ment, especially in terms of financial allocations for development purposes. A considerable element of administrative decentralization exists, but certain national ministries, such as education and health, operate in all provinces in coordination with provincial governors.

One still finds considerable regional sentiment in the various prov- inces, but the development of modern communications connecting all parts of the country is gradually eroding such sectional parochialism. One does not find significant local or regional power plays, although obviously Riyadh, Mecca, and the Eastern Province tend to be fa- vored.

### *Political Participation and the Challenge for Social Change*

Saudi Arabia has to a considerable extent become a social welfare state. While its enormous oil revenues can hardly be said to have been equitably distributed, it should also be emphasized that all Saudis have to some extent benefited from them. Low-cost land and interest-free loans are available to any Saudi male wishing to build his own home. Indeed, construction of all types is one of the most prominent features of the overall Saudi landscape.

In contrast to the public's participation in Saudi Arabia's economic development, its participation in the political process remains limited. No political parties are allowed, press coverage tends to be self- censored, and radio and TV programs are carefully controlled by the ministry of information and monitored by the *'ulama* to ensure that socially unacceptable programs are not aired. It remains to be seen how the newly established Consultative Council will function and whether it in fact proves to be an opening for broader public participation in governance. Gradualism in political reform is likely to continue to be a hallmark of the Saudi polity.

The Saudi political elite is narrow. It consists of members of the extended Saud family (estimated at over 5,000 strong); the religious hierarchy, headed by the Al Shaikh family (descended from the religious founder of Islamic unitarianism); and to a lesser extent, Western-trained members of nonroyal Saudi families, who head major technical ministries. Power is in the hands of the royal family, especially a score or so of its senior members, but King Fahd has developed a highly personalized style of rule. The political legitimacy of the Saud family is rooted in its espousal of rigid Hanbali Islam. The king is expected to rule in accordance with the concepts of the *Qur'an* and Islamic law as interpreted by the Hanbali *'ulama*. The conservative *'ulama* watch closely for any potential signs of innovation or deviation from Islamic precepts. There are some recent indications, however, that King Fahd, while paying proper deference to religious leaders, is slowly but surely reducing their erstwhile power and influence. He still has a long way to go before they can be said to be under control.

It has come to be realized, however, that Islamic law does not adequately cover all aspects of twentieth-century life, especially those relating to high finance and massive economic development. Hence, numerous extralegal royal ordinances (*nizam*) have been issued to cover areas such as mining, some elements of commerce contracting, etc. Such ordinances are invariably drafted with *'ulama* participation to ensure that they do not trespass upon the all-encompassing authority of the Islamic law. Nonroyal members of the elite wield such authority as they have through their ministerial posts, which usually involve limited technical areas. Where sociopolitical matters are involved, it is the royal family and the *'ulama* who determine acceptability or unacceptability. Chambers of Commerce in the major provinces play important arbitral roles in resolving contract disputes between Saudi and foreign firms on issues not adequately covered by traditional Islamic law.

Social reform in Saudi Arabia is developing in slow fashion. In the past four years, and especially since the fundamentalist attack on the Grand Mosque of Mecca in 1979, there have been signs of some social regression. The pace of modernization, many Saudi leaders have concluded, has been too rapid to be readily absorbed by an essentially orthodox Muslim society. This, coupled with concern over sometime public criticism of the Saudi leadership by the Iranian Islamic Republic and the latter's avowed "revolution for export," and by the large number of foreign troops (including women in uniform) during Desert Storm, has brought about a rigidification of the Saudi social structure. Pressures for social change exist, and sooner or later there will again be some relaxation of social standards, but these will be slow in coming.

Many Saudis, both men and women, now travel abroad and are exposed to foreign cultural influences through such travel, through foreign radio or telecasts, and through occasional contact with the expatriate community working in the country. While some Saudis are generally repulsed at their experience with foreign cultures, others would like to see some opening of their rigid social structure, even if this is cast in Islamic terms. This pressure for change presents a major challenge to the Saudi leadership, but as already suggested, not one that is likely soon to explode.

## The Political Cultural Dimension

Saudi society has traditionally been regulated by twin pillars: belief in a single God and the family. As is the case in other Middle East countries, the family in Saudi Arabia is extended rather than nuclear, with the eldest member being the titular head. Peer pressure within the family, whose members are expected to act in accordance with Islamic mores, has in the past been an effective device to assure individual member conformity. Some may travel abroad or attend foreign universities, but when they return they revert surprisingly readily to family-approved norms. The family regulates each member's behavior, offers help and encouragement to its members, and is in general a source of strength to its members.

In recent years, however, the infusion of huge amounts of money into Saudi society has tended to weaken somewhat the influence of the aforementioned twin regulators of social conduct. To the distress of many older Saudis, an element of materialism has inevitably entered the cultural scene. Competition among aspiring Saudi businessmen has become more bitter. As a result, tensions exist within Saudi society as the quest for materialism challenges traditional individual and group behavior.

On another level, materialism is often equated by Saudi traditionalists with westernized modernization, causing the latter and its perceived agents to be suspect in the eyes of more orthodox Muslims. It is the *'ulama* who lead the social battle against westernization and materialism. Language problems aside, it is hardly surprising that it is difficult for a Western expatriate in Saudi Arabia, however culturally attuned he may be to Islamic mores, to engage in meaningful dialogue with orthodox religious leaders or orthodox Saudi believers.

At the behest of the Saudi *'ulama*, and with the acquiescence of the royal family, Committees of Public Morality, a kind of religious police, monitor individual and public behavior. They seek to ensure that Muslims pray five times a day, that shops are closed during prayer times, and that alcoholic libations are not drunk. As such, they represent a religious/communal control mechanism, although many Saudis privately deplore what they often regard as illiterate and narrow executors of this function. At the moment, and especially since the attack on the Grand Mosque in Mecca, the Committees of Public Morality are having a heyday. In pursuit of their responsibilities, as they see them, they often harass not only Saudis but also expatriates. Early in 1992, King Fahd sought to curb them, but they remain a nuisance to Saudis and expatriates alike. Many are corrupt and are bought off with *baksheesh*, or a gratuity.

The Saudi Arabian government, in addition to national and local police forces, utilizes several intelligence organizations to monitor possible dissidence. These intelligence organizations tend to be in competition with one another. Investigatory methods still are often somewhat rudimentary, with rumors often given excessive evidentiary weight. The saving grace in the system is that the Saudi *shari'a* court system, including an appellate and supreme religious court, insists upon strict procedures conforming with Islamic law. Guilty verdicts require adequate evidence. However, evidentiary procedures in Saudi *shari'a* court cases are far different from those in use in the West.

### Potential Sources of Instability

Some destabilizing elements exist in the Saudi polity. Thus, for example, the kingdom's Shi'i minority remains an uncertain factor despite efforts by the Saudi leadership to integrate it into the state. That potential threat has diminished somewhat with the death of the Ayatollah Khomeini in Iran and a reduced Iranian emphasis on "revolution for export."

A second potentially destabilizing element in the royal family consists of divisions within the royal family. Such internecine divisions were prominent in the eighteenth century and led to the collapse of the second Saudi empire when another Arabian family was able to seize power. The present senior members of the Saud family are all strong, self-confident individuals, and it is hardly surprising that they differ on some policy matters. All evidence to date suggests, however, that whatever divergences exist, they are argued out within the closed confines of the Saud family until some kind of consensus is reached. This, unfortunately, can be a time-consuming process, sometimes leaving critical decisions dangling for long periods of time.

## Impediments to Doing Business in Saudi Arabia

Generally speaking, U.S.–Saudi Arabian relations have been and continue to be close. There is a long history, going back to the initial American involvement in petroleum exploration and exploitation in Saudi Arabia in 1934, of economic association between the two countries. American economic planners from the private sector (Harvard, Stanford Research Institute, and others) were prominent in the formulation of the early Saudi Five-Year Development Programs. Since 1974, a Joint Saudi Arabian–U.S. Commission has been in existence, designed to enable the kingdom to draw upon American public and private resources in promoting national development. On the American side, the U.S. Treasury has been the executive agent for such economic collaboration.

Some political differences exist between the two countries. There has been a long history of Saudi perception of excessive U.S. partiality toward Israel in the Arab-Israeli dispute. The Saudis were bitter about the American-inspired Camp David agreements and the subsequent Egyptian-Israeli peace treaty, which they felt divided the Arab world. In the past, the Saudis have considered the United States to be unsympathetic to legitimate Palestinian national aspirations, although the posture of the Palestine Liberation Organization during the conflict with Iraq has created considerable disillusionment among Saudis about Palestinians.

In view of the already-mentioned perceived external threats to Saudi Arabia, dramatically emphasized following the Iraqi invasion of Kuwait in August 1990, and Saddam Hussein's continuing excoriation of the Saudi leadership, the Saudi Arabian dependence upon the United States for security assistance in case of attack has been reemphasized. Yet the public Saudi posture on this matter is somewhat ambivalent. On the one hand, there is an increased realization that, in a pinch, the kingdom will again require direct American military support; on the other, there is a reluctance openly to acknowledge this by entering into formal security agreements with the United States or providing long-term military facilities to the United States, and a preference to have potential American military support as much as possible "over the horizon." Discussions continue between the United States and Saudi Arabia on prepositioning of military equipment in the kingdom for possible future contingencies. There is indeed a "special relationship" between the United States and Saudi Arabia, especially in the security and economic spheres, but it has sometimes been frayed by domestic concerns in both countries.

Among conservative Saudis, especially the *'ulama*, the United States tends to be viewed as anti-Islam, anti-Arab, and as the apostle of promiscuous modernization. In the United States, recurrent congressional efforts to limit arms sales to the kingdom and to require disclosure of Saudi investments in this country have sometimes marred the relationship. U.S. administrators try to appease Saudi Arabia as much as is politically feasible. In connection with Saudi investments in this country, the executive branch of government, supported by the American banking community, has thus far successfully opposed a series of congressionally proposed disclosure bills. There is some evidence that Saudi concern about what they see as persistent congressional harassment is causing a diversification in the Saudi investment portfolio in order to place more funds outside this country.

Although Saudi Arabia nominally remains in a state of war with Israel, and sees Israel as a threat, it has actively supported the current U.S. administration's efforts to revive the long-stagnant Arab-Israeli peace process. Saudi Arabia is not involved in the ongoing series of bilateral talks between Israel, the Arab confrontation states, and the Palestinians, but it did send an observer to the inaugural peace conference in Madrid in 1992 and the kingdom participates in various of the seminars and working groups on "regional" issues that have become part of the overall peace process. It should be noted, nevertheless, that Saudi Arabia is not enamored of any U.S. or other idea of conventional arms reductions. While its general posture toward Israel has improved, and Saudi leaders have in the past year received in the kingdom for the first time prominent members of the American Jewish community, the Saudis for reasons already indicated remain deeply distrustful of Israeli purposes.

Obtaining Saudi visas has long been a problem. Persons requesting visas require a Saudi sponsor and must seek them for working purposes; visa requests must often be approved by Riyadh. They are frequently slow in being issued, even when no possible refusal problem exists.

On the economic front, Saudi Arabia continues to participate in the Arab secondary boycott that was inaugurated after the first Arab-Israeli war in 1948. Its recurrent efforts to require American firms wanting to do business in Saudi Arabia to renounce commercial ties with Israel have over the years prompted several pieces of congressional antiboycott legislation.

In 1965, amendments were passed to the Export Control Act of 1949 and again included in the Export Administration Act of 1969, indicating U.S. opposition to boycotts of friendly countries and requiring American firms to report to the Department of Commerce any foreign demand to participate in such boycotts. Since all foreign firms, including American ones, bid on Saudi contracts are sent boycott questionnaires by the Saudi Arabian Arab Boycott Office, this legislation was viewed by the Saudis as a direct challenge to their sovereign right to determine their own boycott policies.

In 1976, the U.S. Justice Department initiated suit against the Bechtel Corporation for allegedly violating the Sherman Antitrust Act by complying with Saudi secondary boycott requirements, banning contracting firms from dealing with Saudi blacklisted subcontractors (those dealing with Israel) in fulfillment of their contracts. While the case was negotiated out of court in January 1977, its net effect prohibited any U.S. company under contract in Saudi Arabia (or any Arab country) from refusing to deal with firms blacklisted by the Saudis or discriminating against them. American firms were also legally prohibited, under penalty of fines, from replying to Saudi Arabian anti-Israeli boycott questionnaires.

The result of this congressional legislation and subsequent litigation was a standoff. Saudi Arabia refused to budge significantly in easing its Arab secondary boycott procedure; American firms were prohibited from executing boycott questionnaires. In consequence, Saudi Arabia has diversified its foreign contracting activities, and there are complaints that many American firms have lost out to foreign competitors.

A second congressionally enacted obstacle to the provision of American contractual services to Saudi Arabia was the Tax Reform Act of 1976, which requires the U.S. Treasury to deny offenders of antiboycott legislation their right to foreign tax credits, to tax benefits in the United States, and to deferral of taxation on foreign income earned from business in countries participating in a boycott. The Export Administration Act Amendments of 1977, subsequently incorporated in the Export Administration Act of 1979, established rigid procedures for American firms engaged in business in boycotting countries, including Saudi Arabia. Occasional efforts have also been attempted by Congress to enact legislation that would prohibit American firms from refusing to send persons of the Jewish faith to Saudi Arabia, but whether or not such persons can actually travel to the kingdom is, in the final analysis, a function of its visa policies. Only Saudi Arabia can decide to whom it will grant visas. Religion is not indicated on U.S. passports, and applicants for visas at Saudi consular offices must make the decision whether to indicate their religion on the Saudi visa application form.

Still another disincentive to U.S. exports to Saudi Arabia was a 1976 U.S. tax-cut ruling that required the computation of income-tax exemptions for Americans working abroad to price housing at full overseas value rather than equivalent value in this country. This, in effect, discouraged foreign contractors working in Saudi Arabia from hiring Americans because of higher income-tax liabilities and brought about a 30 percent decrease in American employees of U.S. firms working in Saudi Arabia between 1976 and 1980. In order to alleviate the situation, the Congress in 1978 enacted the Foreign Earned Income Act, but IRS regulations construed this so narrowly that it did little to help the situation. Finally, Congress enacted the Economic Recovery Act of 1982, which increased exempted income and excluded from the income-tax computation for Americans working abroad to a phased maximum of $90,000.

A fourth disincentive to American commercial activities in Saudi Arabia has been the Foreign Corrupt Practices Act of 1977, establishing new accounting procedures intended to prevent the concealment in other business expenses of illegal payments to foreign agents or officials who might be involved in foreign government contracting decisions. American firms were concerned about the act, not because they wished to conduct corrupt practices in Saudi Arabia, but because of the inadequate drafting of the law, making it difficult to determine what was and what was not permissible. Moreover, non-American competitors, who could operate without any such restrictions, were advantaged by this legislation. While practices perceived as corrupt in the West, including excessive commissions, have long existed in Saudi Arabia, the Saudi authorities do not condone them and perceive U.S. restrictive legislation as a slur on their reputation.

As a result of these enactments, although U.S. firms still garner just over one-fifth of the Saudi Arabian import market, they have not been able to increase their share of that market. The Saudis have resented the kind of pillorying that they have received in the Congress and from many parts of the American public media as greedy "oil shaikhs" and have demonstrated their resentment by turning to non-American firms for imports wherever possible. There is cause to be concerned that these pieces of legislation, unless amended or more clearly written, will continue to be obstacles to the Saudi selection of American firms for the procurement of goods and services.

## Commercial Conditions: Environment for Investment

Although Saudi Arabia is not in great need of foreign capital investment, it has generally welcomed such investments where they facilitate achievement of Saudi development objectives. Any foreign investment must be approved by the Foreign Investment Committee of the Ministry of Industry. A Saudi agent is required in all such instances, except in armaments, government-to-government, or foreign military sales contracts. In the case of the latter three types of contracts, dealings must be directly with the Ministry of Defense without a Saudi agent. In the case of nondefense contracts, two types of agent exist in Saudi Arabia: the commercial agent and the service agent. The commercial agent operates solely in the private sector. The service agent operates in the governmental contract sphere. There is a legal maximum of 5 percent as an agency fee, although smaller fees are often arranged. The agent has no voice in the management of the company.

The Saudi Arabian government requires registration of all foreign companies operating in the kingdom as a condition of their being permitted to function in Saudi Arabia. Registration (i.e., licensing) is a separate matter from contract conclusion. The signing of a contract by a foreign company with a Saudi Arabian governmental agency does not automatically confer registration. Indeed, it is to the advantage of the foreign company if registration can be accomplished prior to conclusion of contracts. Should this not be possible, registration must be accomplished after contract conclusion if the foreign firm is to benefit from the customary five-year tax holidays generally permitted to such firms.

Foreign firms seeking to do business in Saudi Arabia may enter into "joint-venture" arrangements with Saudi business firms. Any such arrangement, in effect, makes the Saudi participant a partner in the venture, rather than a simple agent. Two types of joint ventures exist in Saudi Arabia. The first type is a contractual joint venture, under which the foreign firm and the Saudi partner agree to bid for and, if awarded the contact, execute the project. In this case, however, Saudi law does not confer juridical personality on the joint venture; hence an agent is still required unless the joint venture's activities are in the defense procurement area. The foreign firm still requires temporary or commercial registration.

The second form of contractual joint venture is the "mixed company." Under Saudi registration, most foreign firms choosing to go this route establish a Limited Liability Company (LLC). Such an organization consists of two or more participants, partners in the enterprise, each of whom has liability limited to its respective shares in the capital of the company. Formation of such LLCs is subject to approval by the Foreign Investment Committee of the Ministry of Industry. The Saudi Foreign Investment Committee usually insists upon initial capitalization of Saudi riyals one million (about $300,000), though higher amounts are sometimes demanded, depending upon the magnitude of the proposed project. LLCs, provided they have a minimum of 25 percent Saudi participation, can apply for five-year tax holidays and also receive bid preference in seeking project contracts. All such joint ventures must be registered and licensed in Saudi Arabia.

There are no legal restrictions on the repatriation of capital and profits, although sometimes bureaucratic procedures may create delays. Nor are there any limits on foreign investment in Saudi Arabia, but a minimum of 25 percent Saudi ownership is required by law. In fact, given the interest on the part of Saudi Arabian firms in engaging in joint ventures, they frequently demand 50 percent Saudi participation. These are matters that must be negotiated between the foreign firm and its expected Saudi associate(s).

Foreign firms operating in joint-venture capacities are subject to corporate taxation after the conclusion of the tax holiday. Corporate taxation has in the past been levied at the rate of between 25 and 45 percent of corporate earnings, with the burden falling on the foreign firm. In January 1992 the Saudi Arabian Ministry of Finance imposed new and additional taxes on foreign partners in joint ventures, effectively making such foreign investments less attractive. If the Saudi government really wants foreign investment, one informed observer noted, it must either lower tax rates or permit higher dividend returns.

Labor availability is a serious problem in Saudi Arabia, especially skilled and/or semiskilled labor. Given the smallness of the Saudi population, coupled with the huge magnitude of the kingdom's development efforts, it is difficult to find skilled indigenous labor. Neverthe-less, the Saudi Arabian government nominally expects foreign firms working in the kingdom to engage at least 75 percent of their labor requirement from Saudi nationals. Since this is frequently difficult, even impossible, it remains more of a goal than a reality, and many foreign firms must perforce utilize less than the prescribed percentage of Saudi labor. Many have had to bring in expatriate labor. But the requirement to hire Saudis before anyone else may be engaged is a significant problem for foreign firms.

Expatriate labor constitutes about two-thirds of the overall Saudi labor force working in Saudi Arabia. The extent of expatriate personnel to be brought into the country, in connection with any particular project undertaken by a foreign firm/joint venture, is a negotiable matter. The Saudi Arabian government carefully monitors expatriate labor brought in by foreign contractors. Any foreign worker must have the sponsorship of a Saudi Arabian national, and entry visas are often extraordinarily difficult to obtain. Saudi Arabian embassies abroad must submit, with few exceptions, names of proposed expatriate workers to the Ministry of Foreign Affairs and the Ministry of Interior, both of which must approve any such visas. Since 1967, this has become a cumbersome procedure. Expatriate workers in the kingdom also often find it difficult and protracted to arrange entry visas for wives and children. Exit visas are also required for expatriate labor, which likewise involve time-consuming procedures. In recent years, the Saudi Arabian government has sought to diversify its expatriate labor and has brought in more technical personnel from Far Eastern countries, such as the Philippines, Sri Lanka, South Korea, and Japan.

Saudi Arabia has no significant record of contract repudiation. There is a history, however, of both Saudi government organizations and private firms frequently interpreting contracts differently from the foreign firms and demanding additional goods and services. Where contract disputes develop, mediation or arbitration by local chambers of commerce is the most accepted practice, although as already indi-cated foreign firms would be well advised to stipulate in contractual agreements how differences of contract interpretation will be resolved. All things considered, however, Saudi Arabia is not an easy or congen-ial place in which to do business.

## The Economic Conditions: Risks and Indicators

Saudi Arabia is one of the wealthiest Third World nations in the world. Its substantial petroleum revenues have over the years enabled the kingdom simultaneously to pursue massive development programs, equally large defense programs, a substantial foreign assistance program, loans to Iraq in the protracted Iraq-Iran war, and maintain sizable investments abroad as well as reserves. Nevertheless, in recent years, largely because of the oil glut and attendant loss of income, Saudi Arabia has found itself in somewhat more difficult financial circumstances. In 1990 and 1991, for example, revenues amounted to $31.5 billion and budgetary expenditures to $40.8 billion. While still substantial, this represented a 60 percent drop from record revenues and expenditures from five years earlier.

Because of the uncertainties of the conflict with Iraq, no formal budget was established by Saudi Arabia for 1991. Instead, the 1990 budget figures were simply continued for the ensuing year. Saudi Ministry of Finance statements indicate that the kingdom spent about $126 billion during 1990 and 1991, or 65 percent more than budgeted expenditures. This included almost $50 billion for costs associated with the Gulf crisis. These special expenses were in addition to estimated $6.7 billion deficits for both 1990 and 1991, which were funded through domestic bond issues. The Saudi Arabian budget for 1992, as published in January of 1992, again projected a budgetary deficit of about $8 billion, to be covered from domestic and international borrowing. Expenditures during 1992 were projected at $48.3 billion, an increase of 27 percent above figures of the previous two years. Revenues were expected to rise to $40.3 billion, or 28 percent. Whether or not this income increase proved feasible depended upon global oil prices.

In the proposed 1992 budget, military expenditures accounted for roughly $14.5 billion, or the regular 30 percent of total expenditures; education was allotted $8.3 billion (or 17.2 percent); health and social services, $3.3 billion (or 6.7 percent); and transportation and communications, $2.1 billion (or 4.4 percent). Recurrent deficits in recent years notwithstanding, Saudi Arabia has no problems borrowing in international financial markets and is considered a good credit risk.

Foreign companies engaged in defense-related contracts are now required to invest (offset) up to 30 percent of the total value of contracts in joint ventures with 100 percent Saudi partners in order to manufacture strategic goods currently being imported. Thus, in the defense sphere at least, Saudi Arabia is adopting an import substitution strategy largely focused on obtaining technology transfers of strategic items.

In agriculture Saudi Arabia is now almost self-sufficient, through heavy subsidies which make its agricultural products cost ineffective. Since so many of Saudi Arabia's goods and services must be imported from abroad, the kingdom has been subjected to global inflation rises. Within the country itself, however, inflation appears to have been only about 5 percent a year. The Saudi Arabian riyal represents hard currency, readily convertible. It is tied to the dollar and, because of fluctuations in the dollar, has recently been devalued on occasion to the dollar. No requirement exists for any radical debt restructuring for Saudi Arabia. Nor have the Saudis been in default on major debt payments, although they have sometimes sought deferred-payment arrangements.

Although Saudi businessmen and the Saudi Arabia government have invested large sums in the United States, Europe, and elsewhere, this is more the result of surplus capital availability than of capital flight. There is some suggestion that the threat to Saudi security posed by the protracted Iraq-Iran war and the 1990–91 conflict with Iraq may have caused some wealthy Saudis to place greater funds abroad, but no accurate figures are available as to the magnitude of such transfers. However, since the successful conclusion of these conflicts, there has also been a considerable return of Saudi capital to the country. Indeed, in contrast with neighboring Kuwait, where Kuwaitis show great concern about the future, Saudis appear to be very confident of their responsibility's future prospects.

## Conclusion

In short, although problems exist in dealing with Saudi Arabia, and time and patience are often required to resolve them, the kingdom remains a promising foreign investment area as long as foreign investors approach such possible investments with caution and legal assistance.

## Select Bibliography

For those desirous of supplementing the above observations, the following select bibliography may be useful:

*Business Laws of Saudi Arabia*, Graham and Trotman, Ltd., London, 1983.

Holden, David, and Richard Johns, *The House of Saud*, Sidgwick and Jackson, London, 1981.

Lerrick, A., and Q. Javed Mian, *Saudi Business and Labour Law: Its Interpretation and Application*, Graham and Trotman, Ltd., London, 1983.

MacKay, Sandra, *The Saudis, Inside the Desert Kingdom*, Houghton Mifflin, Boston, 1987.

Quandt, William B., *Saudi Arabia in the 1980s: Foreign Policy, Security and Oil*, The Brookings Institution, Washington, D.C., 1981.

Safran, Nadav, *Saudi Arabia: The Ceasless Quest for Security*, Belknap Press, Cambridge, Mass., 1985.

*Chapter 7*

# South Africa in Transition: Risks and Opportunities

## Francis A. Kornegay Jr.

The politics of transition in South Africa have become extremely fluid, making possible any number of outcomes that could impact the risk/opportunity equation. This analysis will attempt to examine some of the salient political and economic dimensions of this equation pertinent to corporate investors exploring the possibility of positioning themselves for a long-term commitment in the South and southern African market.

Since the end of May 1992, when negotiations broke down, the political scene in South Africa has become quite unpredictable. By the time this volume is published, one of two broad patterns of events could unfold. Negotiations could resume before the end of the year, by the reconvening of the Convention for a Democratic South Africa (CODESA) where the African National Congress (ANC) and the government already have achieved considerable agreement. A breakaway faction of the Conservative Party (CP) might also join the talks, finally giving a voice to the ultraright. South Africa would then be headed down the road to nonracial elections and a constituent assembly. (Since this was written, the Pan-African Congress [PAC] and Azanian People's Organization [AZAPO] on the left have entered into bilateral "talks about talks" with the government while a breakaway CP faction has formed the pronegotiation Afrikaner Volksunie Party.) Alternatively, the ANC and the government might be unable to restart negotiations in the near future. Violence would continue at current levels or escalate further, taking a steady toll on an already weak economy. President F. W. de Klerk, like Mikhail Gorbachev, would be unable to regain control of events and would be similarly eclipsed, perhaps ushering in a military-managed transition.

The ANC–government-dominated negotiation process, in short, is a delicate phenomenon, susceptible to stresses placed on it by diverse actors. Among them: the security forces, a fragmented right wing, the Inkatha Freedom Party (IFP) and other homeland-based ethnic forces, returning exiles in the military wings of the liberation movements, and township youth of questionable allegiance and discipline. Moreover, the dynamics governing the interplay of these sundry forces are being played out against the backdrop of a protracted recession coupled with the worst drought in the history of the subcontinent. The precarious state of the economy is in turn impacted by a global recession that, in combination with the manner in which the politics of transition are played out, will determine the risk environment for reattracting foreign investment. What follows is an examination of the political dynamics of the transition surrounding the critical issues of central versus regional powers; security; the state of the economy and the unfolding economic debate; foreign trade and investment prospects (including South Africa's "gateway" potential in terms of the rest of the continent); and considerations for corporate positioning in the future.

## Political Dynamics I: The Federation Debate

### *A Comparative Perspective*

South Africa's hoped-for transition to democracy is a peculiarly hybrid process. It is the product of a complex interplay between a reformist "revolution from above" orchestrated by President de Klerk's National Party (NP) government and a mass "revolution from below" against the racial/capitalist system of apartheid. In the vanguard is Nelson Mandela's African National Congress. Unlike the East European upheavals in which anticommunist popular movements successfully challenged totalitarian regimes of the left, the South African case pits left-leaning nationalist movements against a racially based oligarchy (albeit one in which the ruling party is attempting to transform itself into a right-of-center nonracial vehicle of reform). Hence, the comparative difference between the South African and the East European "revolutions" in terms of assessing risks and opportunities. The ideological impetus behind the "revolution from below" in South Africa is socialist whereas in Eastern Europe the thrust has been in the direction of effecting transitions from centralized command economies to market-based pluralist systems. The political challenge in Eastern Europe is to institutionalize a socially democratic capitalism virtually from scratch. Capitalism is already institutionalized, albeit distorted by race, in South Africa. The country's market economy is in the grip of a white political monopoly complemented by an already heavily bureaucratized and culturally compartmentalized state sector. The challenge will thus be one of transforming capitalism to reflect an accommodation between the redistributionist demands emanating from liberation movement constituencies and the preservationist instincts of the white minority to retain the economic benefits that accrued to them under the old order—while generating meaningful economic growth and recovery.

In effect, the de Klerk regime has been attempting to orchestrate a strategic retreat into a postapartheid system from a position of strength that would allow it to dictate, as much as possible, the terms of transformation. The bottom-line: "power sharing" that salvages substantial residual white political/economic power, within the framework of what NP/government officials claim to be an American-style federal system. The ANC alliance (and its rivals in the PAC and AZAPO), on the other hand, advocate the need for a central government. And herein lies the critical point of tension in the South African debate.

Foreign investor confidence would begin to revive pending the outcome of constitutional talks and the nature of the accommodation emerging from the economic debate. The evolution of the political debate toward a compromise between the ruling NP's emphasis on power sharing and checks and balances and the ANC/PAC/AZAPO quest for majority rule under a strong central government is being closely monitored by South Africa's economic barons. Ogilvie Thompson, chairman of the Anglo-American Corporation, the South African-based transnational conglomerate, has cautioned against elections "in order to elect an interim parliament or constituent assembly on a universal franchise" until the issue of "balancing regional against central government powers" has been resolved. It is this issue, more than any other, that defines in broad terms the alignment of political forces in the unfolding constitutional debate: an alignment that this author has elsewhere depicted as a contest between proponents of federalism (whether or not this is a consciously conceptualized policy) and those committed to confederation.

At CODESA, prior to the March 17, 1992, referendum, the ANC and the government appeared to be converging toward a federalist accommodation. The ANC had come to acknowledge a justification for strong regional government while the NP had moved away from its commitment to traditional Afrikaner nationalist notions of group self-determination. The KwaZulu-based IFP, on the other hand, had become aligned with the homeland regimes of Bophuthatswana and the Ciskei and anti-CODESA white conservatives in a movement that will determine current and future risk/opportunity assessments. It is a tension that reflects an apparent fundamental difference and gap in expectations between the incumbent white regime and *some* of its black challengers regarding the constitutional outcome of negotiations. These differences and expectations went to the heart of the breakdown of talks at CODESA. The failure of the talks were further exacerbated by the imbalance in coercive power and resources between the regime and its challengers accompanied by a questionable commitment of the security forces to a negotiated settlement. Between a security establishment under doubtful government control and impoverished black constituencies that may be beyond the control of the ANC and other movements, and whose commitment to protracted negotiations is equally dubious, the capacity for continuing political violence and instability is considerable. The question of politically related violence and the prospects for bringing it under control thus emerges as a major risk factor for close monitoring as the transition unfolds. More on this later.

### *Regional Versus Central Powers*

Aside from the issue of political violence, the risk environment is heavily conditioned by the factor of uncertainty. As this is overcome by the resumption of talks and the eventual installation of a Transitional Executive Council (TEC), the expectation within CODESA to homeland reincorporation should be assessed. It explains the bitter Lucas Mangope/ANC confrontation. Mangope's resistance to reincorporation and commitment to a confederation of states is perceived as inimical to the economic interests of a postapartheid regime; a strategy aimed at denying a possible ANC-dominated central government access to Bophuthatswana's resources and the revenues they could generate to help alleviate the financial squeeze that is likely to accompany a settlement. Or perhaps Mangope & Co. are playing hard to get in the hope of retaining considerable regional powers in a South African federation? The question to be answered is where will conglomerates like Anglo-American, Gencor, and Lonrho come down? And what role will they play, if any, in mediating the regional versus central powers debate?

The ANC, while grudgingly acknowledging the need to accommodate regionalism, nevertheless has allowed its opponents on the right, who favor a neoapartheid confederacy, to seize the federalist designation for their own proposals. Thus, federalism threatens to be discredited as a viable option for the constitutional reorganization of South Africa as it becomes politicized. Yet, federalism is not fundamentally at odds with the ANC preference for a strong centrally governed, united, and territorially integral state. Further, the ANC has an apparent regional interest in an ethnically integrated "Border/Kei entity." This would swallow up the pro-Pretoria Ciskei into a greater Transkeian Xhosa state. Up to now, it appears that the ANC has allowed its maneuvering room on this issue to be proscribed by its alliance partners in the South African Communist Party (SACP) and its rivals on the left, the PAC and AZAPO. The SACP, PAC, and AZAPO appear uncompromisingly in favor of a "unitary" state in which there is a "transfer of power" to an abstract monolithic "majority" as opposed to a transition to democracy that reconciles the realities of cultural pluralism with the ideal of building an inclusive nationalism.

What is yet to be determined is how violently uncompromising are the "unitary inclusivists" prepared to be? To the extent that these and other questions surrounding the issue of "balancing regional against central government powers" remain unanswered, the political stability of the transition will remain in doubt. This is so because the issue of regionalism is intimately linked to the question of the future status of the rural areas (where half of the South African population still resides) and to resolving the problem of politically inspired violence. This is underlined by the violent confrontation between the ANC/SACP alliance and the Oupa Gqozo regime in Ciskei where twenty-eight demonstrators died on September 7, 1992 when fired upon by the Ciskei Defense Force.

One way out of a possible quagmire over the regional versus central powers debate was offered inadvertently by ANC consultant Moeletsi

Mbeki (brother of ANC international affairs head Thabo Mbeki) in the July 24, 1992, issue of *The Weekly Mail*. Although he was not specifically addressing the regional versus central powers issue, he nevertheless floated the idea of a compromise that could defuse its potential explosiveness. Mbeki advocates that the ANC bend on the issue of an elected constituent assembly by having the constitution hammered out instead at a nonelected all-party conference. This might meet the reservations of the Gadja Buthelezi/Mangope/Gqozo trio as well as powerful captains of industry like Ogilvie Thompson who would rather that elections not take place until this issue has been settled. The trade-off for the ANC would be for the government negotiators to accept "the principle of elections by electoral district or constituency" rather than the party list system of proportional representation. Because South Africa still has effective racial segregation, a constituency system means that both racially based and regionally based parties will be assured of representation in parliament. Whether or not this is the approach taken by the ANC or agreed to by its rivals, the Mbeki proposal indicates a method for avoiding violent confrontation in resolving the regional versus central powers dispute.

## Political Dynamics II: The Security Factor

The most serious problem facing the transition is the escalating violence associated with it and the inability to bring it under control. This has had a negative impact on investor confidence after initial optimism that political change was transforming the business climate for the better. Since February 1990 when President de Klerk embarked on his dramatic initiatives, 7,000 people have died in politically related violence. According to Hein Marais, writing in the July/August 1992 issue of *Work In Progress* (*WIP*), these casualties "far exceed that of the preceding eight fiery years of resistance." The collapse of government-ANC talks in the wake of the Boipatong massacre forced to the forefront the issue of political violence as the key problem that would have to be tackled as a precondition to regaining momentum toward a negotiated settlement. Thus far, the elaborate dispute resolution system ushered in by the National Peace Accord of September 14, 1991, has proven a failure. And the impact of internationalizing the quest for a solution to the violence through the introduction of U.N.-sponsored monitors remains to be seen. To gain some understanding of the extent of this problem, it will be examined here at two levels: (1) the problem of political violence "from above" involving the white-led security forces; and (2) violence "from below" emanating from black township youth.

## Violence from Above: The Security Forces

While much of the violence is attributed to the ongoing ANC/IFP power struggle in Natal and throughout much of the Vaal Triangle, attention has increasingly shifted to the role of the security forces and the extent of civilian control exercised over them by de Klerk. In the wake of Boipatong, the extent of this problem began gaining increased press scrutiny. Serious media treatments by Rockland Williams, in a July 11, 1992, Johannesburg *Star* article ("All the President's Men") and John Battersby, writing in the August 24, 1992, issue of the *Christian Science Monitor* ("South Africa's Third Force: A Secret Network to Preserve White Power") as well as ongoing revelations in *The Weekly Mail*, *The Nation*, *WIP/New Era*, and the London-based *Southscan* among others, strongly suggest that de Klerk's control over the security forces is, at best, tenuous; that his actions, as commander-in-chief, appear subject to military veto.

It has become clear that de Klerk's dismantling of P. W. Botha's National Security Management System (NSMS) in the wake of his September 1989 election victory was more form than substance. The decision taken in July 1992 to dismantle Battalions 31 and 32 along with Koevoet is seen in a similar light. Government, in the meantime, has appeared to go to great lengths to protect the security establishment from damaging revelations that might further complicate the transition. Hence, Pretoria's apparent sense of urgency in wanting the ANC to join it in agreeing to a general amnesty covering the security forces and members of the military wings of the liberation movements. This move had strong backing from the United Nations, the United States, and Great Britain in terms of what U.N. Special Envoy Cyrus Vance expressed as a need for the government and the antiapartheid opposition to make a "clean break with the past that would enable a gear-change to a future-directed dialogue." However, the "clean break" had to be based upon full disclosure of past offenses. This the government has resisted. The ANC, as of this writing, is refusing to go along with amnesty unless there is full disclosure of the activities by security forces members for whom the government would seek amnesty.

For Pretoria, the risk is that full disclosure might reveal current cabinet members to have been involved in the assassination of antiapartheid activists during the Botha era. Such revelations could push

President de Klerk into a showdown with his security chiefs if he is pressured to take action against such individuals. The question is whether he will be pushed to this point, and will meet his political demise as a result. Perceptions of de Klerk's weakness in relation to his security commanders has prompted speculation on the possibility of a more active military role in the transition. This is a critical consideration since some of the military/intelligence chiefs and their lieutenants and operatives appear strongly sympathetic to the white ultraright confederalist strivings, including the notion of carving out a white/Afrikaner homeland. Moreover, these influences are becoming increasingly visible in the politics and constitutional planning of the far right. Former chief of Military Intelligence, Gen. Tienie Groenewald, for example, is a prime mover behind the Eenheidskomittee (EK), a far-right "think tank" promoting the Afrikaner Volstaat idea.

The question is, where does de Klerk really stand? He could very well be judged to be an implicit confederalist, or centralist, from his public opposition to "black domination," which most assuredly would result from a negotiated settlement following conventional constitutional notions of democracy, including federalism. Since his March 17, 1992, referendum victory, de Klerk appears to have moved closer to the confederalist camp. Thus, depending on the balance of forces within the Defense Force, the military's restraint in the transition might very well be contingent on de Klerk's ability to deliver a confederal solution, or something close to it, through political means (i.e., negotiations and electoral campaigning).

## *Violence from Below*

Taming the largely youth-driven "revolution from below" presents an equally formidable challenge to securing the transition. It presents a make-or-break test of the first magnitude for the presumptive rulers of the new South Africa. As a challenge, it is compounded by the demographic reality of 66 percent of the African population being under the age of twenty-seven with an official (overall work force) unemployment rate of between 40 and 50 percent. Moreover, this demographic profile is strongly reflected in the heavy youth membership of the mainline black political groupings. Apart from mischief involving the security forces, black unrest in the townships should be viewed against this backdrop. The question is, will the interim and postsettlement regimes have the resolve and the capability to stabilize a largely youth-dominated black South Africa made ungovernable by the cycles of repression and resistance that have unfolded for over well over a decade? This is a tall order given the radicalized culture of resistance that has heavily influenced black youth socialization (political and otherwise) since the mid-1970s. If anything, the de Klerk initiatives of February 1990 added fuel to the fire by unleashing the proverbial "revolution of rising expectations." This has happened well in advance of the political transformation that would provide the ANC and other liberation movement parties with the authority to address the urgent needs and aspirations of their radicalized constituencies. In the meantime, the government, for its part, has not gone out of its way to be helpful to the unbanned movements, especially given the newly competitive political environment and the economic recession.

From both political and security standpoints, the unbanned movements, the ANC in particular, are confronted with a dual task of exerting discipline over their followers and over the township youth population generally. One particularly bright spot in intermovement relations, is the absence of the violent political rivalries among the ANC, PAC, and AZAPO that marked the period immediately following the unbanning of the groups. Moreover, partisan loyalties are mediated by cross-cutting familial and interpersonal relationships. Thus, in spite of apparent tensions among the three (especially between the ANC on the one hand and the PAC and AZAPO on the other), the only openly violent conflict is between the ANC and the IFP. Still, there do exist rumblings of possible war being waged by factions of the PAC and AZAPO against an interim or postsettlement government that represented a compromise on an elected constituent assembly and/or the "one-man-one-vote-in-a-unitary-state" principle. From the standpoint of monitoring political risks, this tension is important.

A serious political security concern confronting the ANC is the issue of control and discipline over township-based self-defense units, including exile returnees in its military wing, Umkonto we Sizwe (MK). (MK is under the joint command of the ANC and SACP.) Prior to the National Peace Accord, ANC-inspired self-defense units were established in response to the outbreaks of political violence in the Vaal Triangle townships in mid-1990 involving followers of the ANC and the IFP. However, what has increasingly occurred has been the development of factional turf battles within the ANC constituency, especially between the defense units and MK mavericks on the one hand and ANC-aligned trade unionists on the other. In 1992 two shop stewards belonging to the National Union of Mineworkers of South Africa

(NUMSA) were executed by MK mavericks. In one instance, the killing came after the ANC had mediated an accord between rival factions, with an executioner quoted as saying "Mandela's peace is not acceptable to us because he is just like a person who irons a shirt without having washed it."

Other incidents have included extortion of businesspersons, threats of consumer boycotts, kangaroo courts with matching "justice," and disruption of legitimate crime prevention. These have prompted ANC and SACP officials into undertaking actions to bring renegade MK members and self-defense units under tighter control. These include an internal ANC commission of inquiry that has publicly criticized the existence and actions of renegade units and MK members and made recommendations for disciplining them. Since the National Peace Accord prohibits political parties from having their own armed units, however, exercising such discipline is expected to be difficult for the ANC. Still, the control of such units is likely to prove crucial to the ANC in establishing its authority at the grass-roots level in townships where unrest has been chronic.

Disbanding the self-defense units has been ruled out since they have saved lives in situations of escalating violence. Moreover, the police are too thoroughly discredited to be considered reliable. Thus reshaping the units into more disciplined and reliable agents of law and order at the community level is the most politically feasible option from the standpoint of the ANC. In light of the strictures imposed by the Peace Accord, political authority over self-defense units could conceivably be laundered through the civic associations that have the potential for emerging as key institutional components in the civil society of the new South Africa. If the self-defense units can be shaped up, then at some point there is the possibility of cooperation with the security forces. This is ruled out for now, given the lack of credibility of the security forces. However, given the actual police shortage (in addition to their lack of credibility), consideration is being given to using conscript troops from the army as police auxiliaries, an idea that is seen as reinforcing the need to move rapidly toward universal conscription or a volunteer professional army drawn from the entire population. In the meantime, as far as the townships are concerned, the taming of the self-defense units may offer the only hope for stabilizing these communities in the short term.

The questions of control and discipline regarding the self-defense units is relevant to the broader issue of defusing and dismantling the increasingly dysfunctional youth-based culture of resistance; a phenomenon that has found expression in many forms within and outside the organizational boundaries of the political movements: in the infantile leftism of the youth wings of these movements where keeping communities in a state of ungovernability is still warmly regarded; the continued chaos in the schools and, to a lesser extent, in some black universities where boycotts and challenges to authority have become the norm; the absence of generational deference to parents and elders, otherwise customary in modernizing and traditional African societies; and the rise, since the Soweto Rebellion of 1976 of the "comtsotsis" phenomenon in which the politically inspired activism of youthful "comrades" has, in some instances, merged with the traditional criminal (or "tsotsis") element in fueling a general sense of vulnerability in township communities.

Prior to the de Klerk initiatives of early 1990, this climate of insecurity steadily gained ground as ungovernability, and state repression responded by creating vacuums in these communities, thereby setting up a situation for the unchecked spread of crime and violence. The impoverishment of the townships and rising unemployment have only exacerbated this climate, which is made even more unstable by the highs and lows of raised and unfulfilled expectations.

There are tangible economic costs to doing business in such an unsettled environment. According to the South African Federation of Softdrink Manufacturers (SAFSM), sales that grew annually by as much as 9.8 percent in 1990 dropped sharply in 1991 to register no more than a 1 percent increase. Although the recession was cited as a major factor in the sharp decline in sales, when it came to the African market, which makes up 76 percent of total soft drink sales, the decline was attributed to escalating violence and unrest, which significantly disrupted the servicing of this portion of the market. This situation may not turn around significantly until the transition evolves to a point where it channels sufficient authority to unbanned movements such as the ANC and PAC so as to allow them to begin imposing a greater degree of discipline, not only over their immediate followers but over township communities generally, especially the youth stratum. However, the lack of a sufficient degree of working unity among the movements has not helped matters. While the ANC, PAC, and AZAPO have apparently managed to reduce and regulate violent rivalries among their followers, the failure to forge a genuine Patriotic Front (or "Parliament of the People") considerably lessens their ability to jointly defuse the youth bomb and rechannel energies into more constructive activities for the benefit of black development. In fact, it could be said that the endemic instability in black communities is a function of the fact that the achievement of unity across party lines has not been an uppermost priority of the black political class currently confronting the government.

As the formal security structures of the new state are transformed and regain credibility, the self-defense units might well evolve into community development brigades with an auxiliary police function. A scenario unfolding along these general lines could considerably transform the resulting risk environment to the point of enhancing the attractiveness of African-populated urban and rural areas as places for both domestic and external investment. In any case, in preparation for the rough economic times ahead that will greet the interim government and its postsettlement successor, it behooves the ANC and other political forces in black urban and rural communities to begin reasserting control over the youth element. For their aspirations are certain to go unfulfilled. This, in turn, will make them a serious threat to the stability of the new political order if they have not been mobilized to become the self-help vanguard for development at the grass-roots community level.

## Political Dynamics III: The Economy

If gaining control of the violence—from the security forces at the top to the youth at the bottom—is critical to enhancing security and stability in the short term, longer-term prospects obviously hinge on the economy. Assuming the ANC's leadership of a future government, youth mobilization for development, transcending partisan lines, should help it buy time politically when the new government is likely to be hard put to satisfy adequately the rising economic expectations of its black constituents. Youth mobilization and black community stabilization, coupled with a revamping of the security forces, could conceivably help the new government lower the risk factors sufficiently to begin reattracting investors, both foreign and domestic.

### *Youth Unemployment*

A major part of the South African risk profile is conditioned by what amounts to a youth unemployment crisis. According to the Bankorp publication *Econovision*, 90 percent of the unemployed are estimated to be under the age of thirty. Of those swelling the pool of the jobless in the 1990s, *Econovision* projects that more than 95 percent will be younger than twenty-five. The importance of addressing this crisis in a major way is increasingly acknowledged in financial, industrial, and union circles, and is reflected in a proposal by Bankorp economists for the launching of a "national community service corps." This idea has been endorsed by the Labor Research Service (LRS) and discussed by the ANC-aligned COSATU as an option for job creation. Because of the lack of skills among much of the unemployed black youth population and the magnitude of infrastructural neglect in black-populated urban and rural areas, proponents of the community service corps and other job creation programs stress the need for a focus on "improving the long-term productivity of the economy by providing basic practical skills to unemployed youngsters, and . . . improving the country's social and physical infrastructure." The work force "would build roads in rural areas and black townships, dams, playgrounds, parks, and community centers." Such proposals amplify the urgent need for black political movements to take the initiative in mobilizing their substantial youth constituencies into a development brigade movement. The incumbent de Klerk government, after all, lacks the legitimacy to initiate such programs, which would need the full backing and participation of the major black political and labor groupings.

### State of the Economy: Implications for Investors

Tackling the youth unemployment crisis would seem to be a politically strategic imperative for managing South Africa's transition. Most economic forecasters see little room for a new government to pursue a strategy of "macroeconomic populism" to achieve a far-reaching redistribution of resources although political pressures to follow such a course are expected to be considerable. Because of balance of payment constraints South Africa needs more foreign exchange earnings, which, over the long term, requires manufacturing for export. Politically, the need is to create jobs. Yet exports are capital intensive rather than labor intensive. Further, manufacturing industry requires lower exchange rates to be competitive internationally whereas mineral exports, upon which South Africa still relies, tend to push up the exchange rate. Still another problem faced by South African manufacturing is that labor costs are high relative to capital, which, according to economist Desmond Blumenfeld (Bradlow Fellow at the South African Institute of International Affairs), produces the "cruel choice" of either pushing down the cost of labor relative to capital or making capital more expensive. Yet, unionized labor is not expected to accept

Third World wages even as minerals have gotten more difficult and less profitable to extract, and this will have serious repercussions for foreign investors.

Apart from sanctions, these economic trends explain South Africa's declining attraction for foreign capital for almost twenty years prior to the watershed unrest of 1976. In short, South Africa has evolved into an essentially raw material–dependent Third World economy with the trappings of the modern world (although the World Bank groups South Africa "with upper middle-income Latin American countries, Hungary and the Republic of Korea"). Of course this evolution was driven by the political decisions of successive governments to promote an industrial strategy that would entrench white privilege. Now that a black-ruled government is in the offing, the inherited structural imbalance in South Africa's relationship with the global economy (resulting from this race-driven industrial strategy) becomes a major obstacle to re-dressing the internal economic imbalance between black and white. Instead, the focus of much of the discourse on South Africa's economic options has settled on the question of "structural adjustment." And here, there are strong arguments in favor of South Africa instituting its own adjustment program rather than having one forced on it by the International Monetary Fund (IMF). For one thing, IMF loans are not expected in themselves to relieve the "cruel choice" between export-led growth and employment creation. Furthermore, IMF loans will have to be repaid ten years down the line, and do not come cheap.

As yet, there is no consensus on the type of structural adjustment program South Africa should undertake. Elsewhere, such programs tend to focus on privatization, and tax and tariff reform, all of which were put on hold or drastically slowed down during CODESA and following its collapse. Compared to Latin America and the rest of Africa, there reportedly is not much in South Africa to be privatized although there is definitely a bloated bureaucracy with which to contend. According to economic commentator Richard Dowden, "white-ruled South Africa has a bureaucracy matched only for size and inefficiency by those of former East European socialist states. State spending . . . has risen in the past two decades from 16 percent to 29 percent." And in the past decade alone, while employment levels in the main industries have declined, "state jobs have increased by 73 percent." Corruption in the state sector has skyrocketed as well. In many respects, the abuses of the security establishment are but one reflection of a much broader problem of what one Johannesburg *Star* editorial described as the "cancer of corruption" pervading the country's public and parastatal sectors.

The patronage pressures that will confront a new government are sure to add yet another dimension to this problem. For under a prospective Government of National Unity—transition and postsettlement—incumbent white civil servants will expect their "kith and kin" in government to protect them from being purged while constituencies of the ANC and other black movements will be expected to be accommodated in the new government. And why not? Thus, those seeking to do business in the new South Africa could find themselves wading through a bureaucratic maze that is a "swollen mix of the old problem and the new" even as separate race-specific departments are phased out.

The unwieldly nature of the South African state is a further complication in the quest for a coherent economic strategy for managing the transition and beyond. Although the internal contradictions in the ANC's economic thinking have been much publicized, "in recent years economic policy has been influenced by a wide variety of institutions and pressure groups, often with divergent agendas. These institutions include the Departments of Finance, Labour, Agriculture, and Mining; the Economic Advisory Council of the State President, the Central Economic Advisory Service, the Ministry for Administration and Privatisation, the Board of Trade and Industry, and the Reserve Bank." Commentators observe that as these organizations do not share the same economic philosophy, their policy prescriptions are more often than not contradictory. The extent to which the major political players in South Africa's transition—and their financial/economic policy quarterbacks—can match the achievement of the internally consistent newly industrialized countries (NICs) of Southeast Asia is likely to impact significantly on the level of investor confidence building that can be generated as a means of attracting foreign capital. To what extent can the new South Africans meet this challenge?

## An Economic CODESA?

The collapse of CODESA and talks between the government and the ANC did produce one major "silver lining." It accelerated momentum toward the convening of the National Economic Forum, which was formally launched in late August 1992. With Boipatong giving greater impetus to the ANC's "Mass Action Campaign," the nation's chief employer body, the South African Coordinating Committee on Labor

Affairs (SACCOLA), and COSATU found sufficient common interest in negotiating a trade-off on the issue of the mass work stoppage planned for early August and the restarting of negotiations toward establishing a transitional government and the electing of a constituent assembly. Although the SACCOLA–COSATU initiative ultimately collapsed, its achievements were significant nonetheless.

The stakes in the COSATU–SACCOLA talks were exceedingly high since both camps were under pressure to avoid the appearance of being co-opted by the other. Yet they did manage, from their dialogue, to fashion a "social charter" that holds out the possibility of an eventual social/economic "compact" emerging from the crucial negotiations in the National Economic Negotiating Forum (NENF). But little is expected from the forum in terms of agreement on the "fundamental restructuring of the economy" until a democratically elected government is installed. For COSATU, the ANC, and other political forces on the left, the objective is to forestall "unilateral economic restructuring" by requiring issues such as the national budget, privatization, tariff policies, the value-added tax (VAT), and other taxes and retrenchments to be discussed and agreed to in NENF prior to changes being made.

In the meantime, the crucial question is whether or not the forum will generate the much-needed thinking through of options that will lay the basis for a business-labor-government consensus on the policy packages needed for adoption and implementation. This may not be an easy task although some optimism has been expressed in government circles that reaching consensus on economic issues may prove much easier than arriving at a consensus on the political/constitutional issues of transition. There are those within the liberation movement constituency who caution against "corporatist arrangements" and instead propose a "multipartite model" based on "guaranteed representation for organizations of civil society" as a counterweight. Indeed there are those who argue that NENF should not be viewed as an arena for drawing up a wide-ranging "Social Contract," which in any case should be avoided since it would imply too much compromise on the part of organized labor. As one South African activist has observed: "The state, even if it is the ANC, will never be neutral in class terms. It will be bound by the capitalist framework within which it works. Social contracts cause demoralisation, demobilisation and division among workers."

## *Economic Issues: Developments the Foreign Investor Should Watch*

Overall, the economic debate on a number of issues of domestic and international import has not advanced very far. Beyond heading off "unilateral economic restructuring," the economic policy postures of the ANC and other movements, for the moment, is one of keeping all options open pending a settlement. In terms of pulling the country out of its current stagnation, there appears to be a major disconnect between economists arguing for home-grown structural adjustment remedies, and all that that implies for wealth redistribution (for example, ANC/COSATU efforts to perfect a "growth through redistribution" model). Yet, according to one scenario offered in the much-quoted IMF occasional paper *Economic Policies for a New South Africa*, by Desmond Lachman and Kenneth Bercuson, achieving a growth rate of 3.5 percent will require raising the ratio of investment to GDP from 19 percent to 27 percent.

Meeting this objective would "need to be supported by a major domestic savings effort, particularly in public savings, even if SA were again to become a significant net user of external savings." Private savings would have to rise from 20.5 percent of GDP in 1990 to an average annual 21.5 percent between 1991 and 2000. Government savings would have to rise from 0.6 percent of GDP to 1.6 percent, which would require a shrinking of the general government deficit from 1.2 percent to 0.7 percent. For that reason, one of the major organs of the corporate establishment in South Africa, the *Financial Mail*, advises the ANC "to inculcate patience into the poor and reduce expectations of a ruinous economic rampage" though recognizing, in the same breath, that this "will be no mean task." Hence, an important question to be asked is what kind of leadership the South African corporate establishment is willing to undertake to lighten the pressure that a new government is sure to encounter when it assumes power in an economically stagnant environment?

While the ANC has backed away from wholesale nationalization, the corporate community has not been very forthcoming in offering alternative formulas for transferring a reasonable share of economic power and resources to the African majority. As an alternative to nationalization, the ANC is considering antitrust laws as a means of spurring the deconcentration of an economy in which, according to the 1977 Mouton Commission, "three or less producers" were responsible for 75 percent of production in over 70 percent of South African industries.

The antitrust possibility has raised the issue of conglomerate "unbundling," which, in the corporate community, is seen as a long-overdue means of making the domestic economy more competitive and spurring foreign investment. Hence, the prospect is raised of "voluntary unbundling" to preempt anticipated antitrust legislation.

However, thus far there is no indication that the corporate community or economists within the liberation movements have proposed options for conglomerate dismantling that would serve redistributive aims, taking into account the urgent need for Africanization and affirmative action to advance black economic empowerment. This is an issue that carries implications that reach beyond the mere promotion of blacks into senior and middle management positions in public and private sectors under circumstances of unchallenged white control. It also raises the issue of how best to satisfy the empowerment demand for advancing toward genuine black control of major economic enterprises.

Political stability will not only depend on addressing the massive black youth/unemployment crisis. It will also require meeting the expectations among mid-level Africans supporting the liberation struggle for the Africanization of management, the promotion of Africans into skilled jobs, the lessening of the skills and wage gap between skilled and unskilled workers, the promotion of Africans in the state apparatus, and institutional power sharing at executive decision-making levels in the private sector. But so far, according to Institute for African Alternatives director Ben Turok, who writes regularly in the *Weekly Mail*, the issue of affirmative action is being "handled with kid gloves in South Africa." The time is ripe to begin planning its implementation in order to "achieve a rapid advance for the previously disadvantaged without doing damage to the running of the country and its economy." But the fact is that there is a substantial, if not growing, resistance among whites across the political spectrum to affirmative action. The tendency in the white community is to adopt the stance that apartheid is already dead and a thing of the past, and that South African society can now start from scratch on a level playing field.

In the South African context, this stance is sure to lead to increasing black middle-class frustration and the fueling of more race-conscious tendencies within, as well as outside, the ANC constituency. This would likely affect the business environment in which foreign as well as domestic business will operate. The potential foreign investor must closely monitor the Africanization/affirmative action debate, particularly in terms of its possible impact on the development of a new investment code affecting foreign firms. An important question that emerges here is to what extent will foreign firms be expected to adhere to affirmative action guidelines, and how will this affect profit margins? This is a critical consideration, because the pressures for Africanization and affirmative action also present an opportunity for the foreign investor seeking to cement long-term commitments in the local and regional markets.

## Foreign Trade and Investment Prospects

Apart from the issue of black economic empowerment within the context of conglomerate dismantling, the urgent need to begin preparing for investment promotion to attract foreign capital is a major impetus for "unbundling." First National Bank senior executive Alex Grant observed (at a June trade and investment conference held in Johannesburg) that because of the high level of concentration of corporate ownership, it is often difficult to operate under normal free-market conditions. "All the major participants will have the same views, resulting in an often one-sided market." Thus, overconcentration is seen as a major obstacle to a new business penetrating South Africa "unless it enters into a venture with a strong South African partner" as in the case of Heinz, when it came close to consumating a multimillion rand investment in partnership with Foodcorp, one of the majors in the South African food industry.

A consensus is developing on the need to deconcentrate the distribution of power in the economy. In opening a South African Institute of International Affairs conference at the end of August 1992, Foreign Minister Pik Botha criticized the inhibiting impact of "growing financial and industrial monopolies" on foreign investment and called for a review to determine to what extent monopolies were preventing foreign participation and competition in the South African marketplace.

Other disincentives to foreign investment are the high cost of capital and, in terms of productivity, the high cost of labor relative to capital. Further, when it comes to foreign trade, the impact of the recession is having a chilling effect on economic thinking. Given the heavy toll that three years of recession have taken on the manufacturing industry, some South African economists are cautioning against quick liberalization moves aimed at decreasing tariff protection. The fear is that with domestic manufacturers operating at reduced capacity, many could be highly vulnerable to international competition. According to

Nedbank chief economist Edward Osborn, "decreased tariff protection could result in elimination of industry." He therefore advises that "any steps towards liberalisation must be very carefully introduced, and really should be delayed until a fair degree of recovery has been achieved." This caution regarding the possible negative impact of foreign competition on South African domestic industries indicates an important level of internal concern over how and at what pace South Africa should open itself up to participation in the global economy. Potential foreign investors will want to know how these concerns ultimately translate into policy under a new government.

There are a host of other questions that potential investors should ask. Will a future government place new constraints on the repatriation of profits? Who will occupy key economic portfolios in an interim and a postsettlement government? What might a new investment code be like, and will it be used as a blunt club or as a means to attract firms to invest in South Africa? According to a survey of "OECD Perceptions of Direct Investment Opportunities in a Post-Apartheid South Africa" conducted by World Bank consultant Whitney Schneidman, potential investors will also be paying close attention to how "foreign firms already in South Africa are being treated during the period in which a new constitution is negotiated and implemented." Though there are serious constraints to a new government instituting an economic policy accenting redistribution, "indications are that business would not balk at the implementation of a broadly supported and workable strategy of redistribution," particularly if it were to increase black consumer power. The question, from a foreign investment perspective, is how will redistribution be approached within the economic constraints confronting South Africa?

We have the questions, but they remain unanswered. This is the key problem for the potential investor. The above questions, along with the crisis of violence, political instability, and uncertainty surrounding the transition, have contributed to a "wait-and-see" posture among potential overseas investors. Would-be newcomers should consult with foreign companies already there.

## Sanctions and Beyond

A major disincentive for U.S. firms weighing the pros and cons of investing or reentering the South African market is the domestic constraint of state and local sanctions. These restrictions remain in place despite the lifting of the federal Comprehensive Anti-Apartheid

Act (CAAA) of 1986. The lifting of state and local sanctions are contingent on the installing of an interim government. Here, several questions emerge: would an interim government, presumably under ANC leadership, send a definitive signal for the lifting of all layers and categories of sanctions? To what extent would an ANC-led interim regime embark on an active campaign in the United States aimed at rolling back state and local sanctions? Here, the situation has become complicated by indications that U.S. state and local authorities may want to regulate corporate involvement in a postapartheid South Africa to enforce potential investor compliance with whatever investment code emerges from a new government. Pending a settlement, the ANC apparently seeks to avoid being pinned down regarding whether or not it will support the involvement of U.S. state and local governments in the enforcement of an investment code adopted by a new government over which it would preside.

In spite of the continued existence of state and local sanctions, the sanctions era is essentially over. The question is whether South Africa will continue to generate U.S. governmental and private sector interest. The seeds of a new relationship based on economic/development assistance programs to "disadvantaged" South Africans continues in effect, but it is as yet unclear how this involvement will evolve, especially since U.S. foreign assistance generally is receiving renewed scrutiny with the heavy political refocusing on domestic issues. At the end of 1991, Rep. Stephen Solarz managed to mobilize an impressive bipartisan coalition of support for a "South African Democracy Aid Initiative" (SADAI) as a harbinger of things to come, inspired by the Multilateral Aid Initiative for the Philippines. The intent was to fashion a multibillion dollar, internationally backed program to finance a postapartheid settlement. However, the timing of the initiative was hardly propitious given the onset of the 1992 national elections and what turned out to be a hemorraging of incumbents leaving Capitol Hill in the wake of the House Bank scandal and electoral redistricting. In addition, there are also serious questions about how much support South Africa should receive at the expense of the rest of Africa. The case for South Africa's receiving the lion's share of U.S.–Africa aid due to its presumed centrality as the potential engine for continental recovery has yet to be articulated. This would require a new global perspective on African development that factors in the potential role of a free South Africa as a guide to future U.S. policy in Africa.

A multilateral aid initiative of the kind envisioned by Solarz would unquestionably go a long way toward improving the risk/opportunity equation in what may be an uphill battle to attract ample foreign investment. A well-targeted bilateral and multilateral aid program would help bring South Africa's human resource potential up to the level of its already world-class material infrastructure; these two, in combination, could have a substantial multiplier effect beyond South Africa's borders. This would guarantee South Africa's attractiveness to foreign investment over the longer term. More immediately, potential investors contemplating entering the South African market will be guided by the Overseas Private Investment Corporation (OPIC) and its companion African Growth Fund (which was set up to attract U.S. venture capital toward promising African investments). OPIC's decision about setting up in South Africa will, in turn, await further advances in the negotiation process.

Finally, whether sanctions are lifted in their totality or not, the conventional wisdom is that potential new and old investors will not be scrambling to invest in the new South Africa. However, there are positive indications to the contrary. Once an interim government is in place and a clear signal is forthcoming on foreign investment, there reportedly are a number of corporations poised for entry or reentry. In many instances, entry/reentry plans are well advanced. If this is borne out by events, the new South Africa's economic prospects would be greatly enhanced. For the pace of South Africa's economic recovery will depend upon whether or not foreign investment accompanies a substantial inflow of bilateral/multilateral aid or instead follows such aid.

### *Economic Opportunity: South Africa As Gateway and Catalyst?*

In spite of current apprehension about the future, from an economic perspective, investment criteria are generally favorable. The weakness of the local economy is seen as being offset by the existence of sound financial institutions and policies that are felt to be pushing the economy in the right direction. The fact that the dual exchange rate system provides a discount in the conversion to the rand is seen as favorable to investors. Note also that the availability of local capital generally can be used to finance up to 50 percent of a particular project. Compared to other Third World economies, South Africa's inflation and general economic malaise are not considered particularly bad. And because it already has a capitalist economic institutional infrastructure already in place, South Africa is considered to have a competitive advantage over economies in other countries undergoing fundamental political and economic change. There are some who consider South Africa's existing economic base and infrastructure to provide it with a much higher investment potential than areas such as Eastern Europe, where it is estimated it will take billions of dollars just to build basic economic foundations. According to an annual competitiveness survey compiled by the IMF international management school in Lausanne and the Geneva-based World Economic Forum, South Africa is ranked eighth among countries considered to have a high business potential.

Assuming that South Africa's political leaders are able to manage its transition over the next few years into a relatively stable society, the country will be well poised over the medium to long term to serve as the engine for developing a subcontinental economy that could conceivably spur a wider African recovery. It is this "gateway" potential that stimulates the economic imagination of local and foreign businesspeople. And it is the reason why the stakes riding on the transition are so high. South Africa's potential for spurring a continent-wide recovery would appear to depend heavily on an export-led development strategy emerging from the economic debate. Investment that targets manufacturing for export would serve as the departure point for opening up the wider African market in southern Africa and beyond in such basic manufactures as agricultural goods, factory appliances, vehicles, medicine, processed food, clothing and textiles, leather goods, furniture, chemicals, and derivatives such as fertilizers and pharmaceuticals. And this would carry with it the revitalization of regional transport and telecommunications networks, thereby speeding up the infrastructural development of the African hinterland in both material and human resource terms.

South Africans see themselves as having the natural resources, the infrastructure, the financial sophistication, the technological base, and the skills to generate such dynamism. According to Andrew Maggs, manager of the South African Foreign Trade Organization's African Trade Intelligence Program, "new and exciting opportunities are emerging throughout the continent and South Africa is poised to play a leading role by grabbing some of these opportunities as far afield as Nigeria and Ghana." Indeed, the business sections of major South African newspapers reflect the upswing in economic development-motivated contacts between South Africa and the rest of the continent. This increasing contact is also reflected in South African trade and investment missions to other African states, and participation in trade fairs (which is emerging as a source of racial tension within the South

African business community as black businessmen complain of being marginalized in such activities).

South Africa's role as a foreign investment springboard into African markets will be facilitated, once the political transition is further advanced or completed, by its entry into the Southern African Development Community (SADC)—successor to the Southern African Development Co-ordination Conference (SADCC)—and the Preferential Trade Area (PTA) for Eastern and Southern Africa. Here, South Africa's entry may help advance the sorting out of regional economic institutional relationships between SADC and PTA and its own Southern African Customs Union (SACU). Thus far, one of the great impediments to subcontinental regional integration has been the turf battles between SADC/SADCC and the PTA typified by SADC's rejection of a proposal from the PTA for the two organizations to merge in launching a Common Market for Eastern and Southern Africa (COMESA)—despite the fact that ten out of the PTA's eighteen member states constitute SADC. Once South Africa officially enters the political scene of regional economic relations, the prospect, according to some sources, is for the eventual emergence of an entirely new subcontinental institutional structuring of interstate relations to replace the existing organizations.

For now, South Africa is little more than a spectator to these politics, although ANC and PAC leaders are generally in attendance at SADC and PTA summits. At the Windhoek summit that saw the formalizing of SADC, ANC Secretary-General Cyril Ramaphosa implicitly dismissed a "gateway" catalytic role for South Africa. He downplayed its being a "locomotive" for regional economic growth by interpreting such a notion as an expression of Pretoria's "new diplomacy"; on the other hand, meetings between the government's and the ANC's foreign affairs departments have reportedly produced a considerable amount of consensus in terms of regional outlook. The ANC's regional economic perspective attempts to play down the notion of South Africa as a regional economic superpower determining the fate of the subcontinent.

For the ANC to take this tack is understandable public relations, since black South African political leaders are at pains to differentiate their regional outlook from what has often been perceived as the regional imperialist pretensions of their white countrymen. Moreover, the ANC, PAC, and AZAPO constituencies remain sold on a "manufacturing for export-based development" strategy. Nevertheless, given the plight of the rest of Africa, it is virtually inescapable, from a foreign investment perspective, that South Africa's "gateway" potential will form a major part of the attraction.

## Conclusion: Positioning for the Future

South Africa's anticipated gateway role could serve as a key factor in guiding corporate positioning for long-term involvement in the South African market. A base in South Africa in effect would serve to open doors to the rest of the continent. Those monitoring market trends in Africa, such as Anthony Hawkins, editor of *Business International*'s Africa Publications, foresee investment decisions in Africa being increasingly regionalized over the next decade. In fact, this is likely to be facilitated by the organizational restructuring of regional cooperation and interstate trade relations that will result from South Africa's official entry onto the political scene after a political settlement. South Africa's emergence from apartheid will reinforce what was a predominant tendency to perceive it as a natural regional hub prior to the launching of the SADCC.

By international standards, South Africa is not a major business player, constituting no more than 1 percent of global business. But, according to Hawkins, it is a market that few multinationals can afford to ignore since it is projected to be the "natural regional focus for Africa in the 21st century." Moreover, it will be useful, in geoeconomic terms, to consider how strategically placed South Africa is for expanding trade relations within a Southern Hemispheric zone extending from the South Atlantic "Southern Cone" of Latin America to the South Pacific. In African terms, South Africa has a marked comparative advantage. In fact, there is concern that the magnitude of this comparative advantage is such that real problems will emerge in developing balanced two-way trade between South Africa and the rest of the continent. This could change, however, if South African firms and/or foreign firms based in South Africa move "upmarket" into high-tech manufacturing and service activities thereby allowing for the importing of some primary goods and basic manufactures from other African producers.

Thus, the foreign investor can benefit from an evolving economic division emerging among and between South Africa and its neighbors. Within this context, over time, foreign corporations investing in South Africa should be well-positioned to benefit from South Africa's emergence as the "capital market center" for the continent, exporting

capital to the rest of sub-Saharan Africa, whose companies and governments, Hawkins predicts, will "raise capital on the Johannesburg
market." But this is not foreseen for several years in light of South
Africa's own capital demand.

In terms of the South African domestic market (aside from the
obvious political considerations linked to the transition), and depending on the size of the firm, corporate positioning should be guided by
monitoring opportunities for joint ventures with a "strong South African partner" as in the case of the Heinz-Foodcorp deal or for opportunities that may emerge out of conglomerate dismantling. The latter
prospect, in particular, should benefit smaller and medium-sized U.S.
firms, including American-based minority business enterprises. Within
this context, the politically sensitive foreign investor is bound to
benefit by approaching such opportunities with a view toward helping
advance the affirmative action and black economic empowerment
agenda of the majority population. For American corporations, there
is the already existing legacy of the Sullivan Principle signatories and
a host of corporate social responsibility–inspired foundations and
trusts that emerged from divestment moves of the late 1980s.

Foreign corporate involvement that promotes a broad range of
educational opportunities and training in skills for black South Africans, that actively encourages promotion into upper-echelon management and decision-making positions, and that supports entrepreneur-
ship will build upon this legacy. More important, foreign firms looking
to develop long-term stakes in the South African market should look
for opportunities that assist black South Africans in the acquisition of
meaningful economic assets and/or the development of viable alternative black-owned and -controlled assets. Within this context, there are
a variety of contractual partnerships and joint-venture arrangements
that are possible, including the linking up of African-American minority businesses with black South African enterprises and/or U.S.-based
minority firms contracting with major South African firms in projects
that involve meaningful black South African participation.

Finally, corporate positioning should be informed by the active
monitoring of the unfolding economic debate. Will the NENF, for
example, result in a broadly acceptable labor-business-government
social "compact" that reconciles aspects of the ANC–COSATU
"growth through redistribution" school with what some see as a desire
by big business and the state to fashion a "newly industrializing
country" (NIC) strategy similar to the East Asian "tigers"? In spite of
a high degree of skepticism, if not hostility, by the ultraleft to the idea

of a compact, there is an important left-of-center constituency appreciation for a scenario that couples a political settlement with a new government's adopting sound policies in making well-targeted social investments while observing macroeconomic constraints, curbing corruption in government, and raising levels of efficiency. The risk/opportunity equation may well hinge on how broad and comprehensive a compact is forged or whether or not the major political camps and interest groups prove to be so internally fractured as to rule out a coherent but broad consensus. There is optimism in some quarters that the NENF may result in such a consensus. In a very meaningful sense, these considerations surrounding the economic debate, coupled with many of the issues raised earlier in this discussion, may suggest the rough outline of a framework for monitoring and assessing the changing risk/opportunity environment in the emerging new South Africa.

*Chapter 8*

# Colombia: Drugs, Politics, and Investment Risk

## Rensselaer W. Lee III

### Overview

Colombia, a turbulent, relatively fast-growing country that contains Latin America's third largest population and fourth largest economy, represents a fascinating case study of investment risk. As many observers have noted, Colombia's economic and (in certain respects) political performance have been enviable by Latin American standards: For example, Colombia's economic growth rate in the 1980s was the best in Latin America—3.4 percent per year on the average compared to the region's average of 1.6 percent. Colombia also escaped the worst ravages of the Latin American debt crisis—it never rescheduled its debts, always made full payments on time, and never experienced severe balance-of-payment problems. Politically, Colombia has had a relatively stable two-party system for the past thirty-five years and this system has produced an outstanding record of elections and peaceful transfers of power among civilian governments. Moreover, manifestations of political instability that have hurt investors in other Latin American countries—such as freezes on repatriation of profits and outright expropriation of foreign-owned assets—have by and large not occurred in Colombia.

Yet Colombia is an extremely troubled country. Violence and lawlessness are rampant: Colombia has one of the highest homicide rates in the world and terrorist acts of various kinds—kidnappings, bombings, and attacks on infrastructure—occur frequently. Though Colombia has a stable democratic system, the Colombian state in fact lacks strategic reach; indeed, in much of Colombia, the state competes for territorial control and political influence with other powerful groups: notably Marxist guerrillas and cocaine-trafficking syndicates. Colombia's internal security and public order problems have distorted the government's spending priorities, forcing the government to spend huge sums of money on the armed forces while leaving vital needs of the population unmet. A further effect of these problems has been to create an extremely high tax burden for foreign and domestic companies alike. In addition, and most worrisome, the inability of successive Colombian governments to establish order and to provide minimal levels of personal security in much of the country has seemed to undermine the legitimacy of Colombian political institutions. Faith in government now appears to be at a dangerously low ebb; for example, in a survey conducted in Colombia in September 1992 by the newspaper *El Tiempo* and the Colombian firm Yankelovich Innova, respondents expressed negative opinions of the Congress, the judiciary, and the presidency by margins of 69 percent, 75 percent, and 61 percent, respectively.[1]

Unsurprisingly, given these depressing circumstances, Colombia has not had a particularly good record of attracting foreign investment. Net inflows of nonpetroleum investments have averaged only $235 million per year in the 1981–91 period—a small figure given Colombia's economic size and its geographical proximity to North American markets. Furthermore, as Table 8–1 shows, such flows have shown a downward trend since the mid-1980s—dropping from $413 million per year in 1984–86 to $197 million in 1989–91. Upsurges in guerrilla violence and the Colombian government's escalating war against the Medellin cartel probably account for much of the decline. Petroleum investment showed a similar drop over the period, from $567 million to $274 million; however, this sector responds to somewhat different dynamics than does the rest of the economy. For instance, the development of the large Caño Limon field, discovered by Occidental Petroleum in 1983, partly accounts for the large investments in the mid-1980s. Similarly, British Petroleum's discovery of the even larger

**Table 8—1.** **Net New Foreign Investment in Colombia (in millions of U.S. dollars)**

| Year | Non-Petroleum Investment | Investment in Petroleum Exploration and Development |
|---|---|---|
| 1981 | 139.74 | 265.06 |
| 1982 | 113.48 | 309.41 |
| 1983 | 117.19 | 189.27 |
| 1984 | 309.84 | 179.43 |
| 1985 | 489.53 | 791.74 |
| 1986 | 440.97 | 728.87 |
| 1987 | 320.55 | 201.83 |
| 1988 | 18.47 | 266.84 |
| 1989 | 259.13 | 271.92 |
| 1990 | 230.28 | 266.04 |
| 1991 | 101.43 | 284.20 |
| 1992 est. | — | 376.33 |

Sources: Ecopetrol; Banco de la Republica.

Cusiana field in Casanare department in the late 1980s will be reflected in increased petroleum-related investments in the years ahead. Still, Colombia's abysmal security situation, as well as certain government policies vis-à-vis the petroleum sector (singling out the sector for special taxation, for example), represent significant disincentives to investment in that sector.

The purpose of this article is to survey the business risks inherent in Colombia's current political and economic situation. The article is not written to cast judgment on the Colombian government or nation or to prescribe a particular strategy for companies contemplating investment in Colombia. After all, corporations attach different weights to different risk factors according to their particular corporate priorities and strengths. Moreover, Colombia's business environment, like that of most countries, differs from sector to sector—banking, manufacturing, and petroleum all present different challenges and opportunities, for example. Yet this article is in some sense designed to alert potential corporate investors to the unique complexities of the Colombian scene and also to analyze the implication of these factors for the stability and security of business operations in Colombia.

Foreign investors in Colombia confront three main categories of risk in Colombia: One category derives from the Colombia's difficult security situation, especially from the "directed" violence of Marxist guerrilla organizations that operate in many rural areas of the country. The guerrilla threat, it is argued, forces the company to increase outlays for security, to bribe local populations, and, more rarely, to make direct payoffs of various kinds to guerrilla forces. The second category relates to organized crime—specifically to Colombia's powerful and well-entrenched cocaine industry. Here the threat is more indirect: unlike guerrillas, cocaine dealers do not have an antiproperty agenda nor do they single out foreign businesses for attack. Yet, generalized violence associated with drug traffic clearly contaminates the working environment for corporations in Colombia, and hence reduces Colombia's attractiveness as an investment prospect. Even more important, there are subtle ways in which the narcotics trade increases the costs of doing business (especially to export industries) and contributes to overall institutional decay in that country. A third source of risk is the Colombian state itself. On the one hand, the weakness of the state increases companies' operating costs—forcing them to assume quasi-state functions in some insecure regions. On the other hand, the private sector confronts an extremely high tax burden—itself a reflection of Colombia's extremely serious public order problems. These three sources of risk—the guerrillas, the cocaine industry, and the Colombian state (which in effect represent three competing centers of political and economic power)—will be described in detail in the following pages.

## The Security Dimension

Colombia's relatively stable democratic system—an advantage from the standpoint of foreign investment—has proved to be an ineffective vehicle for the resolution of social and political conflicts. A manifestation of this problem is that Colombia has a structurally high level of violence. In the late 1980s the country had the third-highest homicide rate in the world (after El Salvador and Zimbabwe). The murder rate in Medellin, Colombia's second largest city, was more than five times the rate of any U.S. city in 1990. According to the human rights group Americas Watch, there were 3,500 political killings in 1991—murders attributed to either leftist guerrillas or right-wing paramilitary groups. Kidnappings have become a major industry in Colombia: during the first eight months of 1992 there were 851 reported kidnappings in the country, an average of almost 3.5 per day. Terrorist attacks on government installations, industries, oil pipelines, electric power facilities, and the transportation infrastructure are common features of the Colombian scene; such attacks are believed to have cost Colombia more than one-half of one percentage point of Gross Domestic Product (GDP) growth during 1992.

The weakness of Colombia's democratic system is also reflected in the inability of the Colombian state to control huge sections of the national territory. Much of Colombian territory is under the control of unofficial armies of various types: ranchers, plantation owners, and emerald mines, for example, all employ gunmen for protection. Cocaine traffickers finance and equip paramilitary groups to protect their land holdings and laboratories. Finally, some 8,000 to 10,000 Marxist guerrillas roam the countryside committing acts of economic sabotage, kidnapping ranchers, businessmen, and local politicians; killing soldiers and policemen; and extracting money from agricultural and industrial enterprises. This suggests that in much of Colombia's hinterland the foreign investor cannot rely on the Colombian state to impose law and order. Furthermore, as the following discussion will show, the requirements of adapting to a hostile environment have sometimes forced companies to act in ways that diminish the authority of the Colombian state and consolidate insurgents' control over particular areas.[2]

From the foreign investor's perspective, the programmatic violence of Colombia's various Marxist insurgent groups presents the most obvious threat. These groups represent an intractable problem for Colombia—a running political sore that has acquired increasingly threatening proportions in the past decade. Colombia has gone to some length to make peace with the insurgent groups; indeed a "dialogue" with the guerrillas underway since 1984 finally resulted in 1989–90 in the demobilization of approximately 3,500 guerrillas comprising four organizations: the April 19th movement, the Army of Popular Liberation (EPL), the Quintin Lamé, and the Revolutionary Workers' Party (PRT). However, the two largest and most important guerrilla organizations, the Revolutionary Armed Forces of Colombia (FARC) and the Army of National Liberation (ELN), as well as a dissident faction of the EPL, refuse to lay down their weapons. (These organizations are now loosely linked in a vague entity called the "Simon Boliviar National Guerrilla Coordinating Board.")

These organizations retain far-reaching political agendas; that is, they want fundamental alterations in the government and the political system. Said one ELN leader in a 1990 interview: "Surrendering our arms is not a consideration; these words are not in our vocabulary. We demand a new government, a new constitution."[3] There are significant practical as well as ideological disincentives to demobilization. Insurgency, like Colombia's other main illegal enterprise, the cocaine industry, is a major economic activity. Total combined earnings of the ELN and the FARC were estimated to be more than 150 billion pesos (approximately U.S. $275 million) in 1991; approximately as much as was earned by Colombia's eighth-largest legal enterprise, Colmotores, in that year. Shutting down the guerrilla enterprise would be a major undertaking, as would the reabsorption of 10,000 guerrilla fighters (who have almost no skills that are applicable to a peacetime setting) into civilian society.

From a foreign investor's perspective, the relevant fact about guerrilla organizations is their hostility to the propertied classes. Guerrillas have developed a financial strategy of exploiting all production assets—oil fields, cattle ranches, coal mines, and the like—in areas that they control. In addition, the ELN guerrillas, more radical than their FARC or EPL counterparts, engage in the gratuitous destruction of property simply to prove an ideological point. Here, foreign enterprises, those involved in extractive industries, appear especially vulnerable. As Manuel Perez, the leader of the ELN, noted in a 1990 interview:

> For more than 30 years, Colombia has been giving away its oil to the rich U.S. transnational oil companies. . . . That is why we want a broad national debate and the only way to start it as to sabotage the refineries and the pipelines. In this country, if you do not press hard, no one listens to you."[4]

Companies operating in areas where guerrilla groups are active, politically and militarily, have responded to this threat in various ways. Such responses comprise legal or officially approved measures designed to strengthen company security or to build a base of support among the local population, and illegal or extralegal measures that involve various patterns of accommodation with guerrilla groups. The former category includes, first of all, direct expenditures for protecting personnel and installations (i.e., the company's own security system). The system comprises a variety of elements; for example, private security guards and armored cars for company executives, and fences, special lighting, and hardened airstrips at oil-drilling sites. An Exxon representative interviewed in Colombia in 1987 estimated that the security precautions required in the Arauca region (an ELN stronghold) add roughly $500,000 to the cost of drilling a well and about $1,500 to the per-kilometer cost of running seismic profiles. British Petroleum, which recently discovered what appears to be Colombia's largest oil field, in Cusiana in Casanare department, pays approximately $6 million dollars, or about 3 percent of the company's annual budget in Colombia, on physical security outlays. This category also comprises payments for additional military and police protection—that is, for a level of protection that the Colombian government is not in a position to furnish. These payments usually are made in kind: for example, the company provides rations, clothing, vehicles, gasoline, and medicine and in return, military and police contingents increase their presence in the region. (This translates into more army patrols in the area of the oil camps and a larger stationary police force in the camps.) Texaco, for example, signed a formal contract with the Colombian military in 1987 (the contract is still in existence today) to provide extra patrols for the company's oil installations in the Middle Magdalena Valley, an area penetrated extensively by FARC and ELN guerrillas.

In addition, oil companies have attempted to establish a "modus vivendi" with local populations and part of this involves making efforts to improve infrastructure and living standards locally—for example, providing roads and elementary sanitation facilities, equipping schools, and delivering medical care. "We believe in raising the living standards of people who live and work around our oil fields and facilities," notes a statement issued by Texaco's public relations office in Bogota.[5] The motivation for such programs is not entirely altruistic. Communities that benefit from development may be less inclined to support guerrilla movements or to cooperate with guerrilla attacks on oil installations—or they may be more inclined to provide the Colombian military with intelligence about impending guerrilla attacks. British Petroleum contributes some $3 to $4 million annually to such "hcarts and minds" activities and Texaco approximately $300,000. Shell and Occidental Petroleum, which operate the Caño Limon oil field in Arauca department (in northeast Colombia), were spending about $5 million per year on various civic action programs in the late 1980s.

However, companies operating in particularly insecure regions—that is, in areas where the state's presence is weak or nonexistent—have sometimes pursued a strategy of direct accommodation with local guerrilla groups. This has meant providing the revolutionaries with money or favors. An oft-cited example concerns the German construction firm, Mannesmann-Anlagenbau, which was under contract with Occidental Petroleum in the mid-1980s to build a 170-mile pipeline to open up the above-mentioned Caño Limon field. (The project was the first leg of a 500-mile pipeline connecting Caño Limon with the Caribbean part of Covenas.) During construction of the pipeline in 1984–85, the ELN guerrillas (who exercised de facto control over much of Arauca) organized work stoppages, carried out several attacks on the company's installations, and kidnapped four of Mannesmann's employees. The company paid a $4 million ransom to secure the release of its employees. However, according to top Colombian military leaders (both the head of the country's armed forces and the commander of the 4th Army Division, based in Arauca), Mannesmann also agreed to pay a monthly "war tax" of $200,000 to the ELN so that the guerrillas would allow construction of the pipeline to proceed without disturbance. Reportedly, the ELN collected $1.2 million in such payments in 1984–88. Mannesmann denied the allegations of payoffs; however, in the ensuing scandal (multinational companies' alleged financial support for subversive movements was for a time a major public issue in Colombia), the company removed its general manager from Colombia. Subsequently, in mid-August 1985, Mannesmann's president, Kurt Schwartzenbach, visited the country and met with Colombian President Belisario Betancur in an effort to repair the damage from the incident.

The Mannesmann scandal was unique—no other case of alleged payoffs to guerrillas has received such publicity. Yet the realities of life in the Colombian hinterland have not changed: companies operating in insecure areas cannot count on the protection of the Colombian state so they are under considerable pressure to make their own arrangements with local guerrillas. The leader of the ELN, Manuel Perez, claimed in 1990 that "since 1986, the ELN has been engaged in 'negotiations' with rich oil companies, forcing them to pay an 'oil charge' (a revolutionary tax) in exchange for [being] allowed to exploit the country's oil fields."[6] An ELN spokesman claims that the movement has amassed a $50 million war chest from such "taxes" over the years. Spokesmen for multinational oil companies deny making cash payments to guerrillas; however, executives interviewed by this writer in Colombia admit providing other kinds of assistance: food, transportation, equipment (such as flashlights, radios, and generators), medicines, and even medical care. Armand Hammer, the late chairman of Occidental Petroleum, once stated, referring to Oxy's oil operations in Arauca, that "we are giving jobs to the guerrillas—we give them the catering jobs and we take care of the local population. It has worked out so far and they in turn protect us from other guerrillas."[7]

Of course, nonpetroleum sectors in Colombia are also targets of extortion. As Table 8–2 shows, both the ELN and the FARC extract money from gold-mining ventures. Of the 240 billion pesos (approximately $400 to $450 million) earned from gold production in Colombia in 1991, the guerrillas collected 7 to 8 percent or 17 billion pesos. In a coal-mining area in La Jagua de Ibirico in southern Cesar department, mine owners reportedly pay the ELN a hefty 480 pesos per ton of coal produced, equivalent to about 7 percent of revenues. (Incredibly, the president of Colombia's National Coal Federation—FEDECARBON— recently told a conference at the Universidad Libre in Bogota that a good way to resolve security conflicts in that region would be to simply turn over a coal mine to the guerrillas.[8]) Guerrillas in addition, collect huge sums of money from cattle ranchers, transport companies, and the cultivation and processing of narcotics crops (opium and coca). Overall, extortion is big business in Colombia. As Table 8-2 suggests, levies obtained from the petroleum and nonpetroleum sectors accounted for the vast majority of the combined ELN-FARC revenues of 151.3 billion pesos in 1991.

Direct accommodation with guerrillas is expedient: it eases pressures on companies in the short run. Yet such a strategy is counterproductive in the long term—payoffs by companies that increase guerrillas' revenues strengthen guerrillas' power relative to the government defense forces; ultimately, the effect is to reduce the government's already tenuous control over the nation's territory, to increase political instability, and to produce a less secure operating environment. Arguably, contributing to guerrillas' coffers merely sows the seeds of future violence. Between 1986 and mid-1992, for example, guerrillas carried out 232 attacks on the Caño Limon-Covenas pipeline, which resulted

**Table 8–2.  Guerrilla Revenues in Colombia, 1991 (in pesos)[a]**

| Source of Revenue | FARC | ELN |
|---|---|---|
| Extortion: | | |
| Gold Mining[b] | 6 billion | 11 billion |
| Oil Field Operations (Arauca department) | — | 7 billion |
| Cattle Ranching | 6 billion | — |
| Coal Mining[b] | — | 8 billion |
| Coca and Opium | 67 billion | — |
| Transport Companies | — | 4 billion |
| Other Extortion | 5 billion | 1.6 billion |
| Kidnapping | 14.8 billion | 14.4 billion |
| Diversion of Budget Revenue | — | 6.5 billion |
| Total | 98.8 billion | 52.5 billion |

(a) Calculate 550 pesos per dollar in 1991.
(b) The ELN is said also to operate some gold and coal mines.

in the spillage of 884,400 barrels of crude oil, incurred repair costs of $41 million, and decreased oil production by 50.1 million barrels, equivalent to an estimated $893 million. For the Colombian economy as a whole, guerrilla terrorism cost an estimated $250 million dollars in 1991—a cost equivalent to almost half a percentage point of Colombia's GDP for that year. To fight terrorism and to reestablish its authority, the government has been forced to impose "war taxes" of its own— levies that have hurt the private sector and (arguably) further diminished Colombia's ability to attract foreign investment.

## Cocaine

Colombia is by far the most significant producer of refined cocaine (cocaine hydrochloride) in the world. At least 70 percent of the cocaine sold in international markets originates from refineries in Colombia; most of the rest is produced in Peru and Bolivia (countries that also account for the lion's share of South American suppliers of coca leaf). The business of refining and distributing cocaine is dominated by two loosely articulated coalitions or syndicates of criminal families centered in Medellin and Cali, Colombia. The Medellin and Cali coalitions, often somewhat misleadingly called "cartels," comprise numerous individual trafficking groups that engage in different phases of production, transportation, and distribution. Also, within Colombia, 20 to 30 percent of trafficking is controlled by independents. The Medellin and Cali coalitions possibly have exported some 500 to 600 tons of cocaine into international markets in 1991; some of these exports comprised cocaine transshipped from Bolivia and Peru. These syndicates' gross revenues from cocaine in 1991 could have been as high as $10 to $15 billion, which dwarfs the value of Colombia's legal exports in that year—$7.6 billion—and which represents roughly two to three times the combined sales of Colombia's five largest corporations in 1990.

The Medellin and Cali syndicates are highly professional organizations that employ a range of specialized personnel, such as pilots, chemical engineers, accountants, lawyers, and financial managers. A former money launderer for the Medellin mafia, Ramon Milian Rodriguez, described the "stereotypical cartel member" as "college educated" and "reasonably sharp"; members of the management team, he said, all have "advanced degrees in their specialty." The syndicates also incorporate the most modern forms of air and sea transportation and state-of-the-art communications networks, including satellite radios and encryption devices. The Medellin cartel has also hired foreign military specialists, including former Israeli Army and British Strategic Air Services institutions, to train traffickers' private security forces in such subjects as self-defense, weapons, camouflage, intelligence and counterintelligence, and communication.

Drug trafficking syndicates differ from legal businesses in certain respects: for instance, syndicates employ professional assassins and regularly use murder and torture against competitors. Additionally, syndicates make enormous outlays to create networks of accomplices and informants at all levels of government. Finally, trafficking organizations keep their internal structure and internal communications flows compartmentalized for security. Legal enterprises, by contrast, are more inclined to encourage communication flows among different parts of the organization. The cocaine industry is not an organizational model for the legal economy in Colombia. Yet, cocaine is a business nevertheless—one with far-reaching ramifications for Colombian economic and political life. Cocaine profits exert significant influence over the economy; moreover, traffickers' enormous wealth, their logistical resources, and their private armies have allowed them to co-opt or supplement the power structure in many parts of Colombia.

What kinds of risks does the Colombian cocaine industry present to foreign investors? How does the industry affect the stability and security of the company's operating environment in Colombia? At first glance, the threat would seem to be minimal. For example, unlike guerrilla organizations, traffickers do not boast a revolutionary political agenda: they are not interested in redistribution of wealth, the nationalization of productive assets, or the expulsion of foreign capital from Colombia. Traffickers do not target foreign businesses, or their employees, in Colombia. Furthermore, drug dealers as property owners— traffickers maintain extensive real estate holdings and operate some legal businesses—are themselves vulnerable to extortion by guerrilla organizations.

Perhaps more than other business groups in Colombia, cocaine dealers have taken an aggressive stance against leftist guerrillas. In Colombia's unprotected rural areas, traffickers finance and equip paramilitary forces to protect their farms, ranches, and laboratories against extortion and also to persecute the guerrillas' civilian supporters. The paramilitaries have succeeded in wiping out the guerrilla infrastructure in certain areas. As one Colombian official put it, "The truth is, where there are paramilitaries with money from narcotrafficking there are no guerrillas. The paramilitaries are well trained, well-paid and blood-thirsty and the guerrillas respect that.''[9]

If the cocaine industry presents no direct political or ideological threat to the business community (and, by implication, foreign inves-tors), it does disrupt business operations in other ways. One important negative effect derives from the repatriation of cocaine profits—esti-mated to be as much as $2 billion per year or more than 25 percent of Colombia's 1991 legal imports. These revenues return to Colombia mostly in the form of foreign exchange and imported goods (both legal imports and contraband). This inflow hurts legal businesses operating in Colombia more than it helps them. The appearance of large quanti-ties of dollars in Colombian financial markets means that dollars become cheap relative to the local currency, reducing the competitive-ness of local products both in foreign markets and in the domestic market. Companies manufacturing products for export can be caught in an economic vise: they receive their revenues in (relatively) cheap dollars but they must pay their domestic operating costs (such as labor, raw materials, and certain taxes) in overvalued Colombian pesos.

Recent financial policies in Colombia have aggravated this problem: These include the government's decisions in 1991 to turn exchange transactions over to private financial markets, to allow Colombian citizens to own foreign-currency bank accounts, and to allow Colom-bians to repatriate any amount of capital on a ''no questions asked'' basis provided that they pay the government an upfront fee of 3 percent. These decisions produced a veritable avalanche of foreign exchange—much of it money from illegal activities, including cocaine trafficking—pouring into Colombia. Official foreign exchange reserves increased from approximately $4.6 billion in 1990 to $7.5 billion in mid-1992. Such inflows raised the value of the peso by approximately 10 percent in 1991. This situation is a tough one for exporters: At least one economist (Eduardo Sarmiento Palacio of the University of Los Andes) predicts that Colombia's nontraditional exports (i.e., those other than coffee, oil, and coal) will decline during 1992, largely because of the influx of narcodollars and speculative capital into the Colombian financial system.[10]

Narcotics exports also hurt the legal economy by stimulating im-ports. Contraband financed partly by drug earnings has depressed domestic industry as the cheaper goods crowd out legitimate manufac-tured goods. The Colombian Merchants Association (FENALCO) estimated the value of contraband merchandise, which by definition is not taxed, to be $1.1 billion in 1988, slightly more than 20 percent of

Colombia's legal imports in that year. Estimates of the shares of the domestic market held by contraband during the 1980s ranged from 40 percent for such items as automobiles, spare parts, and hardware to 90 percent for liquor, jewelry, watches, and cigarettes. Legitimate manufacturers and retailers, of course, suffered severely. At times contraband textile imports drove the textile industry—the centerpiece of Medellin's economy—to the brink of bankruptcy. A General Electric factory producing portable radios went out of business because its products could not compete with a flood of illegally imported radios. According to FENALCO, an estimated 300,000 jobs in the legal retail sector were lost in the late 1980s because of inflows of contraband.

In 1990–91 the Colombian government, as part of its "apertura" (economic opening) policy substantially reduced tariffs on imported goods. Incentives for smuggling diminished as a result. Between December 1989 and February 1992, the average tariff rate on imports declined from 43.7 percent to 11.8 percent; duties were eliminated on categories of products (for example, alcohol, cigarettes, and electrical appliances) that had entered the country largely as contraband in earlier years. Also, import licensing requirements were eliminated for most product categories. Such moves apparently benefited legal importers and retailers while increasing manufacturers' exposure to international competition. Of course, narcotics earnings continue to finance imports—if now largely legal imports. However, there is an additional problem associated with the repatriation of narcodollars: Drug dealers are not primarily concerned with making a profit from importing goods. Rather, they see imports as a means both of converting dollars to pesos and of "laundering" (disguising the origins of) their illicit earnings. "Traffickers now import goods legally and sometimes sell them in Colombia at prices even lower than paid in the United States," said Joseph Finnan of the Colombian–American Trade Council in Bogota. Finnan cited an example of a legal company importing goods to sell in Colombia being undersold by another importer that was apparently linked to narcotics traffickers.[11] Given the tremendous influences of cocaine profits on the Colombian economy, the government's new "apertura" policy could have devastating consequences for importers and manufacturers alike.

Foreign companies contemplating investment in Colombia must take into consideration the social and political effects of the narcotics trade. In general, these effects are to undermine government and the rule of law. Murder, terrorism, and corruption have been the vehicle for this process. For example, in 1991 more than 400 Colombian policemen were killed in the line of duty, many assassinated by traffickers' contract killers or killed during counternarcotics operations. Also in Colombia, 242 judges and court officials were killed from 1981 through 1991, according to the judicial workers' union. Under these circumstances, police are afraid to make arrests and judges are reluctant to preside over trafficking cases. Moreover, the Medellin mafia in recent years has selectively targeted and murdered high-level Colombians— among them a justice minister, an attorney general, a supreme court judge, an editor of a major Bogota newspaper, and at least one presidential candidate—who supported the extradition of Colombian drug lords to the United States or who otherwise crusaded against the cocaine industry.

In 1989–90, the Colombian government initiated a major crackdown on the Medellin mafia following the assassination, apparently by traffickers' henchmen, of a leading Liberal Party candidate, Luis Carlos Galan. Elements of the Medellin mafia calling themselves the "Extraditables" (the government had extradited a number of Colombian traffickers to the United States during the 1980s) issued a communiqué declaring a "widespread and total war" against the Colombian state. The result was a wave of bombings, murders, and kidnappings that claimed the lives of more than 1,000 Colombians, many of them bystanders, and caused hundreds of millions of dollars in damages to buildings and to industry. Colombia's tourist trade—as reflected in hotel occupancy rates, restaurant sales, and passenger air miles flown—suffered a precipitous decline during this period. New foreign investment also declined, although not as much or might be expected (only 11 percent) given the pervasive violence in Colombia during this period. The Medellin mafia's campaign of narcoterrorism clearly took its toll on the Colombian public. A poll conducted for the Bogota weekly *Semana* in November 1990 concluded that more than 60 percent of Colombians favored granting amnesty to drug dealers and that more than 90 percent were disposed to accept an accused "Extraditable" as a cabinet minister if such steps would bring peace to Colombia.

In response to such pressures, the government initiated what amounted to peace negotiations with leading Medellin traffickers— offering them reduced jail sentences and the chance to avoid extradition to the United States (the fate that traffickers feared most) if they surrendered voluntarily. Several drug kingpins accepted the government's offer and turned themselves in during the period from December 1990 to June 1991. Moreover, in June 1991 Colombia's Constituent

Assembly, a body created to draft a new constitution, wrote a clause into the new constitution that definitively outlawed extradition. With the surrender in June 1991 of a top cocaine kingpin, Pablo Escobar, the Medellin mafia formally called an end to its war against the state. As a result, generalized violence associated with the narcotics trade has diminished significantly. However, Escobar and several of his colleagues unfortunately escaped from prison last July and are still at large; moreover, the Colombian cocaine industry as a whole continues to prosper, especially the organizations based in Cali, which, by all accounts, have expanded their export operations dramatically in recent years.

Currently, the Colombian government is in an unenviable position vis-à-vis the cocaine traffic. Should the government again prioritize the struggle against cocaine, the result could be a new wave of mafia-sponsored violence in Colombia; on the other hand, to pursue a policy of tolerance or inaction vis-à-vis the drug trade could have serious consequences domestically and internationally: the further decay of Colombia's institutions, the deterioration of Colombia's image abroad, and possibly retaliatory sanctions by the United States (now the market for at least 80 percent of the cocaine exported by the Colombian traffickers). Currently, the Colombian state is, in a sense, "muddling through"—navigating between the extremes of tolerance and violent repression. In the past year and a half, the government has seized large quantities of cocaine, destroyed many processing laboratories, put a number of traffickers in jail, and tightened controls over money laundering. However, such action has had little effect on the leadership structures, trafficking networks, and financial operations of the Medellin and Cali coalitions. Indeed, these coalitions may be stronger, more professional, and better entrenched in Colombian society than ever.

In general, the relations between the Colombian government and the cocaine industry present a discouraging panorama for foreign investors. For example, official corruption, a long-standing practice in Colombia and other Latin American countries, becomes more onerous where the cocaine industry thrives. Because traffickers are able to pay vast sums for protection, the effort is to generalize the practice of demanding bribes—to produce a hypertrophy of official greed—and probably to increase the size of the typical bribe. The larger issue, however, is the threat of narcocorruption to the integrity of Colombia's political and economic institutions. Here, there is much cause for concern. For instance, drug money represents an important underpinning of the entire democratic process in Colombia—a Liberal Party senator from Antioquia department estimated in 1989 that some 40 percent of the legislators in the Colombian congress have accepted contributions for their political campaigns from drug dealers.[12] Cocaine money finances intelligence and protection networks in all key national institutions and at all levels of government. The financial inducements to cooperate with the drug lords are enormous by Colombian standards: For instance, a police private on the trafficker's payroll may receive $255 a month and a police captain $5,000; the official monthly salaries earned in their ranks are, respectively, $128 and $180.

The impotence of the Colombian state vis-à-vis the cocaine industry is remarkable by any standard. Take, for example, the continuing saga of Pablo Escobar. Escobar, reputedly the top figure in the Medellin cartel, for years managed to elude the Colombian authorities, despite a series of encirclement campaigns conducted by thousands of Colombian soldiers and police troops. In June 1991 Escobar turned himself in voluntarily under a plea bargain deal negotiated with the Colombian government. The terms of Escobar's imprisonment, however, made a mockery of the criminal justice system. Escobar reportedly paid for the construction of the prison, "La Catedral," in the trafficker's home town of Envigado near Medellin (the funds were channeled through the Envigado municipal treasury); he bought the land on which the prison stands several months prior to his surrender; Escobar and his men controlled the security arrangements inside the facility; and the prison itself—equipped with cellular telephones, fax machines, and computers—apparently served as a command post for running Escobar's cocaine operations.

Last July, when the government attempted to move Escobar to a more secure jail, the trafficker and several associates managed, incredibly, to slip out of the Envigado compound past a surrounding cordon of 400 heavily armed soldiers. Needless to say, Escobar's escapades create the impression of a government that is not in charge. Unsurprisingly, Colombia's President Cesar Gaviria suffered considerable political damages from Escobar's escape—polls taken immediately before and immediately after the escape showed that the percentage of Colombians holding a negative opinion of the president jumped from an already high 45.1 percent to an even higher 59.1 percent.

From an investment perspective, the cocaine industry should be seen as a "wild card" that has enormous potential for destabilizing Colombia's political and economic life. In effect, tremendous resources of the narcotraffickers are a sword of Damocles over Andean governments. Governments in the hemisphere as well as foreign multinational corporations must always take into consideration that the drug lords will let drop this sword. Colombian economist Francisco Thoumi argued in an unpublished manuscript in 1991 that the Colombian traffickers might have accumulated a net worth of between $39 billion and $60 billion by 1989–90, based on cocaine profits and earnings from investing these funds in legal activities. He argued,

> The scale of narco-wealth is very threatening to the Colombian power structure, since it suggests that the narco-capitalists may well have a combined drug and capital income that is enormous relative to the size of the country's economy. . . . Narco-capitalists [have] as much capacity to invest in Colombia as the entire private sector of the country. . . . Narco-business income is so large in relation to some key economic variables in Colombia that narco-capital could easily alter the status quo of the economy. . . . The full impact of this wealth has yet to be felt. It could be truly dramatic, and narco-capitalists could eventually become the dominant economic group within Colombia.[13]

The drug lords could mobilize resources on a scale to challenge the authority of Latin American governments. For instance, the traffickers could finance large and well-equipped private armies, purchase large sections of the bureaucracy, or engage in destabilizing speculation against the currency. Moreover, they could use their economic power to drive legitimate enterprises, including foreign-owned ones, out of business; alternatively, they could convert such enterprises into conduits for cocaine shipments and illegal money flows.

## The State

External governmental factors—generalized violence, guerrilla extortion and terrorism, and the corrosive effects of the cocaine economy—significantly increase the risks of doing business in Colombia. However, multinational corporations must consider another important source of investment risk in Colombia—the Colombian state itself. There is some irony in this assessment: Colombia has a proinvestment history, "a long tradition of respecting the rights of the foreign investor," as a document published by the Colombian Embassy in Washington, D.C., puts it. Furthermore, Colombia has liberalized its foreign investment regimes in recent years: foreign investors now have the same rights as Colombian investors, there are no limits to profit remittances, and there is complete freedom to invest in nearly all sectors of the economy. Yet, the favorable investment "rules of the game," touted by Colombian government spokesmen do not in themselves make the case for investing in Colombia—these rules must be juxtaposed with certain fundamental realities of Colombian political life. One such reality is that the state's authority itself is suspect. As argued earlier, the state is only one of three centers of power in Colombia. (The others are the active guerrilla organizations and the major drug trafficking syndicates.) Furthermore, as will be shown below, the state—largely because of the violence and lawlessness plaguing Colombia—has adopted an increasingly predatory stance vis-à-vis the business community.

Our previous discussion has suggested that part of the investor's risk derives from what the state does not do well or, in some regions, do at all: maintain public order and the rule of law. Symptomatic of this problem is the enormous private security industry in Colombia, which consists of some 80,000 operatives (almost 1 percent of the Colombian labor force). The Colombian government sees the industry as an extension of its own frail powers, as "a support for the authorities in their struggle against crime," as Colombia's defense minister, Rafael Pardo, puts it. In outlying regions of the country, as noted earlier, companies find it necessary to perform quasi-state functions; they provide an array of security and welfare services within their operating spheres. In exceptional cases, companies may have to make their own deals with local guerrilla forces. Whether or not these various costs are perceived as acceptable depends very much on the company's size, its operating rules, its anticipated profits, its experience with security-related problems, and the intestinal fortitude of its management team.

Yet it is the actions of the Colombian state, not its failure to exercise authority, that cause the greatest concern in the business community. As one foreign oil executive remarked in a recent interview with this writer: "The government is a bigger problem for us than the communist guerrillas." The government may be weak but it is also predatory. Colombia has introduced no less than eight tax reforms in the past twelve years with the result that the government now has one of the highest effective tax rates on foreign corporations, 43 to 45 percent, in Latin America. (In Mexico and Venezuela, for example, the rates are respectively 35 and 30 percent; it may be noted that investing in Mexico and Venezuela under a proposed free-trade pact linking the three countries could provide as much access to the Colombian market as investing in Colombia itself.) As of 1993, according to the latest (June 1992) tax reform, companies operating in Colombia will pay a 30 percent income tax, a 12 to 15 percent tax on profit remittances, and a 25 percent income tax surcharge. (The combined taxes mutually offset each other somewhat so the actual tax is in the 43 to 45 percent range.) However, in addition to the above levies, there are special taxes levied on production of oil, coal, natural gas (even "associated" gas that is not used or flared), and ferronickel alloys.[14] Also, companies are required to invest the equivalent of 25 percent of their 1991 income in Colombian government bonds—a requirement that is in effect a forced loan because the bonds, which mature in five years, do not pay any interest. The petroleum sector is singled out for especially heavy taxation: not only does the industry pay the production taxes mentioned above, it also pays a higher remittance tax than non-oil industries: 15 percent compared to 12 percent. In subsequent years, according to the new tax code, the disparity becomes even greater: From 1993 to 1997, petroleum remittance taxes will decline from 15 percent to 12 percent; nonpetroleum taxes from 12 percent to 7 percent.

High taxes, of course, are largely an indirect cost of Colombia's civil war and (to a lesser extent) of the country's problems with the narcotics industry. Indeed, the above-cited surcharge and production tax were imposed as "war taxes" by the Gaviria government in 1991 and enacted into law in June 1992. The petroleum industry, which already makes substantial outlays for physical security and "hearts and minds" activities is especially resentful about the new levies. (Unfortunately, oil is a politically vulnerable sector in Colombia as in other Latin American countries. A wide spectrum of political actors from the ELN guerrillas to the late Liberal Party leader Luis Carlos Galan have favored nationalizing the industry. Such sentiment accounts partly for the discriminatory tax treatment that the industry receives.) The tax situation seems unlikely to ease anytime soon. Colombia's armed forces budget—an astonishingly high 10 to 14 percent of government expenditure—will continue to be a drain on the economy as a whole and on the private sector in particular until an accord is reached with the guerrillas. But such a possibility seems remote, at least in the near term. Defense Minister Rafael Pardo warned last summer that the nation faces "a prolonged war" against the guerrilla movement[15] and talks between the government and the FARC and ELN representatives are in suspension as of this writing. Furthermore, the cocaine business appears to be a relatively permanent feature of the Colombian landscape. While the decline of "narcoterrorism'' has reduced after mid-1991 Colombian's outlays for counternarcotics operations, the government still spends tens of million of dollars yearly wiping out drug crops, destroying clandestine laboratories, and seizing cocaine shipments. As noted in the beginning of this chapter, Colombia is a country in turmoil; certainly, the additional economic burden imposed by violence, drugs, and insurgency will continue to plague the government's relations with the private sector, including foreign companies operating in Colombia, for many years to come.

## Postscript

There is always a danger of exaggerating the risks of investing in a high-profile country such as Colombia. Certainly, aspects of the discussion of major risk factors presented in the above pages can be qualified somewhat. For example, the direct costs of coping with antigovernment guerrillas are perceived as manageable by large multinational corporations—at least this is the impression conveyed by this writer's interviews (over several years) with representatives of BP, Occidental, Exxon, Shell, and Texaco in Colombia. Also, Colombian government spokesmen claim, probably correctly, that few, if any, foreign companies have been driven out of the country by the guerrilla insurgency per se. With respect to the threat from the cocaine industry, repatriated narcodollars may have good as well as bad economic effects in Colombia; the former include increasing demand for goods and services, preventing balance of payments crises, and perhaps facilitating Colombia's repayment of its foreign debt. Finally, the Colombian government—though obviously beleaguered—is firmly committed to encouraging new foreign investment, and sees such investment as playing an important role in Colombia's future; this means that the government is amenable to persuasion and bargaining. Still, our basic contentions—that there are significant risks associated with doing business in Colombia, that the risks are to some extent interrelated, and that Colombia's problems of violence and insecurity are likely to persist for a lengthy period—are widely accepted by observers of the Colombian scene. Also, the government's political authority and its ability to command the allegiance of the population are cushioned only by the trickle-down effect of narcodollars and, in this setting, the tax burden in the business community (after all, a highly visible target for the taxing authorities) may continue to escalate. Still, there are indications that foreign investment, especially portfolio investment, will increase in 1993. Certainly, politics and economics in Colombia may eventually become less forbidding and more predictable, but until they do, Colombia's hopes of attracting large inflows of new foreign investment, even with the new "apertura" policies, do not accord with our analysis here of the harsh realities.

## Notes

1. "Poll shows decline in Gaviria's popularity," *El Tiempo* (Bogota), September 7, 1992, pp. 1A, 8A.

2. Mark Ludwig and Patricia Olney, "Guerrilla Terrorism and International Bureaus in Latin America: The Threat and the Response," University of Miami: Center for International Business Education and Research, 1992, p. 25.

3. "ELN Leader Vows to Continue Political Violence," *Voz* (Bogota), September 27, 1990, p. 3.

4. "ELN Leader on Recovering Oil Resources," *La Prensa*, September 11, 1990, pp. 10, 11.

5. Interview, Texaco (Bogota), October 9, 1992.

6. See note 4.

7. Youssef Ihrahim, "Discovery in Colombia Paints Up Big Change in World Oil Picture," *The Wall Street Journal*, May 13, 1985, p. 12.

8. "Fedecarbon propose acuerdo con guerrilleras," *El Tiempo*, September 4, 1992, p. 8A.

9. Douglas Farah, "Cartel Enforcer Linked to Massacre," *The Washington Post*, May 6, 1990, p. A21.

10. Eduardo Sarmiento Palacio, "The Decline of the Colombian Economy," *Colombian Economy*, no. 177, September 1992, p. 7.

11. Interview, Colombian-American Trade Council, Bogota, October 9, 1992.

12. Jose de Cordoba, "Colombia's Narcos Find Brute Force Yields Little Entree," *The Wall Street Journal*, October 5, 1989, pp. A1, A4.

13. Francisco Thoumi, "The Economic Impact of Narcotics in Colombia," unpublished manuscript, pp. 18–21.

14. The taxes established were 600 pesos (about 80 cents in 1992) per barrel of light crude, 350 pesos per barrel of heavy crude, 20 pesos per million cubic tons of gas, 100 pesos per ton of coal, and 200 pesos per pound of ferronickel alloys. See "*Reforma Tributaria 1992. Ley 6 de 1992*," Bogota, Peat Marwick Ltd., 1992, pp. 1–3.

15. "Colombia Power Crisis Points to Zero Growth," *Colombia Economy*, no. 175, July 1992, p. 5.

*Part Three*

# Calculated Risks

*Chapter 9*

# Political Risk Insurance: Conservative if Costly, a Back-up Option After Identifying Serious Vulnerabilities

## Felton McL. Johnston III

If we disregard the activities of banks—and bankers will tell you, rightly, that they have "insured" political risks for centuries—modern political risk insurance is an infant phenomenon. It has great potential for growth, but in the meantime it has problems of capacity, availability, and cost. We are in the fairly early evolutionary stage of the market for political risk insurance and correspondingly for those who sell it and those who use it. This chapter will describe what political risk insurance is, its utility, what is available, and who offers it in various marketplaces. Also described are the motivations and constraints that influence those insurers and what they provide, and how the practices and performance of the marketplace seem likely to develop. In conclusion some suggestions will be offered about how to approach the marketplace, what for, and when.

### What the Markets Offer

In general, potential political risk losses are categorized by insurance buyers and sellers by the type of exposure to loss—sales and contracting overseas, and investment—and by the type of coverage available for such exposures. The accompanying table of insurable perils (Table 9-1) provides a general description of these exposures for which coverage is available, all of which are generally one form or another of loss due to (a) inconvertibility or transfer risk coverage, (b) expropriation, confiscation, or other "wrongful" behavior by a government, and (c) various forms of political violence along a spectrum from international war to strikes, riots, and civil commotions. If it occurs to the reader that the latter two categories of risk are not peculiar to other people's countries, this simply confirms the reality that "political"

### Table 9—1.  Insurable Perils

I. Selling and Contracting Abroad
   A. "Wrongful" calling of bid, performance, advance payment, and similar guaranties or other "on demand" instruments posted by a seller in favor of a buyer.
   B. Contract frustration: action taken by a government, not allowed by terms of the contract itself, including:
      i. contract repudiation
      ii. export embargo/license revocation
      iii. import embargo/license revocation
   C. Nonpayment or other default due to
      i. currency inconvertibility (active or passive)
      ii. political violence
   D. Loss due to other causes:
      i. confiscation or deprivation of equipment or inventory
      ii. damage or nonpayment due to political violence

II. Investment Abroad
   A. Currency inconvertibility due to active or passive measures (devaluation protection is generally unavailable). Coverage may extend to repatriation of capital, earnings, debt service, and various contractual payments.
   B. Expropriation
      i. nationalization or confiscation of an enterprise or of assets without adequate, effective, and timely compensation
      ii. "creeping" expropriation (e.g., confiscatory taxes or price controls)
      iii. other governmental action or condonation of actions, resulting in deprivation of the investor's assets, rights, or ability to operate
   C. Political Violence
      (Coverage from private entities generally excludes land-based war, although strikes, riots, and civil commotion are generally covered, and coverage for losses due to civil war and insurrection may be selectively available.)
      i. damage loss
      ii. nonpayment or default
      iii. other losses consequential to political violence
      iv. kidnap and ransom (available from private carriers only)

risks are not peculiarly foreign by nature. Nevertheless, that is the way the market, for the most part, treats them.

## The Market Players

The markets for political risk insurance can be divided into the private versus the public official markets, and the private markets in turn are separated by location (Europe [principally Lloyd's] versus America), and by the philosophies and motivations of the players. All are evolving in relation to each other: they are obliged to adapt their policies and practices to each other even though their separate existence is likely to continue.

The official markets are made up principally of the export credit agencies whose purpose is to facilitate the sale of goods from their countries to others. While these agencies principally serve to offset export risks rather than investment risks, many offer protection against the latter instances, and of course "investment" and "export" risks are not mutually exclusive categories. These agencies tend to pursue the same aims in much the same ways, although important differences do affect what may be obtainable from them and the terms on which it is offered. They are to be found in every industrialized country and in many less-developed countries.

Most of these agencies will insure—on a whole turnover or a more selective basis—a domestic manufacturer's export receivables against political risks and, in some cases, commercial risks as well. (See Table 9–2 for a list of the principal agencies.) They may—and often do—provide political or comprehensive risk protection for term loans as well; indeed, they may make the loans themselves. The scope of their political risk coverages is generally described in Table 9–1 under "Selling and Contracting Abroad." They may in fact be private entities doing business both for their own account and for the account of their governments.

These agencies, or in some cases other national agencies in the same countries, may offer insurance, guaranties, and loans for overseas projects in pursuit of additional objectives, either to secure access to goods and resources or to promote economic development in third countries. These objectives are of course not mutually exclusive. Thus the export credit agencies of many capital-exporting countries or associated agencies now cover "investment" risks as well.

An important recent addition to the ranks of public agency invest-

**Table 9—2.  Principal Official Agencies Insuring Export and Investment Exposures**

| Country | Agency | Export coverage? | Investment coverage? |
|---|---|---|---|
| Argentina | Compania Argentina de Seguros de Crédito a la Exportacion S.A. (CASC) | Yes | No |
| Australia | Export Finance and Insurance Corporation (EFIC) | Yes | Yes |
| Austria | Oesterreichische Kontrollbank Aktiengesellschaft (OeKB) | Yes | Yes |
| Belgium | Office National du Ducroire (OND) | Yes | Yes |
| Canada | Export Development Corporation (EDC) | Yes | Yes |
| Cyprus Republic | Export Credit Insurance Service, Ministry of Commerce and Industry (ECIS) | Yes | No |
| Denmark | Eksportkreditradet (EKR) | Yes | No |
| Finland | Valtiontakuukeskus (FGB) | Yes | Yes |
| France | Compagnie Française d'Assurance pour le Commerce Extérieur | Yes | Yes |
| France | Société Française d'Assurance Crédit (SFAC) | Yes | No |
| Germany | Hermes Kreditversicherungs-Aktiengesellschaft (HERMES) | Yes | No |
| Germany | Treuarbeit Aktiengesellschaft (TREUARBEIT) | No | Yes |
| Hong Kong | Hong Kong Export Credit Insurance Corporation (HKEC) | Yes | No |
| India | Export Credit Guarantee Corporation of India Limited (ECGC) | Yes | Yes |
| Indonesia | PT. Asuransi Ekspor Indonesia (PT. ASEI) | Yes | No |
| Israel | The Israel Foreign Trade Risks Insurance Corporation Ltd. (IFTRIC) | Yes | Yes |
| Italy | Sezione Speciale per l'Assicurazione del Credito all 'Esportazione (SACE) | Yes | Yes |
| Italy | Società Italiana Assicurazione Crediti S.p.A. (SIAC) | Yes | No |
| Jamaica | National Export-Import Bank of Jamaica Limited (EXIMJ) | Yes | No |
| Japan | Export-Import Insurance Division International Trade Administration | Yes | Yes |

|  | Bureau, Ministry of International Trade & Industry (EID/MITI) | | |
|---|---|---|---|
| Korea | The Export-Import Bank of Korea (EIBK) | Yes | Yes |
| Malaysia | Malaysian Export Credit Insurance Berhad (MECIB) | Yes | No |
| Mexico | Banco Nacional de Comercio Exterior S.N.C. (BANCOMEXT) | Yes | No |
| Netherlands | Nederlandsche Credietverzekering Maatschappij N.V. (NCM) | Yes | Yes |
| New Zealand | Export Guarantee Office (EXGO) | Yes | Yes |
| Norway | Garanti-Instituttet for Eksportkreditt (GIEK) | Yes | Yes |
| Portugal | Companhia de Seguro de Créditos, S.A. (COSEC) | Yes | Yes |
| Singapore | ECICS Ltd. (ECICS) | Yes | No |
| South Africa | Credit Guarantee Insurance Corporation of Africa Limited (CGIC) | Yes | Yes |
| Spain | Compañia Española de Seguros de Crédito a la Exportación S.A. (CESCE) | Yes | No |
| Spain | Compañia Española de Seguros de Crédito y Caución S.A. (CESCC) | Yes | No |
| Sri Lanka | Sri Lanka Export Credit Insurance Corporation (SLECIC) | Yes | No |
| Sweden | Exportkreditnämnden (EKN) | Yes | Yes |
| Switzerland | Geschäftsstelle für die Exportrisikogarantie (ERG) | Yes | Yes |
| Switzerland | The Federal Insurance Company Limited (FEDERAL) | Yes | No |
| Turkey | Export Credit Bank of Turkey (TURK EXIMBANK) | Yes | No |
| UK | Export Credits Guarantee Department (ECGD) | Yes | Yes |
| UK | Trade Indemnity plc (TI) | Yes | No |
| USA | Export-Import Bank of the United States (EXIMBANK) | Yes | No |
| USA | Overseas Private Investment Corporation (OPIC) | No | Yes |
| Zimbabwe | Zimbabwe Credit Insurance Corporation Limited (ZCIC) | Yes | No |
| Multilateral | Multilateral Investment Guaranty Agency (MIGA) | No | Yes |

ment insurers is the Multilateral Investment Guaranty Agency (MIGA), a World Bank–affiliated agency whose purpose is to supplement or fill the gaps in the national agencies' coverage. MIGA insures investments independently in cooperation (as coinsurer or reinsurer) with national agencies.

The private political risk (nonbank) insurance market had its origins at Lloyd's of London in the "marine" market centuries ago. Nearly two decades ago, syndicates at Lloyd's began reinsuring the inconvertibility and expropriation portfolios of the U.S. Overseas Private Investment Corporation (OPIC) and commenced offering policies directly to companies doing business abroad. More recently, U.S. firms, led by AIG, Citibank, Chubb, and a few others, and PanFinancial out of London and New York, have developed broad programs for insuring firms' export and investment risks against political perils. Additional non–U.S., as well as new U.S., participants in this market may be anticipated.

It is now possible for an American firm, for example, to cover its sales and investment risks not just with government agencies such as the Export-Import Bank of the United States (Eximbank) and OPIC, but in the private domestic and Lloyd's markets also. Still, the ability of that firm to obtain the desired protection may be constrained in both public and private markets, in different ways and for different reasons.

## Motivations and Constraints of Political Risk Insurers

Although many of their goals and interests are common, public and private sector entities do have distinctive motivations and operate under separate constraints. The distinctions between these two markets will continue, although each is increasingly coming to share some of the other's approaches.

Public entities are not involved in political risk insurance *primarily* to make money (although they are increasingly interested in enhanced revenue generation, loss avoidance, and loss control). Their involvement principally serves national or international objectives—export promotion, international economic development, and other foreign policy goals. They commonly also have subsidiary objectives or interests that may favor the investor or not. For instance, most public entities will do business with smaller domestic firms on terms at least equal to those offered to larger firms, even though the smaller firms' business is not profitable. The public entity generally will be willing to consider insuring individual items (i.e., to be the victim of adverse selection) if those items otherwise fit its criteria. And the public entity may be willing to assume some (but not all) risks the private market would shun for underwriting or other reasons, and to write business at rates below "market." Also, other terms and conditions may be more favorable in the public sector market. For instance, investment insurance is commonly available in public markets for up to twenty years but is generally limited to up to three years in the private market. Some of these differences for "investment" risks are summarized in Table 9–2.

The private insurers' motivations, while exclusively commercial, are not simply to make the most possible money from any particular transaction. Their willingness and ability to respond to the needs of businesses operating abroad reflects, in any instance, a variety of considerations, including particularly:

1. *The absolute limits on the insurer's capacity to insure political risks.* Any insurer is constrained by regulations imposed by governmental authorities, rules of voluntary associations (such as Lloyd's Council), and by its own board and management. Since the overwhelming practice in insurance (and especially in catastrophic lines like political risk) is for a primary insurer to reinsure his own risks and retain only a portion of them, an insurer must be sure that individual items underwritten and cumulative exposures fall within the terms of his reinsurance; otherwise, he must be sure that he is willing and able to retain them for his own account. If a particular transaction or group of transactions does not fit within the insurer's reinsurance "treaty" (the agreement covering a broad range of transactions for which the insurer does not need to have the reinsurer's individual approval), then he may seek to arrange "facultative" reinsurance for the transaction(s). Finally, the insurer will have a set of rules by which he governs his own behavior generally. For instance, while he may be able to lay off 90 percent or more of a given risk with reinsurers, he may nevertheless be unwilling to retain 10 percent of a risk that individually or in combination with other assumed risks will cause his exposures (with respect to countries, perils insured against, industries, or other categories) to exceed some level with which he is comfortable.

2. *The insurer's attitude toward political risk insurance and his reasons for being in the business.* What the insurer is willing and able to do has much to do with his reason for underwriting *any* political risks. It is a simplification, but a valid one, to say that there are two basic reasons why insurers will assume political risks, given the

"catastrophic" nature of those risks and their unpredictability, which causes most insurers to shun them. The first is simply that there is money to be made, and in an industry characterized for the most part by low margins (and, at the bottom of a cycle, by no margins or worse), earnings and earnings growth may be found in new, exotic, and perceived higher risk products such as political risk insurance. In these lines, where there are fewer players, demand generally exceeds capacity, and insurers may be willing to pay handsomely to hedge their exposures, the attraction for some insurers is obvious.

The other motivation (which does not necessarily exclude the first, of course) is competitive. To retain valuable business in their other (especially) property and casualty lines, some insurers may feel obliged to be in the political risk business, like it or not. This is particularly true for insurance companies catering to firms that are heavily engaged in international trade and investment.

3. *The insurer's relationship with the business seeking insurance and with the broker, if any, representing the insured.* An insurer's view of a particular transaction or group of transactions is obviously colored by his view of the prospective insured. Is the company one with which his firm does a large volume of business, or is the insurer seeking to win new business from this company? Is that business particularly desirable? Conversely, is the prospective insured not a regular customer, merely shopping for the lowest rate, seeking to cover only his worst risks, and perhaps known to be a troublesome or accident-prone insured? A new or irregular customer not particularly sought after may nevertheless obtain reasonably priced cover for an acceptable risk, especially if he is represented by a skillful, vigorous, and influential broker; but other positive elements can have an important bearing, especially in marginal situations.

4. *The insurer's view of the particular transaction and related business, and how it fits his overall book of business.* Naturally, if an insurer has an opportunity to insure a broad class of business—such as the expropriation risk associated with a company's investments in eight countries—the insurer will normally find that opportunity more attractive than the risk on any one of those investments, not just because this brings him more business but because it helps him to develop a broader book of business and avoid adverse selection. Accordingly the insurer may offer a blanket or "global" policy: the insured pays premiums on some investments he considers "safe" and might not otherwise insure, but his average cost per dollar of insurance coverage obtained is brought down. In this case, the company's

confidence in its own judgment about what is or isn't safe (and, of course, whether coverage is reasonably available otherwise for what is considered unsafe) may determine whether a global policy is chosen. Otherwise the insurer looks at the potential opportunity and the inherent risks it poses, much as the prospective insured should, except that the insurer focuses on the likelihood of loss, the value insured, and the prospects of salvage, with less regard for the overall effects of loss on the insured.

## The Future Development of Political Risk Insurance Markets

While it is not easy to predict the future evolution of political risk insurance markets, evidence and logic point to certain likely political risk market trends.

First, while there have been retrenchments by some active participants and continued unwillingness by most companies to become involved directly in political risk underwriting, over the *long* haul the private market seems likely to grow in overall capacity, to attract more participants, and to offer broader and more effective protection. For sheer competitive reasons, this should be true at least for large companies seeking to obtain coverage; and as the market develops to serve and retain these important customers, its ability and willingness to serve less-favored buyers is likely to increase generally, although not correspondingly.

How smoothly and rapidly this market development progresses will depend in large part on the experience insurers enjoy. Major losses will always drive some participating insurers and reinsurers from the field. Very profitable experience will attract new participants—and increased involvement by existing ones—as will the threat of losing an important customer to more aggressive competitors.

The growth of the private market is already having an impact on public sector underwriters—both in political and commercial (credit) risk fields. The private market has focused on export (versus investment) risks, as have the public agencies. Although lacking the advantage of the fiscal backing of the state, private insurers are correspondingly free of many of the constraints imposed by the state and some of its bureaucratic burdens. This has enabled private insurers to capture markets that might otherwise be served exclusively by public agencies, even though those agencies in general offer coverage at lower rates. At the same time, as they have suffered extraordinary losses, the public agencies have come to recognize that their official role and support of the national interest does not assure unlimited tolerance for their losses, and since the debt crisis of the 1980s most official agencies have been obliged to review critically their terms and conditions and their strategies for reconciling public policy goals and their own commercial interests.

It is likely that public entities will strive increasingly to conduct their affairs on a sounder commercial basis. This may mean less generous terms for insureds in some instances, but more flexible and otherwise beneficial terms for others as those agencies seek to preserve markets and market shares. Over the long term it seems likely that public and private entities will develop not just in competitive reaction to each other, but that new and interesting arrangements for cooperation between them will be found. This is true already where major projects are involved and neither public nor private market capacity alone is sufficient to accommodate insurance demand. The prospective demand for large amounts of insurance, cumulatively per country and for individual projects in the former Soviet Union and other markets is likely to spur increasing cooperation among public and private insurers.

## Approaching the Marketplace

A broad and important set of issues relates to the process by which a company assesses political risks and decides what to do about them. Although there is no single, correct methodological approach to assessing political risks nor a single correct approach to dealing with those risks, there can be no doubt that every firm doing a substantial part of its business overseas should have an articulated, coherent, and effective process for recognizing and coping with overseas political risks. The absence of such an approach is likely not only to expose the company to risks it should not assume and that might cost it dearly, but also to result in bad decisions about risk taking generally (including foregoing opportunities that could safely be seized) and less than optimal solutions to risk mitigation and control. And although larger companies are more likely to have the resources and sophistication to assess and address political risks, their bureaucratic complexity may be an obstacle to an effective process. Whether or not the firm has such an approach may determine not just what and how effective a role political risk insurance plays in the firm's efforts to cope with risk, but how beneficial that insurance is, and at what cost. Given the practices and motivations of insurers, companies that take a careless, casual, or simply episodic approach to purchasing political risk insurance are not likely to obtain the best terms and conditions the marketplace offers.

It is fundamental that a company having major exposures in overseas markets not only consider the role of political risk insurance at an early stage of decision making, rather than as an afterthought or a last-ditch solution to political risk problems, but that the company consider it as part of the risk environment itself. This is not to say that every firm needs to have political risk insurance—larger firms with a broad spread of risk may well be able to self-insure most if not all risks—or that other solutions to risk problems, including various financial techniques, may not be superior. But a strategy for analyzing and coping with political risks that does not take carefully into account the availability of political risk coverage and other techniques for coping with risk will at best be a flawed strategy. It will either involve the company in risks that could and should be avoided, or dispose the company to avoid risks that could, with the proper measures for protection, be undertaken profitably.

What is suggested is a continuous process by which the company considers and reconciles its general business strategy, the associated political risks, and its approach to those risks. The company may, for instance, decide that a blanket political risk insurance policy is well suited to its overall strategy, and that negotiation of such a policy, if it is available on reasonable terms, could permit the firm to undertake substantial risks that otherwise it would have to avoid. It may discover that the incremental cost of insuring some risks is so great that they should either be self-insured or avoided altogether.

Such a process is no less important for a firm whose overseas exposures are more concentrated or otherwise less suited to a blanket or global insurance policy. Even a firm with a single overseas exposure—an investment in one factory abroad—needs to contemplate the present and future implications of that investment and its associated risk. What does the investment mean to the company? What is the true sum of the company's risk exposures associated with that investment—both current and contemplated? What would its loss or the prolonged interruption of its operations imply for the parent firm? What means are available to mitigate those exposures, and what does that imply for that investment in the future? How should the invest-

**Table 9—3.  Public and Private Markets for Insurance of Investment Risks**

| | *General and Principal Distinctions* | |
| --- | --- | --- |
| | *Private commercial markets* | *Public agency markets* |
| Perils insured | While limited revolution, insurrection, or civil strife coverage may be obtained from selected sources, it is generally unavailable for events on land and immobile assets | Generally no exclusions for loss due to any warlike event. |
| Terms of commitment | Although rarely beyond 3 or 4 years, established operations will normally roll coverage forward annually, and will renew, at some price, even when adverse conditions have developed. | Up to 15 or 20 years from many entities. |
| Cost | Highly variable, based upon underwriting judgments, relationships with insured, capacity considerations, reinsurance arrangements, etc. | Varies widely among national agencies, but generally below those of commercial insurers. |
| Capacity | For individual projects, perhaps up to $250 million, but limits are highly variable among insurers and with respect to individual insureds, and market conditions. | Varies widely by agency or program involved. |
| Geographical availability | In theory, anywhere, but subject to reinsurance restrictions, country capacity limits, and underwriting judgments, and likely to be more elastic for buyers of global or blanket coverage. | Generally limited to "friendly" countries with which special arrangements have been reached governing rights and salvage, or to those having "acceptable" legal regimes or practices. Attention is often concentrated on former colonies or other countries with which there are special economic relationships. "Global" coverage is generally unavailable. |
| Investor eligibility | No particular requirements; regular customers are favored. | Nationals of the agency's country and companies domiciled therein, in some cases with national ownership requirements. For MGA, nationals of member states. |

| Investment or project eligibility | Normally no distinction as to new or existing investment. | Coverage is generally available only for new investment (including earnings reinvestment) or for creation or expansion/ modernization/improvement of an existing one. Projects may be ineligible for various public policy reasons; e.g., adverse domestic economic effects, military implications, etc. Correspondingly, undertakings having particular benefits (especially economic) for the agency country are often favored, and such benefits may actually be required for coverage to be available. |

ment be structured and financed? Should its profits be reinvested, or should they be remitted home promptly?

Early consultations with insurers and brokers may cause the firm either to lower its sights or raise them. An insurer may be willing to combine, on an attractive basis, political risk coverage with the insured's overseas property and casualty coverage. "Manuscripted" policies with terms and conditions designed for the insured's particular needs and concerns might be negotiated. No coverage may be available for some exposures. It may be possible to obtain expropriation or contract frustration coverage, but inadequate coverage for transfer risks associated with the same project(s).

Insurers may offer more than the mere plug to fill the risk gap. The insurer (or the broker) may help the company to identify and cope with risks it has not previously recognized. Over time, some of the more sophisticated insurers will likely be providing, on a regular basis, assistance to companies in risk identification and in loss control, as they now regularly do in property and casualty insurance lines. Public sector insurers in particular may, by their very association with the project, discourage harmful foreign governmental actions or enhance the potential for recovery when they occur—an especially important element when the investment's operations are intimately and significantly linked to those of the insured.

But insurers may also offer less than what is appropriate, or simply the wrong thing. A buyer of insurance (and his broker) needs to look closely and critically at the policy he is offered. What are important exceptions and limitations? Is the deductible appropriate? What are the insured's duties and rights in the event of loss? An insured can pay for coverage and be in a position to collect, and yet have to forgo compensation because actions required to collect are inconsistent with other corporate interests in a given situation. It is also necessary to consider the motives and behavior of the particular insurer. What is the claims experience others have had? How prompt, flexible, and efficient is their claims management? How strong a company is the insurer? Why are they in this market? Can they be counted on to renew the policy regularly on reasonable terms, even if the risk environment worsens? What is the insurance company's overall relationship with the insured?

## Summing Up

Political risk insurance is a risk transfer tool whose availability from both public and private entities is increasing. Nevertheless, the market for this insurance is fragmented, in the early stages of its development, and characterized by capacity constraints and relatively high costs. The availability of insurance varies not just with the perceived risk of a particular investment, but with the specific character of the insured and the insurer, and their relationship. A wise company will not merely utilize political risk insurance to cope with particular problems as they arise, but will continuously incorporate political risk insurance and other risk transfer and control devices into its business strategy and planning.

*Chapter 10*

# Conclusion

Take calculated risks;
that is quite different from being rash.
—Gen. George S. Patton

In an era of so-called "globalization," a trend has been developing for intermediate-size corporations to expand their frontiers overseas, and even take a close look at some of the less well-trodden areas. For an American company, learning to adjust to an international environment (particularly one of the less-developed countries of the Third World, Eastern Europe, or the former Soviet republics) is a matter of commitment, patience and the flexibility to appreciate that other people and systems may behave differently from ourselves in the negotiation and implementation of business transactions.

The new international topography of less-developed countries (including the former socialist countries of Eastern Europe and the former republics of the Soviet Union) varies in ways that this book and the illustrative in-depth case studies in Part Two have tried to demonstrate. The international businessperson should never forget his or her role in representing his or her company. He or she should assume the characteristics of neither explorer nor missionary. Most important, international businesspeople—whether planners or marketing officers— should not perceive themselves as scaling the Matterhorn—either for glory or profit.

Be circumspect and look at each new and unfamiliar market through the sort of prism that we have tried to present here. Apply the principles well and let some intuition and cross-cultural sensitivity temper the numbers and hard facts. Political/social risks should not be represented as a "red flag" from which to run. In fact, we rarely like to use the term "political risk." But you will notice from Robert Ebel's Chapter 5, on the former Soviet Union, or Commonwealth of Independent States, that oil companies and other industries that require a lot of front-end capital and a longer term for development in the country are always prepared for a damaging political or social crisis. They make it part of their business, one way or another, continuously to monitor events that could jeopardize their enterprise and be prepared for an accident of their own that might generate bad publicity. Further, at the negotiating phase, they do not mind talking explicitly with their "opposite numbers" in a prospective host country about the trade-offs between risk and return.

Our use of the concept, "business environment conditions," is meant to be interpreted broadly. It is meant to be relatively neutral emotionally and in concert with the general process of rational corporate strategic planning and good marketing savvy. If the marketing executive can think in terms of our framework, retaining a knowledge of the implications of the discussion of such issues as political legitimacy and elites in an elitist country, for example, or inflation and a drain of the country's hard-currency reserves, he will put himself in a better, more informed position. Not only will he be reacting to problems or catastrophes in the social/political milieu or economic/commercial sphere in a knowledgeable manner, but he gradually will be able, under certain circumstances, to take the necessary actions to help shape the outcome for his particular foreign enterprise.

How might the corporation establish a mechanism for keeping watch on the business environment in several different countries? Given a specific region of the world, how can senior management intelligently select one particular country perhaps for a dual purpose: to serve as the first regional recipient of foreign direct investment and also to act as a fulcrum for additional investments and trade in neighboring countries? The well-heeled outside consultant can provide the general picture, but his or her report will still have to be reinterpreted in-house. Otherwise, it is unlikely to have much impact on corporate decisions or actions in the field. One former foreign service officer now at Texaco does use an outside consulting service for the more comprehensive jobs (a group of Oxford dons) but then has to compose his own short memorandum applying their conclusions to the company's needs, and affix it to the nicely packaged, more general, and untailored report.

In our opinion, the following guidelines ideally should be followed if the reader in senior management wants to steer a course with a compass, instead of "worry beads," in hand.

First, one must put together a small in-house department, comprising individuals with a solid background in comparative politics or international relations and in economics and finance. A balance between the two disciplines would be good, and they should *interact* wherever appropriate. The department should become genuinely interdisciplinary.

Second, it is crucial that the international business environment people try to establish a communications flow within the corporate entity that will ensure that the real needs of the corporation are being served. It is important that this special support staff at corporate center leave their desks and do a personal selling job on behalf of their program with operational officers in the subsidiaries and abroad (even if one of the staff must fly to Johannesburg to meet with the African marketing executives); a give-and-take exchange must ensue over the utility to the marketing people of the environment analysis services and what factors are most meaningful. "Environment Analysis" must be sure to maintain its program as an integral part of strategic planning and its selection of target markets overseas. The department also should coordinate with the treasurer's office concerning foreign currencies and their transfer, and work with the insurance office whenever political risk cover is involved.

A formalized channel of communication might be established on an uncomplicated level with regional operations officers: for the purpose of eliciting input on a given country, getting feedback on the analysis submitted, and just "involving" the operations officers in the process. The central purpose ought to be to educate, not to predict the future! The best sort of education always involves a two-way flow. Many larger corporations have mapped out future target markets, strategies for penetrating them, and ways to reduce the need for, or avoid, political risk insurance on the basis of proper environmental assessments.[1] If proper channels of communication and a working relationship cannot be established among different departments at the corporate center or between the international business environment department at headquarters and the field areas internationally, many interesting reports might be written, but corporate needs will be fulfilled inadequately.

Third, more data are now available—from newspaper accounts to daily terrorist reports—from on-line computer services. But the analyst still must garner the information and build files to be able to answer a question about the present with the advantage of hindsight. Beyond the written resources, the analyst must learn how to "work Washington." Regularly cultivate good relationships with people at the Department of State, the Department of Commerce, the Department of Treasury, OPIC, Capitol Hill committee staffers, and the senior staff of the National Security Council, as well as regionally specialized academicians and the key officers in embassies and international banks. One can more effectively submit a tender for a project on a dam in Sierra Leone, for example, simply by making the appropriate phone calls to the State Department and the World Bank. On one occasion, this author was asked for a country environment background report on Brunei. Panicked because of a tight deadline, he phoned a number of academicians in the field and finally found one who, as editor of a scholarly journal, had just turned down a piece on Brunei because he "didn't believe the subject was big enough to warrant coverage." After a few phone calls to the writer, a Ph.D. student in Southeast Asia, we were able to piece together a report in less than a week.

From a positive standpoint, we have noted that many multinationals have incorporated country analyses into the process of strategic planning—targeting international markets and developing strategies for positioning the corporation in that market.

Sometimes, the process is informal and responsive on an ad hoc basis. The country business environment department should be ready to tackle questions from the legal department or troubled marketing people in the field concerning such matters as the backgrounds of local personalities, the history of a specific airport under construction in Indonesia, or the implications of a political change.

Ultimately, the midsize corporation that wishes to expand internationally will be in greatest need of country business environment analyses as a first indication of whether to proceed. When war, insurrection, civil strife, and expropriation or default become real, potential threats, the corporation may opt for political risk cover or avoid the business opportunity altogether. A survey commissioned by OPIC some years ago noted that firms "whose strategy and structure is global" and have a greater and more diversified spread of international operations may well decide to absorb the cost of risk because of the diversity of the portfolio of its subsidiaries.[2] But what about the smaller-scale, newly internationalizing corporation? The key to deciding early in the game whether to avoid a particular international opportunity, whether to choose one opportunity over another, or just what strategies to pursue to protect oneself is at bottom good intelligence and more good intelligence. Country business environment analysis and the access to the right political and economic information on the spot might not reduce the risk of running into difficulty, but it can reduce uncertainty and allow the company to think through its options.

## Notes

1. "A Study of OPIC Assistance to U.S. Private Direct Investment in Developing Countries," an unpublished paper for OPIC by Arthur Young & Co., May 28, 1982, II-17.

2. Ibid., II-22.

# Index

249

# About the Author/Editor

David M. Raddock, a specialist in Chinese politics, comparative communism, and developing countries, currently is principal officer of David M. Raddock Associates in Brooklyn Heights, New York. Formerly, he was director of international political affairs for ENSERCH Corporation and a managing partner of one of the country's larger public relations firms.

Dr. Raddock received his undergraduate degree at Cornell University in Asian studies and government and received his doctorate in comparative politics from Columbia University. He has conducted research in East Asia, Southeast Asia, Africa, the Middle East, and Latin America. He began his career on the faculty of the Graduate School of International Management at the University of Texas (Dallas).

Dr. Raddock has been a frequent contributor to such academic and popular publications as the *New York Times, Journal of Commerce, Far Eastern Economic Review, Arts Magazine, Art News, Newsday,* among others. His first book, *Political Behavior of Adolescents,* discussed social change in the People's Republic of China at the time of the Cultural Revolution.

# About the Contributors

*Robert E. Ebel* is senior fellow at Georgetown University's Center for Strategic and International Studies. Formerly, he was the international vice president of a major corporation. In government, he was affiliated with the Central Intelligence Agency and the Department of Interior.

*Hermann Frederick Eilts* is chairman of the department of international relations at Boston University and has served in government as the U.S. ambassador to Egypt and Saudi Arabia.

*Guocang Huan,* an accomplished political analyst while in the People's Republic of China, now works for J. P. Morgan Company. He has been a research fellow at Columbia University. He received his Ph.D. from Princeton University in international political economics and has been a contributor to *Foreign Affairs* and other prestigious journals.

*Francis Kornegay Jr.* is manager, program development, at the U.S.–South Africa Leadership Exchange Program. He did graduate work at the Johns Hopkins School of Advanced International Studies and contributes regularly to the *Washington Report on Africa*.

*Rensselaer W. Lee III* is president of Global Advisory Services in Alexandria, Va. He received his doctorate from Stanford University and his B.A. from Princeton.

*Felton McL. Johnston III* is vice president of the Overseas Private Investment Corporation.